The Daily Telegraph

SMALL BUSINESS GUIDE TO

STARTING YOUR OWN BUSINESS

Also by Michael Becket

An A–Z of Finance

Bluff Your Way in Finance

Computer by the Tail
(with Hamish Donaldson)

Economic Alphabet

How the Stock Market Works

Office Warfare:
An Executive Survival Guide

The Daily Telegraph

SMALL BUSINESS GUIDE TO

STARTING YOUR OWN BUSINESS

MICHAEL BECKET

MACMILLAN

First published 2003 by Macmillan
an imprint of Pan Macmillan Ltd
Pan Macmillan, 20 New Wharf Road, London N1 9RR
Basingstoke and Oxford
Associated companies throughout the world
www.panmacmillan.com

ISBN 1 4050 0677 3

5 7 9 8 6 4

A CIP catalogue record for this book is available from the British Library.

Typeset by SX Composing DTP, Rayleigh, Essex
Printed and bound in Great Britain by
Mackays of Chatham plc, Chatham, Kent

Contents

Read this first

There are good and sensible reasons for starting your own business. They include finding a gap in the market; recognizing a shortage of goods and services that you would pay good money for; spotting a group of people with an unsatisfied need or one that is not being adequately catered for – and the knowledge that in any of those cases you could plug that gap.

There are many bad reasons for going it alone. The commonest are discontent with the current employer, redundancy, and an abstract desire to be rich. Quite a few people develop a conviction that all other managers are such fools that they are bound to be better. It is also hopeless to get an itch for independence without any real dedication to any specific area of business, merely searching for some sector or idea. The idea must come first.

The emotion-laden rhetoric from all directions can so easily confuse people. We are surrounded by lures and cajolings about the wonder of running your own business. Government ministers go on ad nauseam about how important entrepreneurs are; newspapers are intermittently stuffed with stories of people barely out of their teens making millions from floating their miraculous companies; and the bookshops overflow with enticing promises of easy wealth.

There is much less about the dedication required, yet starting and running your own company is often painful, always hard work, and seldom leads to great riches.

Do not misunderstand – these words of caution are intended to be a warning that starting a business is more complicated and harder work than you imagined and than the publicity suggests, but this is not intended to put anyone off. There is something enormously satisfying about creating your own business, in making it happen, and being your own master. And if it turns out as you had hoped – and with hard work, careful management and luck, it can – you may earn a decent living and just occasionally become rich. Even on the most pessimistic assumptions and if many things go wrong, the odds are a heck of a lot better than winning the National Lottery jackpot.

In recent years there has been a steady process of re-evaluation as companies decide to focus on what they understand best, and one result has been the disposal of some subsidiaries. This has produced a big market for people buying the portions no longer wanted by the major corporations. That process of buying out an existing business is much less problematic: there is an established organization and structure, known markets, existing staff, established products and so on. That is why venture capitalists love them. This book is not for them. If you are lucky enough to be involved in a good management buyout, your path is clear and you have the experience of running the business you have bought, although the chapters on management and financial controls would still be helpful.

This book is primarily for people with the ambition to create a company from scratch. It is also helpful for anyone who has inherited or taken over a very small business without much experience of the sector – just skip the bits about setting up and registering.

Chapter 1 is the psychiatrist's couch – and here you are both the patient and the healer. Be brutally honest in your self-analysis to decide whether you are temperamentally suited to starting and running your own business. This is the necessary prelude to Chapter 2 which focuses the mind on whether that ambition is really practical or a short cut to financial suicide. In other words, whether the planned enterprise is realistically a goer.

Much of the rest of this book assumes the aim is to set up a business. If the planned work entails something simpler, like doing freelance or casual work, or operating from home, some of it will still be useful, but in a different way. The first chapter applies above all because it takes a special sort of temperament to operate alone, without external directions or targets. In addition, Chapter 2 on deciding whether the venture will keep you solvent is obviously still important. Chapter 8 covers financial control and Chapter 10 marketing; any manager needs that sort of information whether a one-person venture from a back bedroom or a substantial and growing company.

Heaven knows there is no shortage of information and advice on starting and running businesses. Government departments pour out booklets and set up endless organizations to provide guidance; banks promote their services through information packs; there are several magazines for the small business; and the bookshops have countless books on what to do. The problem is that much of this seems to come from people who have written about it, lectured on the subject or advised on it rather than done it themselves. Although most of the material contains useful tips and sound theoretical guidelines, practical input is also needed.

A concomitant difficulty for a starter is not digging out material and advice, but finding something that is sensible and useful. One of the themes of this book is the advice to treat all information and guidance, from whatever source, with caution and scepticism. That also applies to facts and statistics, even when they are apparently authoritative.

This is not just a confirmation of the old aphorism that there are lies, damn lies, statistics and seasonally adjusted figures. It goes deeper: even reputable public sources use unjustifiable figures and base guidance on unverified assumptions. So, question all sources of advice, including this one.

If there were perfect and infallible answers to the question of how to create a wonderful business, all those people writing tomes on how to be a millionaire would be far too busy sunning themselves on their own Caribbean island to slave over a hot computer keyboard. My own little publishing company would by now rival Murdoch and Bertelsmann. Alas, it is not quite as easy as that. In the absence of guaranteed answers, this book will provide many of the right questions and ways of judging the responses.

After that, all you need is unremitting hard work, enormous skill and endless luck.

- Any organization or publication mentioned in the text is listed with details in the Appendices (p.263).
- If the text anywhere refers to he, that is because saying he or she every time is verbose and clumsy, and always going for the plural makes the writing difficult or ungrammatical. No slight on women is intended – they represent almost half the new businesses being started, and tend to have a slightly smaller failure rate than men.

1 Can you really hack it?

Despite centuries of protestations by the rich, research has finally established that money does buy happiness. No, really. University researchers have carried out the surveys. Ambitious people have long suspected it – encouraged by the sight of very few wealthy people disposing of riches to increase their happiness. Money is certainly one of the reasons that motivate many to set up their own business.

The previous, introductory, section tried to sound a word of warning that it is seldom this straightforward. When working for yourself you have a difficult boss, whether demanding and intransigent or slack and lazy – there is no compensation for personal weaknesses. Even in so-called lifestyle companies, set up to give the owner an adequate income and independence without too much hassle, the hours are often long and unsociable, the pressure sometimes intense, and the conditions of work deplorable. Surveys are notoriously unreliable but it is salutary to note that one recent study suggested a quarter of entrepreneurs with new businesses spent over 65 hours a week at work. That is over nine hours a day, seven days a week. Even allowing for a margin of machismo, that is pretty onerous.

Therefore, before embarking on such a demanding course, stop and think why you are doing this. Negative reasons such as being unemployed or dissatisfaction with bosses are not enough. Being a craftsman fed up with working for someone else is not a very good reason either. If the business becomes successful, craftsmen stop doing the craft work which is what they are good at and presumably enjoy, and are forced into administration which may be less fun and is a separate skill in which they have neither training nor experience. Any of these motives are insufficient to carry one through the decisions and life changes that being an entrepreneur entails.

MOTIVATION

Motivation for going it on your own is crucial, but it takes honest insight to establish. What do you want? That is different from asking what you would like. We would all like to be rich, beautiful and loved, but what you really want is what you are prepared to strive very hard for. So consider the question. Do you want to be obscenely rich? It may be surprising but studies suggest the ambition to amass huge wealth is relatively rare as the main motivation. Your motivation may be to get 'sod-off money' – enough to enable you to feel no obligation anywhere, not beholden to anybody. Perhaps even more common is a slightly less insistent version: a desire for independence and to take orders from no one. Other variants include a preference for flexible working hours, sufficient cash to keep a roof over the family home without having to endanger one's digestion and arteries in ulcers and heart attacks. Not all of these motivations are compatible with running your own business, and some of them only apply to certain types of venture.

Most people will have several reasons. Even so, it is wise to be clear about all of them and to set them in some sort of explicit mental priority list. That way, the type of business and the commercial targets will not conflict with the entrepreneur's real ambitions.

What is important is not the choice of ambition, but recognizing what it is you really want. It is only once this has been established that the type and organization of the business will be compatible. Many people are dissatisfied because business life is not what they had quite hoped for, but that is only because they had failed to do the original planning and did not look at their true aims.

SUITABILITY

Can you honestly cope with working up to 12 hours a day, right over the weekends, failing to have more than the occasional word with your spouse, scarcely seeing your children, and being under continuous pressure and on your own, for, at a minimum, the first four years? That may be what it will be like in the early years. It may not get much easier after that if the business survives, but you can normally share some of the worry with others if the business is successful.

It is important to choose a sector you really love and are interested in because you may be focusing on it for 60 hours a week.

Scott Adams, creator of the Dilbert cartoon strip character, says in his book *Dilbert and the Way of the Weasel*: 'a retarded chimpanzee can drink a case of beer and still perform most management functions'. However, he is referring to large corporations that carry a large consignment of placemen and incompetent wafflers. You cannot afford to be either when running your own small business.

A recent survey found 90 per cent of small business owners said they do not regret going it alone. That may be misleading, however, since the ones who did regret it, and grew to hate financial insecurity, stress, loneliness and long hard work, got out. A frequently-quoted statistic is that one-third of small businesses cease within the first three years. The usual implication is that they have gone bust, but in fact a large percentage of the businesses wound up because the owner reckoned the rewards were not worth the effort. Those people go back into employment and are unrepresented in the figures.

CHECKLIST

This is not a scientific personality test, merely a way of focusing the mind on whether one's general approach, family circumstances, finances, skills and social preferences make setting up a business a realistic proposition. It is not infallible, and people impatient with such self-test checklists can skip the section. However, even they should at least glance through it to get an indication of the sort of questions they ought to be asking before totally changing their life. Respond as honestly as you dare.

1 *I have:*
a lots of stamina and can work long hours at a stretch
b the energy to get the work done
c a preference for doing things at my own pace
d a need for regular breaks and changes of pace in my work

2 *My health:*
a is pretty robust – I am hardly ever ill and remain resilient
b I can cope with most infections and frustrations fairly efficiently
c the occasional bout of flu, bronchitis or migraine apart, I can cope
d I catch infections but I am careful to take precautions

3 *Stress:*
a is not a problem, I thrive on it
b occurs from time to time but I cope with it easily
c begins to tell on me after a bit
d causes me distress and physical problems

4 *Socially:*
a obviously I enjoy being liked, and generally I am, but I do not work very hard at it
b making the effort to get on with people has become second nature
c I tend to keep myself to myself
d I am a loner and find socializing difficult

5 *Risk taking:*
a does not cost me sleep but I like to calculate the odds first
b I think it inevitable but best avoided
c really makes me worry and I prefer to avoid it
d is part of my nature – I really enjoy a gamble

6 *Self-confidence:*
a is part of my nature; I can do anything if I set my mind to it
b can usually be summoned up for most challenges
c is usually bogus for most people faced with something difficult
d for me it is limited to the few things I have mastered from youth

7 *My experience of business:*
a is extensive at managerial levels in a variety of specializations
b covers several aspects and I have watched managers at work
c is limited but I am a quick learner
d does not yet exist but I have bought some books on it

8 *When disappointments or obstacles stop me:*
a I generally reorganize the strategy quickly and start all over again
b I punch my way through regardless
c I try something easier and more achievable instead
d I stop and start a new round of planning and wait for a more propitious moment

9 *My family:*
a is really keen for me to have a go, and will muck in to help as needed
b has accepted my ambition to go it alone
c is reluctantly prepared to tolerate my choice
d is opposed to my starting a business

10 *I take decisions:*
a easily and quickly on the evidence available
b after a long and detailed consideration and extensive research
c only in consultation with everybody who can have a useful input
d reluctantly, and I like to wait until it is absolutely necessary to see which is likely to be the best course

11 *I am loyal to people:*
a as long as they do not abuse my trust
b for a very long time, even if they do not always justify it
c come what may – loyalty is vital
d only when it is convenient

12 *On personal ambition:*
a I have always had a pressing urge to be first and a winner
b I really like to win but not at too high a cost
c success is good for the ego, but not indispensable for a balanced individual
d a pleasant lifestyle and good family life are the best things one can have

13 *I can get on with people:*
a almost all the time and with almost all types
b if they are the types and have the attitudes I can get on with
c at any time no matter what they are like
d after reasonable acquaintances when I have found out what they are really like

14 *Encountering setbacks:*
a it is a challenge to find a way round or through
b is demoralizing but after a bit I usually persevere
c stops me in my tracks for a long time to reconsider
d makes me wonder if I am doing the right thing

15 *I seek help and advice:*
a on most of what I do, if only to act as a check on my judgment
b readily when I am out of my depth or on a subject I know little about
c occasionally, or when nothing seems to have worked
d pretty rarely

16 *Leisure time is:*
a completely unimportant to me, I would not know what to do with it
b enjoyable but not nearly as important as the business
c as important as getting on with the work all the time
d more important than working all the hours God sends

17 *When afflicted with serious problems:*
- **a** I am always a survivor
- **b** I can recover given time
- **c** the result depends on the problem
- **d** I like to get my head down and take time about rethinking

18 *Insecurity:*
- **a** is a stimulant – I thrive on it
- **b** I can cope with it
- **c** is to be minimized whenever possible
- **d** worries me and I try to avoid it

19 *I think success:*
- **a** is what you make it – it is always the person's own performance
- **b** comes from having the right product
- **c** demands ruthless dedication to your own goals
- **d** is mainly the result of luck

20 *Criticism:*
- **a** is not a problem; I take it in the spirit intended
- **b** is useful if constructive
- **c** helps depending on where it comes from
- **d** makes me wonder why that person is attacking me

Score four points for A, three points for B, two points for C, and one point for D.

- If you have scored 80, you are almost certainly lying, have a peculiar personality, and/or you will be a millionaire within five years.
- If your score is between 65 and 79, you probably have much of the temperament and many of the attitudes to go it alone in a successful business.
- With a score of 50 to 64, it might be wise to get several expert and experienced managers on board to help, even if you have a very good idea for starting a business.

- A score less than 50 suggests that being an entrepreneur is probably not the ideal course for you. It may be too stressful and too much against your attitudes and preferences to make it a sensible choice.

This checklist is merely an indication of psychological suitability. A high score does not automatically mean certain success in business. Many other things are needed for that, most notably competence in running a business, which is much harder to determine. Common sense and scepticism are indispensable, and the rest of this book will provide some of the tools to help you apply them methodically to the right problems.

There is no point in cheating on this checklist because the person cheated is yourself. The reason that about one-third of new businesses close down in the first three years is often not because the ideas are stinkers, but because the people running them are just not suited to the job. It takes a mixture of temperament and talents, and without them the chances are that the venture is unlikely to survive. Even after running through the checklist, consult family and good friends and double-check whether they agree with the responses. Not many of us are granted accurate self-knowledge.

Looking back at the list will show the type of personality needed to survive, much less prosper, as an entrepreneur. The most vital characteristics are the abilities to work long and hard without succumbing to pressure, and to bounce back from rejection and lack of success. Be sure you have them in abundance or the enterprise will fail, and the financial and psychological costs are high.

FILLING THE GAPS

Assuming you have convinced yourself that you really do have what it takes to survive with a new business, it will have become clear from the checklist that, like everybody else, you have limitations.

Without experience of how to run a business, the enterprise starts with a major handicap. Either the entrepreneur has to be unusual in having the innate talent and instincts for doing the right thing, or these knacks and techniques have to be learned fast and accurately. The alternative is deep trouble.

If the enterprise is to start as a potentially growing business, rather than as a hobby or a one-person pursuit, there will be several people aboard either at the start or very soon after. These others should have talents complementary to those of the entrepreneur. In other words, the company needs sales and financial competence, administrative talent and, for manufacturing, a range of other specialist functions. There is nothing shameful in not knowing about some aspect of business, but there is great shame in not admitting it. Having acknowledged a gap in experience or competence, the sensible thing is to fill it. This aspect is explored a little further in Chapter 3 under 'Directors' (p.49). However, below directors in the organization, there will be the need for a range of managers.

This book gives a preliminary overview on how to fill the gaps. The following chapters raise most of the important points, but a single book can only skim the surface and act as a reminder of the main factors an entrepreneur needs to remember. Experienced managers keep much of that information in their heads. Novices can start here, but with trepidation. This book warns about most of the dangers, but nothing can take the place of common sense.

2 Can the idea make money?

HAVE YOU GOT AN IDEA?

Most people, by the time they have read this far, have at least the outline of an idea for their new business. That is just as well, because books cannot do that for you. Books can teach you how to fan the flames, but the initial spark has to come from the person setting up. This is vital, and so is the enthusiasm that goes with it.

As already noted, whatever sector or type of business is started, it had better be something you really enjoy doing and feel strongly about. Preferably it should be an area you already understand and have experience in; otherwise the extra learning puts another hurdle in the way of business success. Entering a sector of business that the managers do not already know from first-hand experience makes potential backers nervous. It is not impossible to change tack even in middle age, but it is hard to make it work. Money men may profess to admire management guru Charles Handy's exhortations to lead a 'portfolio life' – he advises that one should regularly start a new career – but mistrust it in practice. They prefer people applying accumulated expertise. They worry about untried novelty. It takes a lot to persuade backers that somebody who can manage a shipyard can also manage toothbrush making or book publishing. Managers inexperienced in their chosen sector for starting a business begin with a handicap.

The other requirement, and the one that really matters, is that the new business has to be profitable, and this chapter shows how to find out. This is where facts replace hopes. However, it is not about writing a business plan – that will come later if this works out, and is a much more elaborate document – this is simply a set of calculations to see if the proposition can make a profit, in all normal circumstances.

WILL IT MAKE MONEY?

The first rule is that not every good idea makes money. Not even if it is a very good idea. Not even if it is a very good idea and it generates extensive sales.

When doing a serious assessment, as opposed to a back-of-the-envelope wishful thinking summary, the questions to ask are:

- Who will want to buy this product/service?
- How many such people are there?
- How many of them are likely to try the product?
- What sort of price are they prepared to pay?
- What is the competition?
- What will it cost to provide it (including manufacture, storage, distribution and marketing)?

The rest of the evaluation is a sophisticated elaboration of these questions plus supplementary calculations to see if they hang together.

Novelty

It helps if the underlying notion of the business is something new because that gives it an automatic USP – unique selling point (a much-loved advertising attribute). It is not indispensable, however. As the joke goes, the early bird may catch the worm but the second mouse gets the cheese.

If you have a new technology, being first is important because a dozen giant businesses will immediately check to see if it is worth their while emulating the new product and fighting for the market.

Then, getting a market share and establishing a name and lead counts. Being first is also good if the position is defensible. If the product is an improvement or a new twist on an established idea, the more important factors are superiority, value and image.

If, on the other hand, you have a new way of selling (e.g. the Internet), a new spin on an old idea, or you are making something better, there is less advantage to being first; the important factor is being better.

Who will buy it?

It is nice to come up with a good idea for a new product or service – that eureka moment. And in the first flush of enthusiasm, it is easy to get carried away with the brilliance of the idea. But the first question must always be: who will buy this product or service? This applies whether it is a book, a new piece of machinery or a sophisticated service. The answer comes in four stages. The first question is how many people are likely to be interested and/or use some inferior supplies at the moment. The second is whether the new notion is novel enough, a big enough improvement (including in price), and likely to be remarkable enough for people to realize it is better. The third question is to try to calculate how many of the target market will have heard of the product and will get a chance to purchase it. The final question is to estimate how many of the interested group you can realistically expect to abandon their current purchases (see 'Sales', p.22).

Research your market: talk to people who might use the product and to people working in related industries about its potential. Trade and specialist publications can help in working out the size of the target market and their advertising rates will give figures for the cost of initial publicity.

A really sensible calculation of these factors can scupper many a happy dream. Which is rather the way T. H. Huxley famously described science: 'the slaying of a beautiful hypothesis by an ugly fact'.

Cash-flow forecasts

This data will then be incorporated into the absolutely vital cash-flow forecast. It is worth buying a computer, if only to use its spreadsheet program to create cash-flow forecasts. This work is indispensable and, as this section will show, a painfully iterative process. It can, however, be done on a really cheap computer – one that need not cost more than a couple of hundred pounds.

The cash-flow exercise is vital from the start of planning, and regularly after that, on alternative assumptions. A first shot can be produced over a weekend on a computer's spreadsheet program. This may show that half the information you need is not to hand, and a couple of weeks of research must follow. And slowly the forecast will come together.

Told to create financial forecasts and a business plan, most people starting out thinking it is impossible. Their first instinct is to say it cannot be done; crystal balls are not available. We do not know the future and never can, they say – after all you cannot know sales of a new product in advance and the best one can hope for will be a wild guess. Novices assert theirs is a new idea, a different product, an unknown quantity, an untested area, and so on. Therefore, by definition there is no information on how well it can do.

If it really were that impossible you would be in real trouble – the venture would be a greater gamble than betting your home on the result of the 3.30 at Kempton Park.

Fortunately, it is not nearly as bad as that. Although the future is unknowable, it is possible to make an educated guess. Even if your guess turns out to be inaccurate, doing the calculations and seeing the alternative figures help. In fact, once you start the exercise the picture becomes steadily clearer and, even more surprisingly, it gets easier the longer you do it. You begin to realize you know more about the market and potential costs than you initially thought.

1 Cash flow

CASH FLOW 2001		Jan	Feb	Mar	Apr	May	June
Drink 1	Volume in Cases	–	–	–	–	–	–
	Sales Revenue £	–	–	–	–	–	–
	Cost of Goods £	–	–	–	–	–	–
	Gross Profit £	–	–	–	–	–	–
	%	–	–	–	–	–	–

REVENUE 2002		Jan	Feb	Mar	Apr	May	June
Drink 1	Volume in Cases	906	1,055	1,255	1,455	1,655	2,005
	Sales Revenue £	15,823	18,419	21,910	25,402	28,894	35,004
	Cost of Goods £	9,516	11,078	13,178	15,278	17,378	21,053
	Gross Profit £	6,306	7,341	8,733	10,125	11,516	13,952
	%	40	40	40	40	40	40
Drink 2	Volume in Cases	–	–	–	–	160	660
	Sales Revenue £	–	–	–	–	1,853	7,643
	Cost of Goods £	–	–	–	–	1,258	5,188
	Gross Profit £	–	–	–	–	595	2,455
	%	–	–	–	–	32%	32%
	Total Gross Profit £	**6,306**	**7,341**	**8,733**	**10,125**	**12,112**	**16,407**

OVERHEADS 2001		Jan	Feb	Mar	Apr	May	June
Marketing	Brand Development of Drink 2 £	–	–	–	–	–	–
	Design £	–	–	3,000	–	–	–
	Market research £	–	–	–	3,000	–	–
	Sampling costs £	–	–	–	–	–	–
	PR/Publicity £	–	–	–	3,000	2,000	1,000
	Advertising/POS £	–	–	–	–	–	–
	Web site/E-commerce £	–	–	–	750	120	120
	Sub total £	**–**	**–**	**3,000**	**3,750**	**2,120**	**2,120**

July	Aug	Sept	Oct	Nov	Dec	Total
384	448	512	576	1,007	1,092	4,019
6,509	7,594	8,678	9,763	17,069	18,509	68,122
4,032	4,704	5,376	6,048	10,574	11,466	42,200
2,477	2,890	3,302	3,715	6,495	7,043	25,923
38	38	38	38	38	38	38

July	Aug	Sept	Oct	Nov	Dec	Total
3,006	3,186	3,366	3,546	3,291	3,450	28,177
52,480	55,623	58,765	61,908	57,461	60,237	491,926
31,563	33,453	35,343	37,233	34,559	36,228	295,857
20,917	22,170	23,422	24,675	22,903	24,009	196,069
40	40	40	40	40	40	40
384	1,140	1,380	1,620	1,860	2,100	9,304
4,447	13,201	15,980	18,760	21,539	24,318	107,740
3,018	8,960	10,847	12,733	14,620	16,506	73,129
1,428	4,241	5,134	6,026	6,919	7,812	34,611
32	32	32	32	32	32	32
22,346	**26,411**	**28,556**	**30,701**	**29,822**	**31,821**	**230,680**

July	Aug	Sept	Oct	Nov	Dec	TOTAL
1,000	1,000	1,000	1,000	1,000	1,000	6,000
–	–	1,000	–	–	–	4,000
–	–	3,000	–	3,000	–	9,000
1,000	1,000	1,000	1,000	1,000	1,000	6,000
150	150	150	150	150	150	6,900
–	–	–	–	–	–	–
120	120	120	120	120	120	1,710
5,270	**5,270**	**2,270**	**2,270**	**5,270**	**2,270**	**33,610**

1 Cash flow continued

	OVERHEADS 2001	**Jan**	**Feb**	**Mar**	**Apr**	**May**	**June**
Administration £	Rent		–	–	–	400	400
	Stationery/Print		3,000	–	–	–	–
	Warehousing		–	–	–	–	–
	Car/Travel		100	100	100	250	250
	Accom/Subsistence		50	50	50	200	200
	Entertaining		200	200	200	200	200
	Office equipment		–	–	–	4,700	–
	Furniture		–	–	–	1,000	–
	Telephone		–	–	–	600	–
	Set-up Costs/Legal		3,000	–	–	–	–
	Postage/Couriers		50	50	50	50	50
	Accountancy		–	–	–	–	–
	Insurance		–	–	–	–	–
	Miscellaneous		200	200	200	200	200
	3 Directors' Salaries		12,075	12,075	12,075	12,075	12,075
	Employees' Salaries		–	–	–	2,000	2,000
	Sub total		**18,675**	**12,675**	**12,675**	**21,675**	**15,375**
	TOTAL OVERHEADS £		**18,675**	**15,675**	**16,425**	**23,795**	**17,495**
	OPERATING PROFIT£		–18,675	–15,675	–16,425	–23,795	–17,495
	Servicing Finance £		–	–	–	–	–
	Tax £		–	–	–	–	–
	Dividends £		–	–	–	–	–
	Sub total £		–	–	–	–	–
	NET PROFIT £		–18,675	–15,675	–16,425	–23,795	–17,495

July	Aug	Sept	Oct	Nov	Dec	TOTAL
400	400	400	400	400	400	3,200
3,000	–	–	–	–	–	6,000
150	150	150	150	150	150	900
250	250	250	250	250	250	2,300
200	200	400	400	400	400	2,550
200	200	200	200	200	200	2,200
–	–	–	–	–	–	4,700
–	–	–	–	–	–	1,000
–	400	–	–	600	–	1,600
–	–	–	–	–	–	3,000
50	50	50	50	50	50	550
–	–	–	–	–	2,000	2,000
–	3,000	–	–	–	–	3,000
200	200	200	200	200	200	2,200
12,075	12,075	12,075	12,075	12,075	12,075	132,825
2,000	2,000	2,000	2,000	2,000	2,000	16,000
18,525	**18,925**	**15,725**	**15,725**	**16,325**	**17,725**	**184,025**
23,795	**24,195**	**17,995**	**17,995**	**21,595**	**19,995**	**217,635**
–21,318	–21,305	–14,693	–14,280	–15,100	–12,952	–191,712
–	–	–	–	–	–	–
–	–	–	–	–	–	–
–	–	–	–	–	–	–
–	–	–	–	–	–	–
–21,318	–21,305	–14,693	–14,280	–15,100	–12,952	–191,712

Sales

There are many ways to find out the size of the potential market. To begin with, one needs to discover how many people are interested in the subject matter, and that is relatively easy in our much-researched society.

From here, you have to make a reasonable guess at the percentage of potential customers that it is sensible to assume will hear about the new product in the first year, and all subsequent periods. No matter how wonderful the goods or service, not everyone who hears about it will buy, so you have to make another guess at the proportion that would. That will entail some research on the method and route of sales, distribution, access to the market, the need for and cost of publicity. Yes, much of it is a stab in the dark and guesswork, but the longer you analyse the available data, the closer you will approximate to something reasonable.

For instance, if the product is a new magazine for lawyers, it is possible to find the total potential audience by asking the main trade associations/trade unions for the sector, the Bar Council, and the Law Society, for the numbers of barristers and solicitors. There are also the Employment Lawyers Association, Solicitors Family Law Association, Computer Lawyers Consortium, Association of Personal Injury Lawyers, Forum of Insurance Lawyers, and probably a dozen others. On top of that are magazines such as *The Lawyer*, *International Financial Law Review*, *Commercial Lawyer*, *Legal Times*, *Legal Business* and *European Corporate Lawyer*. As if that were not enough, there are two massive tomes listing most lawyers in the country with their specialisms: *Chambers Guide to the Legal Profession* and *The Legal 500*. If even that proved insufficient, you could turn to The College of Law, the Solicitors Complaints Bureau or the lecturers at university faculties of law. These sources should provide a set of lists and totals with which to start.

For finding small businesses, there are the various organizations representing the sector and component parts of it, and the government's Small Business Service to get an estimate of the organizations in the field.

For instance, to find how many people are in the market for a healthy soft drink, one can look at comparable sets of parallel products, including other health drinks, and the number of outlets selling them.

In a similar way, there is somebody comparable or competitive in every field of endeavour, ready to produce statistics of the total universe, as market researchers call the totality of potential consumers in a market.

Stop and think a moment – who would have information on the collection of people you will be pursuing? It could be government, trade associations, market research companies, trade unions, clubs and associations. There will almost certainly be a trade magazine covering at least part of the field, and perhaps a specialist or hobby magazine. Reference libraries, especially business libraries, are a good place to start. They have lists of trade associations to contact in addition to the normal range of reference works. In most fields there are also acknowledged experts, sometimes academics, sometimes freelancers. No matter how eminent, these experts are generally helpful and kindly, and prepared to provide information and advice surprisingly readily. There are probably specialist reports on the sector from companies such as Mintel and Corporate Intelligence Retail. The major research reports usually cost a small fortune, but most of the larger business libraries have access to them.

Then there is the web. That can be frustrating because typing in the relevant words and their alternatives into a search engine (Google, Alta Vista, Jeeves, Lycos and the like) may yield 300,000 websites from each of the search engines, of which 299,987 are likely to be useless. It is a long, boring and irritating task, buoyed up only by the hope that the other 13 sites may provide enormous amounts of useful information beyond the specific need that prompted the look, the number of potential customers.

All that work is merely to establish the total population in the target market. If the new product is a free journal sent to every member of the target audience it will also provide the final total. If something is to be sold, the next step is to ask how many of the potential audience will buy it. At this point you have to consider competition. There is no such thing as a unique product or service. Even if precisely what you are doing has not been done, there are alternatives and substitutes. That means customers have to be weaned away from other suppliers. At the very least it will take time and money to reach the market or the retailers who sell to the market, and also to publicize the product.

You also have to consider distribution, which itself is a major challenge. You have to calculate whether, for instance, you can get the product to the retailers dealing with the area. If they are supermarkets, the demand will be for bulk regular deliveries. Who can do that is the next question. If retailing is through small outlets, can you get round to them in your own car and, if not, how much will the distributor take off your profit?

That is the approach from the top down. You start with the overall population of potential buyers and make a guess at how many might be interested. Then you ask how many of those would be prepared to buy, and so on.

Alternatively, you ask them. Not all markets demand market research outfits to ask thousands of people. A week on the telephone ringing round can, in some cases, provide a good picture. It may not be statistically sound, but it could provide a pointer.

There is a different approach which can be used in parallel. Take a new project such as publishing a book. There is no way of knowing how many people will buy it, but experience in the field can help to make a guess based on previous products. That will provide a start. Then you test your guesses. Start with a reasonable figure. It might sell around 8,000 in a year. Feed that figure into the cash-flow tables which already contain costs, and see how it looks. Will it be a regular sale every month? Probably not; it will rise initially and then tail off. So try 500 in the first month, 1,000 in the second month, 800 in the third, 500 in the fourth, and so on. Once you have it down in black and white, the reaction is almost immediate: no that does not look right, the experienced publisher says very quickly. So you try again. And then try again. Gradually it will look more convincing to the experts. It is hardly scientific, possibly not even reliable, but it helps to get the figures started.

After some massaging of the figures, a picture starts emerging, and that picture will reveal where the danger lies: if the book (or whatever) does not sell 5,000 in the first four months it will probably lose money and, in any case, the project will be £8,000 in the red by June. This is the sort of conclusion thrown up immediately and it prompts the next step: asking how likely the book is to sell 5,000 in four months. Really likely? Really, really likely?

Be viciously realistic about this. The sales figures cannot be hopes, but must be expectations. Otherwise the whole exercise is worthless – more to the point it will not convince backers (see Chapter 5). If the new product is a health drink with organic contents and all sorts of beneficial effects, it will still need to fight for shelf space at Tesco, Sainsbury, Safeway, Asda and the rest. It will compete not just against other health drinks, but against all the other ways of quenching your thirst from gin and tonic to cola. It will also contend with the inertia of the retailers who are not keen to disrupt their systems for a new business that could go bust within a week. The calculations must include what is needed to persuade your buyers: some retailers may demand cash for shelf space at the start, and have requirements on how it is to be stocked. This may require specialist distributors to get round all of them, and they cost money too.

To return to the magazine for lawyers, have there been others in this field who have failed? If so, why? Who would want to advertise in it? First check on what other magazines charge for similar markets and circulations, and then spend weeks of frustration on the phone to all the potential advertisers, trying to get them to give a guide on whether they would buy space if you achieved various levels of circulation. Do not believe them, however. People, on the whole, do not want to tell an eager young entrepreneur they would not touch the new product or service to save their lives, and are probably also trying to get rid of you so they can get on with some work. So they may say they will stock the goods or advertise in the magazine. But when it comes to the crunch, and they are expected to gamble with some money or give up remunerative shelf space, it may be a different story. Thus, apply a discount factor to whatever people say.

It is quite useful to do a spot of one's own market research. This does not necessarily involve hiring organizations such as Gallup or Mori at huge fees, and at first need not even be statistically reliable. It may just involve contacting a dozen of the biggest buyers in the business and putting a carefully phrased suggestion to them to see how likely they would be to buy. Do not accept a straight answer even if they say yes. Follow up with questions about what they think would be an appropriate price and at what point they would think it too expensive, what they would order if it cost twice that, how many they would order in the first instance, where their own preferences are and so on. Treat the answers with care. It is difficult to envisage what one would do when it actually comes to handing over money. Assume the results of such an unscientific personal survey are on the optimistic side.

Time factors

When entering the figures into the spreadsheet do not make the mistake of assuming payment is immediate. If things go well or it is in a prompt paying industry, the money might come in within 30 days, but for most cases it is safer to assume a wait of 60 days. This is close to average in Britain. By definition, however, that means some trades and some customers pay much later than that.

Another consideration is the seasonality of some products and services. For instance, people eat less ice cream and have fewer soft drinks in the winter, jobs are not advertised between the third week of July and the second week of September, toy and book sales boom in the run-up to Christmas, and construction work slackens in winter.

Costs

For people intimidated by the whole process of producing cash-flow statements from a position of ignorance, the easiest place to start is with costs because it is easy to get figures for those, complete with most of the alternatives. For instance, in a service company with no manufacturing premises, you work out how many staff you will need, how many square feet of office space that entails, and ring estate agents covering the area you plan to move into.

Staff costs are similarly easy to deduce from job advertisements. The first step is to establish the pay levels. Then, if the business is a professional firm, for example accountant, solicitor, some form of consultancy, or a repair type of outfit like plumber or electrician, you know the people are charged out by the hour. For instance, if you pay a worker £12 an hour for a 40-hour week, the cost for a 47-week year is £22,560. National Insurance plus other costs bring the cost of that employee to around £27,000. If the employee carries a share of the overheads and back-up services (everything from the office staff to vehicle and tools) that could add another £8,000. A careful analysis on the spreadsheet will provide a pretty exact figure for this.

This calculation has the advantage of showing that if that worker is charged out at (earning money for the business) 80 per cent of his time (pretty good going in most cases) you have to charge customers over £23 merely to recover the costs. If you want to make a profit and allow for sicknesses and periods of low demand, it would be foolish to charge under £30 an hour. By starting with labour costs, you have arrived at a plausible figure for pricing.

For a different sort of costing, let us imagine a new business that will launch a magazine in a part of the market currently empty or at least inadequately catered for. Costs are fairly easy to establish: there is paper, printing, distribution, rent, rates, wages, postage, photography, legal costs, auditors and so on. The first step is to enter each of those headings into a spreadsheet (see p.68).

That is the easy bit. Go down to the local newsagents and look in magazines to see what companies print those similar in type and size to the one being planned and ring them up. A few days on the telephone to these printers and their paper suppliers will produce production costs. Employment agencies, sellers of second-hand office furnishings, et al will generate masses of other figures.

Unfortunately, it is not quite that easy because even at this point the costs will be affected by a range of other factors. For instance, the costs of paper and printing depend on the circulation. When you become more sophisticated with this work, it will be possible to link the cells on the spreadsheet; a change in the assumption of circulation will automatically adjust the demand for paper and the printing costs. In the initial stages, however, printers and paper merchants have to work on the range of options you give them – ask for a set of prices based on the optimistic, pessimistic and realistic figures. Do not worry about that, they have done it before.

The launch of the product, and indeed later marketing pushes, may have to be signalled by direct mail shots to the target audience. That means buying mailing lists, printing publicity materials and posting it all. It also involves persuading newsagents who are already short of shelf space to stock another product about which they know nothing. (You may begin to see the point of some of the self-assessment questions in Chapter 1.)

For a product going into supermarkets, you may have to buy initial shelf space, and there will be distribution and publicity costs, quite apart from the manufacturing and packaging. As with all physical products there will be set-up costs such as designing the product.

All these items can be costed. Britain is knee-deep in data; it is just a matter of finding it which takes a little ingenuity and quite a lot of common sense. The government collects Himalayas of information from the Registrar General's population figures, through the Department of Trade's surveys to the family expenditure surveys. There are censuses of population and of distribution, and there are Business Monitors for various sectors of the market. There are commercial directories, trade associations, professional bodies, university theses, trade directories, *Yellow Pages*, specialist libraries and trade journals.

One approach to this sort of research is to start with an acknowledged expert and ask who else is knowledgeable on the subject. The expert could be a trade journal, found from *Willings Press Guide* or *British Rate and Data*, available from most public libraries, or the trade association (there is a directory of those as well). And this is before you have even tried the Internet. Type the area of interest into Yahoo, Lycos or Google and there is a good chance that in under two seconds it will find nearly half a million sites. All right, so most of them may be useless, but that still leaves many sites which have some information. In other words, there is absolutely no excuse for saying the information is unavailable.

Pricing

How much people buy will also depend on the price. This is known in economics as elasticity of demand. For people not already working in the specific industry, pricing is an especially troublesome concept. So much so it might be best to take external advice. Young companies almost always underprice and make too slim a profit to thrive or to reinvest for growth. Pricing is an arcane art and depends mainly on what the market will bear. You can introduce other factors into setting the level, but that will not be a commercial decision. For instance, Morgan Cars for many years set the prices as low as it could because it wanted people who loved the machines to be able to get them. The result was a chronic shortage of money for reinvestment. Similarly, the Gandolfi brothers produced handmade, beautiful mahogany and brass cameras tailored to the owners' hands and specifications for probably 25 per cent of the market value of the cameras and, consequently, lived in something approaching dire poverty.

There may be well-established margins in the sector. Retailers, whether clothes shops or supermarkets, have clear policies on margins for various product categories, depending on speed of turnover, danger of being left with unsaleable product, and so on. Book chains like WH Smith might demand a 60 per cent discount from marked retail price, baked beans might only have a 10 per cent mark-up. Restaurants add something between 50 and 150 per cent to the cost of wine. All of which needs to be factored into the calculation.

As the preceding paragraphs have suggested, fundamentally there are two approaches to finding the right price. One of them is to start with the numbers that are known, such as:

- the cost of raw materials
- manufacturing cost
- if production is subcontracted, that profit margin
- storage
- distribution

- marketing: publicity, salesmen etc
- minimum profit margins for survival.

If the product has a finite lifetime (all this applies to service as well as physical products), as most do, the costs of entry, of setting up and of marketing will all be written off during that period.

In some sectors that is all. Defence contractors have traditionally worked on a variant of this – simply a cost-plus basis. Some publishers have forms with the total cost of printing, number of copies, type of book cover and so on with a formula to produce an automatic price result. This sounds a scientific version of this approach, but in practice the market often obtrudes and a senior publisher may look at the result and say it will never go at that price, take £3 off it. The publisher realizes that is uneconomic but justifies it on the grounds of wanting to sell the book which is in the list because it is worthwhile and will enhance the company's literary prestige. But then large parts of publishing have remained an inefficient but gentlemanly cottage industry.

The second approach is to see what consumers will pay by checking the price of competitors. Then work back from there. You deduct retailer and wholesaler margins and find out how the two results compare.

If the result shows costs to be higher than the market will bear, one option is to decide that this is not a commercial proposition and to try something else. Another is to consider alternatives, such as selling to the outlets to by-pass the wholesaler, or direct to the consumer to cut out both wholesaler and retailer margin – though that is not without cost.

There is a third option. If the product is sufficiently differentiated from the competition it may command a premium price. That would require superior-quality product, exemplary after-care service, or a prestige cachet. This is a form of market segmentation.

Professional advice may be needed to get at the elasticity of demand. If you sell 1,000 products at £100 each, what would happen if the price rose to £150? If the answer is that you would sell 800, the obvious reaction is to do it because the revenue would rise from

£100,000 to £120,000. In fact, you would probably be keen to investigate further, to see whether £200 might increase the overall income still further.

By the same token, if the result were that at £150 the sales would fall to 400, bringing revenue down to £60,000, the idea would be less appealing. In that case, the sensible strategy would be to ask what would happen if the price could come down to £80. Once again, if the overall revenues rose (indicating, in economists' language, elastic demand) that is clearly the way to go if you can manage it. All of which is rather more straightforward in an established market than with a totally new product where the best you can manage is to calculate for something relatively comparable.

Sometimes the results of such an exercise will be surprising. Raising the price for some categories of upmarket goods has paradoxically increased demand, much to the astonishment of inexperienced marketers who did not expect the prestige of the items to rise sufficiently to appeal to a snobbish category of customers.

There are other factors to be considered. For instance, setting a high price will attract competition into the market. On the other hand, a high-price prestige product may be in a specialist niche, resistant to market fluctuations. The smaller output also reduces production problems.

In real life the elasticity of demand calculations are never quite as straightforward as textbooks suggest – varying the quantity of output also alters costs. It is rare for unit costs to remain constant with substantial changes of volume – raising production usually provides falling unit costs from the economies of scale. On the other hand, there may be additional storage and distribution costs, plus more administrative needs. Some of this will also apply to services and the number of staff required may change as customers become more numerous.

Funding

Going through the exercise of checking whether the idea will make a profit also shows the funding needs. It will show, not only from month to month but cumulatively through the year, just how big the Micawber gap is between income and expenditure. Few businesses are fortunate enough to break even, much less make a profit in their first year. Indeed, most backers are suspicious of any plan that purports to show the venture in positive cash flow in under three years, and even more doubtful if it claims to start producing a profit in that time.

This point, incidentally, stresses the huge difference between positive cash flow and profits. The former is when current money inflows are greater than current spending, while the latter is when the inflows are enough to cover the initial costs, capital expenditure, depreciation, and so on.

The gap between income and spending will then suggest how much equity capital and how much overdraft will have to be introduced.

Having made those assumptions and worked out the necessary loans, you have to do the calculations again because, quite apart from anything else, the overdraft must be serviced with regular interest payments.

What if?

When all the work has apparently been completed and the spreadsheet cells are all filled in, you start the 'What if' exploration. What if rents rise, sales drop, raw material prices rise or fall, postage increases, inflation alters? Every single set of figures is changed by reasonable levels to test the effect. The technical term for this is sensitivity testing. This is because it checks how sensitive the economic model – your spreadsheet is in effect an economic model – is to changes in the assumptions.

It is part of that iterative process mentioned earlier and, although tedious and time-consuming, the task has two major benefits. First, it teaches where the main dangers lie, which will be invaluable when the business is running. If you know that the magazine can be made unviable by a 12 per cent rise in paper prices, or that a soft drink cannot be made profitably if the price is forced down by 10 per cent, then either you make sure that the contracts are secure or that you can take evasive action at the first hint that paper is liable to become more expensive or drink retailers more pressing.

With revenue sensitivities one can construct different types of calculations allowing for a range of outcomes. Not only can one use alternative sets of assumptions, but also make different phases last varying lengths of time. So one can see what happens if it takes three months or nine months to build up sales. The important thing is that the figures will in future, when the business is up and running, provide early warning of trouble ahead, which is the only way any business can stay solvent.

The second benefit is that one learns intimately how the model works and what the company can do, which is invaluable when negotiating with backers, and will be a boon in the long discussions with potential investors and their specialists because they tend to ask a lot of 'what if' questions. Anybody contemplating putting cash into the business, whether it is a business angel or a venture capitalist, is going to quiz the manager thoroughly. And some of the most pointed questions are precisely on this sort of topic. They will ask how vulnerable the business is to changes in the financial environment or its costs, and if the entrepreneur has all the information immediately to mind with exact and quantified answers, they will be much reassured.

Break even

To get a full measure of viability will need at least one more calculation, separate from the spreadsheet. This finds out when the enterprise breaks even – what is the level of sales at which it survives. (See also Chapter 8).

This calculation requires the total fixed costs – the things that have to be paid whether you make a single penny from sales or not, such as rent, rates, management salaries. Variable costs depend on what you do and how much you use, such as raw materials and direct labour.

The break even is when the margin on the product equals the

overheads. Or to put it in accountants' language, you divide the total fixed costs by the selling price minus the variable cost per unit.

It takes a bit of concentration to work through this, but it is worthwhile, so here goes. Let us say the rent, rates and salaries for a small toy company are £25,000 a month and the bank interest on the overdraft is another £5,000 bringing the total fixed costs to £30,000. You are selling 10,000 toys and it costs £200,000 in total for the manufacture, selling, distribution, etc. That means the variable cost per toy is the £200,000 total variable costs divided by 10,000 items sold, which is £20 per toy. Let us say you are selling them at £30 a go so the margin per toy is £10. Divide that into the overheads of £30,000 and the answer is 3,000. Which means you have to sell 3,000 toys to cover all your costs – or break even. Any more sales over that and you are in profit.

That then suggests the question: is it likely that you will sell more than 3,000 of those toys a month. And, if so, how many more?

You can do a similar calculation for a service industry which charges for the time taken on a client's job. The calculation in this case is how much you need to charge to prevent starvation. The maximum you could reasonably work would be an average 40 hours a week for 48 weeks a year. That does not suppose much in the way of holidays, and allows only a little time for marketing, administration and the like. No service business achieves anything like that ideal – customers do not queue end to end so conveniently.

Then tot up how much it costs to live. That includes rent or mortgage, council tax, telephone, gas and electricity, food, clothes, life insurance, travel, stationery, computer depreciation, car running costs and depreciation, professional magazines, bank charges, income tax, National Insurance plus sundries and emergency reserves. If that comes to £32,000, you have to earn a minimum of £667 a working week to stay alive and you have to charge your time at £17 an hour at a bare minimum.

If you then gear that to a more realistic level of chargeable hours per week – and this applies for a plumber or a barrister – it will rapidly increase the hourly rate. The calculations can be done the other way round – by discovering the going rate for a marketing consultant or computer technician and working back to see how many hours you need to charge before the overheads, personal and professional, are covered. Then realistically consider whether it is reasonable to expect such a level of demand and if payment can be sustained.

CONCLUSION

The point of this long and demanding exercise is to discover whether a particular business idea or project will make money. And not just any money, but enough to recompense the participants for doing it and the investors for putting in their cash, and in reasonable enough quantities to make it worthwhile. That means checking not only whether the cash flow turns positive within a measurable time, but that the business also makes a healthy margin of profit, which is not quite the same thing.

As a double check, it may be worth running a set of dummy profit and loss accounts from the accumulated information to see what might be presented to positive venture capital investors who frequently want sample accounts.

There is no point in going through all this elaborate work of research and calculation if you refuse to accept the results. Or, to put it another way, it is pointless to look at a spreadsheet which presents a picture of something between unpromising and disastrous, and then say 'but it has to be better than that'. It is no good trying to massage the figures to bring them closer to an instinctive feeling that the notion has to be a winner, or tinkering with the cash flow until you get the result you want, if this is done at the cost of distorting probability.

Emotional commitment is all very well, but not to the point of financial suicide. If the figures show the project will indeed make a profit, but you could make at least as much by putting the cash into a bank deposit account, it would be folly to press on. Every new venture carries a risk and its returns have to be substantially higher than you can get elsewhere to compensate for that. On top of that you have to add yet another premium to compensate for the hard work and stress in starting and running the business.

Take the advice of W. C. Fields: 'If at first you don't succeed, try again, then quit. No use being a damn fool about it.'

FRANCHISING

Much of this work becomes unnecessary for a franchise. For a start, there is a business format or product that has been tested in the market and found to be successful. You start trading with a name that is already established and may be getting advertising backing. The system operator provides all the costings, the likely level of outgoings, including the licence fee and royalties, and will even help with estimating income. An established operation has outlets in similar circumstances and can call on experience to give a fairly accurate forecast of how the business will run. It may not be cheaper to set up as a franchise operator than starting one's own business from scratch, but it does remove many of the dangers and possibilities for expensive mistakes.

Greater detail on how to go about setting up and operating a franchise, and how to pick the right system, is given in Chapter 3.

3 How to set up a business

A few lucky people hit on a scheme that enables them to continue in existing paid employment while building up their own business. Once they reach the point when the new venture is reasonably self-sustaining, they can resign without starving. Sometimes this can be made easier by having a family member help in the early periods. It makes the transition a lot less painful.

Although safer, even that course has dangers. For one thing, there is the risk that the new business remains a hobby, and the cautious person is reluctant to cut the umbilical cord which supplies a steady and predictable income. In addition, it is unlikely that without full-time commitment the new venture will ever take off to become an independently viable enterprise.

There is nothing wrong with a hobby that makes money, just as there is nothing culpable about running a 'lifestyle' business which is never intended to be a worldwide corporation. Indeed, with the growing trend for part-time work, it is all becoming very much easier. But you do have to be honest with yourself and tailor the enterprise accordingly; a mismatch of ideas and practice can be painful.

A second difficulty is that a paying hobby or part-time enterprise for pin money has to be run in the evenings and at weekends, which takes much energy and stamina. Considering how hard most people work – we are constantly being told how subject to overwork and stress the population of Britain has become – most people will be too exhausted to give the new venture the full attention it needs. Eventually they may abandon the whole thing from sheer tiredness. Paradoxically it may be abandoned when it is doing reasonably well because that is when it demands the most effort.

In any case, there are not many types of business that can be successfully run when nobody else is at work. Contacting clients and suppliers becomes tricky. It can be done, but the odds are against you. There are a few occupations that can be done during those hours, but they are more likely to supplement an existing income than turn into full-time businesses. These include craft occupations like designing Christmas cards or potting, doing typing or book-keeping for a local small business, writing or graphic arts, or personal services such as acupuncture and hairdressing.

This book is about setting up a business that will be more than a hobby – it takes you all the way to making trade acquisitions and obtaining a public quotation on the stock exchange. Chapter 1 established whether you are temperamentally capable of coping, Chapter 2 that the planned project can make a profit, and now this chapter is about how to create the organization to make it happen.

GOVERNMENT SUPPORT

Practically every politician regularly kowtows to small business. Cynically, one might say that is hardly surprising, considering there are 3.7 million of them. With spouses and employees, they probably represent at least 10 million votes. In addition, it is the small businesses that are reckoned to be creators of employment, although the Trades Union Congress has recently questioned that assumption. Whatever the reason, ministers make frequent speeches in support of small business and devise countless schemes, funds, and advice organizations to help. So does the European Union (EU).

It would obviously be foolish to reject all this largesse or the free advice and assistance that go with it. But it can be almost as hard work getting this support as doing without it. Some of the schemes are so arcane hardly anybody knows about them, and others require such rigorous application screening that management time may be better spent elsewhere. To be fair, the system is being made easier – the forms are shorter, the number of funds is smaller and the sources of information better armed. At the very least it is worth investigating whether you are entitled to get something. Business Links and the

Small Business Service may help (see Appendix for addresses), and all the major banks have starter leaflets or packs of advice.

The choices

Businesses can set up in five basic ways: sole trader, partnership, limited liability partnership, cooperative and incorporation. There is no absolute necessity to decide right from the start which suits you best because the decision is reversible, although changing in some directions is a bureaucratic hassle and can cost additional money. There is no reason to go through the process twice if you can settle it at the outset.

Despite the avowed desire of government to reduce red tape, there is a terrifying tangle that can almost strangle a young business or at the very least come close to immobilizing it. Various organizations campaigning for small businesses have pointed out that bureaucracy adds billions of pounds to their costs and yet the only answer is more regulation, and Brussels is manufacturing more as you read this. In addition to the structure of the business, there is a growing list of permissions, licences, approvals and certifications from an army of tax-funded bureaucrats. Here is a random selection:

- The premises have to be for business rather than residential: Certificate of Lawful Use or Development.
- If you sell alcohol, the local authority has to approve the management, premises and organization.
- Hotels sleeping more than six people need a fire certificate from the local fire brigade.
- Taxis are licensed by the local authority.
- Tobacco sales require a licence.
- Nursing homes require an annual licence.
- Restaurants need permission from the local authority to put tables outside.

- Alteration to the structure or appearance of a building needs planning permission from the local authority plus possibly from English Heritage.
- Vehicles which can carry more than 3.5 tonnes need an operating licence.
- If you keep personal data on people (customers, mailing lists, etc.) you must register with the Information Commission.

If you think that looks intimidating, there is a nasty surprise to come. There are hundreds of these, possibly thousands. The old legal Latin tag is *ignorantia legis neminem excusat*, meaning ignorance of the law is no excuse. Or as a senior judge ruefully pointed out, everybody is presumed to know the law except judges and they are subject to appeal. Appendix D (p.279) provides a long but not complete list of the laws businesses are presumed to master.

Setting up an office in the back bedroom can legally be done only if there is no restrictive covenant to the contrary in the deeds, and will probably need a change of use approval from the local authority's planning department. If the approval is granted – and often it is not – the premises may be re-rated as a commercial site – you may have to pay the high business rates on the premises. Many people do not bother and if it is a quiet unobtrusive service provided from a desk at home or a virtual company with no real location anywhere, the local authority is unlikely to know about it. Strictly speaking this is illegal, somebody may complain, and it is not a good basis for starting a new business which is expected to become something substantial.

This section is intended as an outline warning rather than as a complete guide to the regulatory aspects of business. Even comprehensive manuals on law for small businesses dodge this issue of licensing, permissions, inspections, etc. Obviously some of the licences are trade-specific, but in addition to pre-registration requirements there is a mass of legislation to which businesses must conform, much of it connected with employment (see Chapter 7). Professional advice may be needed.

BUSINESS STRUCTURE

Sole trader

The simplest business structure is sole trader. It is neat and tidy and requires practically no initial organization, though you should tell the Inland Revenue which passes on the details to Customs and Excise in case you need to register for VAT. Even if you do not trade under your name, it must appear on the letterhead. In fact, the label of sole trader is slightly misleading, since not only people working on their own count under this heading. In legal or tax terminology, it means that one person is the complete owner of the business and of all the profits from it. If there are any losses, that person is also responsible for those.

Since you are the business and the business you, any losses come back to the owner. In other words, you have unlimited personal liability and creditors can in theory come after you for every debt down to, in the conventional phrase, your last cufflink or earring. Creditors can seize all personal assets including house, car and furniture to pay debts and the owner-manager can be made personally bankrupt. In practice, they can make a person living in ostentatiously lavish premises move to a smaller home but even the most flinty-hearted creditor cannot leave a person without a shelter and some minimal personal belongings.

To encourage entrepreneurial activity, the government is keen to encourage the unlucky or the feckless to start again while penalizing bankrupts who are criminally siphoning off creditors' money. It will still be unpleasant.

While that feels dangerous, there is the advantage that a sole trader requires minimal administration. There is unlikely to be any great demand for initial capital – sole traders are almost invariably service businesses and even when craft-based set-ups, the capital requirements are likely to be well within the ceilings set by banks for overdrafts. No accounts have to be filed at Companies House, there is no requirement for an audit, there is no corporation tax to calculate separately and so on. There is VAT to pay when the business revenues top the threshold, but that is about it. The problems will arise with success. The transition to employing somebody can be painful. For that aspect, see Chapter 7 on staffing and Chapter 12 on expansion.

It is relatively easy to turn any business from, say, a sole trader or partnership into an incorporated company. It can be more complicated and expensive to go back, though one can disincorporate. Do not become a company for short-term expediency.

Partnership

There is in theory no need to establish a partnership at all. The business just works that way so it is one. The tax authorities should be notified because, for instance, the VAT thresholds now apply to the whole partnership as opposed to each person in it. In addition, the Inland Revenue requires a tax return for the partnership as a whole. But that is about all that is needed by way of administration. On the other hand, if there are any disputes either among the participants or with the tax authorities, it is easier if there are indicators such as a partnership agreement and a separate bank account. To prevent later acrimony, it is wise to include in the agreement:

- when the partnership starts
- what its business is
- who the partners are
- if there is a senior partner, who it is, and how it is chosen
- how partners can be added
- how partners can leave
- what happens to departing partners' capital
- how much capital each partner is putting in
- whether partners may carry on other business outside the partnership

- the distribution of profits and attribution of losses among partners
- how any surplus is to be distributed
- who owns how much of the capital
- what happens on death or retirement
- how disputes are resolved.

Without a written agreement, the law will follow the rules set out in the Partnership Act 1890.

All the partners are 'jointly and severally' liable for all partnership debts. That means not only unlimited personal liability as for the sole trader, but also that each partner is responsible for the actions of the others. If one of the partners makes a misjudged commercial decision, the debts fall on everyone, and if one of them cannot pay, that share of the liability falls on the others.

Partnerships have advantages. One is a lower rate of National Insurance cost, and since this tax is increasingly burdensome, that has been enough to ensure that the major accountancy firms have remained partnerships. Another benefit is secrecy. Companies must file annual returns at Companies House so their directors and finances are open to inspection by anybody. Partnerships need disclose nothing. The Dutch clothing retailer C&A is a partnership wherever it trades because the owning family wants to discourage prying eyes.

Limited liability partnership (LLP)

To avoid the insecurity of having unlimited personal liability and being obliged to meet other partners' debts another structure was devised. It has most of the benefits of partnerships, including the tax advantages, but limits the liability of each individual partner.

Limiting the partners' liability carries a penalty. To create an LLP you have to fill in an incorporation document and pay £95, and register the name at Companies House. It will also demand an annual return to be filed.

Cooperative

Unlike a partnership, where there can be a senior partner, the cooperative has all the employees as owners and everybody is equal in law. They need to register and adopt a series of forms, and the Industrial Common Ownership Movement and Cooperative Development Agency help with setting up the formalities (see Appendix A, p.263).

Incorporation

There is nothing to stop someone setting up as a sole trader or partnership and deciding to incorporate at a later stage. It is much easier moving in that direction than the reverse. Indeed, there are even some tax benefits. For instance, selling the goodwill of the existing businesses to the new corporation for, say, £30,000 after two years as a sole trader means that after taper relief there is no tax to be paid.

There are many advantages to being a company, and only one disadvantage: cost. It costs more to set up, though that is minimal; it costs much more to administer, including perhaps auditing and filing accounts at Companies House; and it can cost more in tax (e.g. employer and employee National Insurance which can be four times the amount paid as a sole trader). The rate of corporation tax has been reduced at the bottom end, but that is unlikely to make much difference except to businesses so small they cannot support an owner and cannot be commercially justified.

On the other hand, the owners of an incorporated business are not liable for any of the company's debts and if it goes bust they can lose only the money they sank into it in the form of loans or share purchase. Directors or others who have given personal guarantees for the debts are of course still liable, and there is a wide range of penalties for fraudulent or negligent directors, including personal liability, fines and jail.

Among the additional enticements produced by the government to incorporate are reduced starting rates of tax. The tiddlers have to pay tax at only 10 per cent, small companies at 20 per cent, though in practice anybody who falls into such low levels of profit should be able to adjust the financial decisions to eliminate taxable profit altogether. It is certainly an uneconomic level of return, if genuine, which suggests that the tax concessions are more of a political gesture than constructive help to real business.

A company is also more flexible in what it can do and the government has been pushing people towards limited liability companies by steadily eroding the benefits of other forms of organization. For instance, there are tax benefits in selling a company. Finally, it gives the business a certain cachet – it is up there in the big league with the centuries-old traders.

That, anyway, is the theory. In practice, despite the law about limited liability, the directors of a new business are likely to be asked to guarantee its overdrafts, leases, rent and supplier credit. Bang goes the benefit of limited liability from incorporation. That is only at the start though and, as the business grows and acquires assets of its own, the directors should get shot of those liabilities even if it means an argument with the bank.

There are in fact several types of company, including unlimited, and limited by guarantee, but in reality the one most people use is the ordinary limited liability company with shares. This is the one with Ltd after its name. There is also a superleague for large corporations that graduate to the more expensive plc status, but that is not the province of this book.

Incorporation entails certain formal obligations. For instance the certificate of incorporation needs to be displayed, and the company's stationery show the full registered name, the names of either all or none of the directors, place of registration (England or Scotland), registration number, and both the registered and the trading address (young companies often decide to have the auditors' office for their registered address). The name of the company must be displayed outside the premises. Companies must also file annual returns at Companies House and, above a threshold level, those figures have to be audited. They must hold annual general meetings of shareholders which decide whether to approve the annual report and accounts, and elect directors and auditors.

A company can have just the one shareholder, and has to have at least one director, plus a separate company secretary (though even that is being reconsidered). Neither of the roles needs any qualification or experience, but both have a wide range of legal obligations. Those include acting in good faith (putting what is best for the company first, and avoiding conflicts of interest), ensuring the company keeps good accounting records, preparing annual accounts, getting them audited (if it is necessary and required by law), and sending them to shareholders and Companies House. Breaching some of the obligations can make directors personally liable for losses – another exception to the limited liability. They can also be prosecuted, fined and imprisoned.

If the company defaults on its debts, members of the board can be disqualified from acting as directors for a time and a public record is kept of those people. For wrongdoing, the directors are responsible even if they did not know what was going on – the law takes the view that it is their job to know and they should take the trouble to find out. That is, incidentally, a good reason for not lightly taking on non-executive directorships or leaving the running of the business to someone else. There are insurance policies to cover claims against directors on the grounds of breach of duty (see the section on insurance in Chapter 6).

Companies are owned by their shareholders. Shareholders have not lent the company money, they have bought a piece of it. That gives them a raft of rights, including election of directors and appointment of auditors, but does not automatically entitle them to any return. The company pays them a dividend on shares when it decides it can afford to.

People who set up personal service companies (a one-person company through which they provide their work) can come under the Inland Revenue's IR35 rules. These regulations treat them as if they were employees for tax purposes without providing them with the benefits of being employed, unless the people can demonstrate by a number of strict and difficult criteria they really do have an independent business and are not using a company merely as a ploy to reduce their tax. The IR35 catches people such as consultants, software specialists and other experts such as engineers who work on long-term contracts for one company. To find the rules, visit www.inlandrevenue.gov.uk/ir35 or one of several accountancy advice sites.

Registration

Creating a company is simple. The actual documents probably need a professional to draw them up, but they are not complicated. Companies House has a 'starter pack' for people prepared to try a spot of DIY lawyering, and legal stationers have packs of a standard memorandum and articles of association. The documents run to a formula and are easy to get accepted. The requirements and the cost are small: Companies House charges a mere £20 for normal registration, which can take up to a fortnight, and even the faster registration procedure costs only £80.

An alternative route, which is even quicker, is to buy an existing company off the shelf. Organizations like Jordans or F.D. Registrars register them wholesale and will sell you a complete package, including memorandum and articles of association and company seal for £50 to £120. It does not matter if the name is something like Lakebird or Brassfield, which is not the name you have chosen for the business – for a further £10 fee to Companies House the name can be changed. In theory, that also requires an extraordinary general meeting of shareholders passing a special resolution, but for a week-old company that procedure can usually be circumvented.

Memorandum

The company needs a so-called memorandum listing the name (for choosing the name of the business see p.51) and the country (England or Scotland). The memorandum also specifies the objects of the business (i.e. what trade it plans to pursue). It is best to be a little vague in drafting this section. The current aim may be to set up a magazine publisher, soft-drink manufacturer, producer of a new form of hypodermic syringe, marketing adviser, design consultancy or whatever, but a couple of years later you may want to extend the range. The design consultancy may want to help customers test the products and so move into market research; the magazine publisher could be drawn into books, printing, distribution or even advertising; the soft drink company may want to set up its own shops. To avoid acting *ultra vires* (beyond your stated and permitted range), the company would have to ask lawyers to reformulate the document, have it approved by at least 75 per cent of shareholders through a special resolution, and re-register it with Companies House. All this is a bore and an expense. So put in vague clauses in the document saying that anything the directors consider suitable is what the company does.

The memorandum also specifies the nominal and authorized share capital. The registered capital does not have to be paid up or issued so there is nothing to be lost by making it large enough to allow for expansion and the possible need to issue more of it at a later stage. Even the shares that are issued do not have to be paid in full. Therefore, if the three directors of a new business take up £1,000 nominal shares (i.e. they are issued with 1,000 £1 shares – although as the name nominal indicates, that is the face value rather than the price somebody else might pay), they do not have to pay for them in full. They may in fact pay only £100 each at the time. It does mean, however, that if the business collapses they have to put up the rest.

Articles of association

In addition to the memorandum, registration requires an 'article of association', which is the document setting out the company's individual rules. It covers things like the appointment of directors and holding general meetings. It also specifies the procedure for issuing shares, and this is the time to insert safeguards. For instance, you can insert that any additional issues should be offered first to existing shareholders in the proportion of their existing holdings. That can prevent some of the shareholders ganging together to dilute the holding of somebody. Like the memorandum, this document is composed primarily of 'boilerplate' clauses (which lawyers lift unchanged from previous documents).

The Stationery Office booklet on setting up a company has a sample set of articles of association adapted for small businesses.

Other details

Form 10 from Companies House contains the list of directors and secretary together with their occupations, nationality and any directorships held in the previous five years.

Implementation

Once the certificate of registration has been received, the owners take up their shares, the company holds a meeting to appoint directors and secretary, decide the registered office (often an accountants' premises for convenience) and, if necessary, to appoint auditors.

Directors

There may be some renaissance all-round geniuses equally at home composing a symphony, discussing quantum mechanics and tax law, writing theses on plate tectonics, and earning a PhD in molecular biology, but they are probably not reading this book. The rest of us, if we are lucky, have a useful talent which can produce a living. Few indeed are the managers who have a competence, much less a talent, for more than one of the areas required for running a business. There is no shame in being ignorant of finance or a complete duffer at marketing. If you have a knack for selling, you need not be an expert in production, or vice versa. The shame is not admitting to shortcomings. Successful business people happily admit, without a sense of failure, that they needed a brilliant finance expert or sharp production manager to enable them to succeed. Depending on the type of business, one needs to bridge the gaps by hiring good senior managers, getting together with the right sort of people and making them directors, or recruiting the best sort of people as non-executive board members.

An entrepreneur needs enough self-knowledge (see Chapter 1) to recognize weaknesses and gaps in experience. Having the idea that starts a business is in itself quite an achievement, but it will need all sorts of unrelated abilities to make it happen, and an even greater variety of talents to make it succeed. That is why selecting the board and the senior management is vital. Many a young company fails because the person starting it either lacked the talent or the time to do all the jobs.

Entrepreneurs are generally a bit bashful about attempting to recruit senior experienced people on to their boards. That is a mistake. It is astonishing how ready really quite distinguished and successful people are to help out a promising young enterprise. They too are human, and even the most senior and widely acclaimed people at the tops of their sectors have a core of insecurity that responds to flattery. They are flattered to be asked for their advice, and they like being told it is helpful. A surprisingly large number of successful managers also have a sense of wanting to do something for the community which gave them so much. So do not be afraid to ask experienced figures to act as non-executive directors, even if the acquaintanceship is slight. If the worst comes to the worst, they may say they are too busy. If you are lucky, they may consider it a challenge, a way of repaying something to the community, and may take it as a means to return to the basics of business which they left decades before.

There is no point in selecting worthies or placemen. The idle nonentities likely to accept the jobs as a sinecure will not enhance the prestige or reputation of the company. It is also an increasingly passé concept. The old City joke runs: what is the difference between a non-executive director and a supermarket trolley? The answer is the supermarket trolley has a mind of its own.

All directors owe what the law calls a duty of care to the company, and this involves knowledge, skill and diligence. They must act in the best interests of the company as a whole and have regard for employees and creditors. They must also stick to what the memorandum of association specifies, although this is more flexible both because the memorandum can be worded to give almost infinite flexibility and even if it is not, shareholders can ratify actions outside the limits. Failure to do the job conscientiously has nasty legal consequences.

Name

A lot of fuss is occasionally made about naming companies, usually by specialist outfits creating and registering corporate images, to drum up business from major corporations. In fact, the only sensible requirement is that the name be memorable without seeming silly, and the legal requirement is that it should not be confusable with an existing business in a similar territory. The name of the company need not be the same as its products or even as the trading entity. For instance, being called Diageo does not prevent the company selling its porter under the Guinness brand. And who knows what Arcadia or Kingfisher do? Does Shell seem a good name for an oil company, or Bass for beer?

The concern about choosing precisely the right name tends to derive from the feeling that you must create the right image. That assumes customers fall for some carefully burnished gloss, irrespective of what the substance is like underneath (see Chapter 10 for the fallacies in this). Yet it is worth noting at this stage that the company creates the image by what it does, and it will enhance its name with its reputation. It never works the other way round for long.

Some people suggest using a synthetic, nonsense word. George Eastman did it a long time ago with Kodak, but it is dangerous territory, especially if you plan to export. What is just a random collection of letters in Britain may be something obscene in parts of Asia. There are companies specializing in researching this sort of thing, but they do charge a lot for the service and this is, in any case, inappropriate for a start-up. It is probably best to avoid anonymous initials. Yes ICI, IBM and GKN etc. get by, but initials lack character for a new entity.

If the business is to be an incorporated company, then Companies House will ensure there is no clash with existing names. It will also turn away names that contain any of about 130 words proscribed, except by special permission. Anything intended to mislead, criminal or obscene, is banned, and words like Royal, Charity, or anything suggesting it is part of government. The same applies to the addition of labels such as International to the name. The Bank of England has to approve you before you can call yourself a bank. If a proposed name looks or sounds similar to another, it will be turned down. There is the facility to do a name search on the Companies House website or by phone. It may be wise to check with the trademarks registry as well on the same website.

If the enterprise is a partnership or sole trader, an existing corporation may still require its name to be dissimilar or it could take out a legal injunction to prevent passing off. Even in that case, however, it would have to prove that the two were likely to be confused. For instance, the *Daily Star* tried to prevent a tabloid being called the *Star* but the judge ruled that few people were likely to confuse the journal of the Communist Party with a different shaped paper full of pictures of semi-clad girls. The television station Granada failed to prevent Ford launching a car with the same name and, when Warner Brothers tried to stop the Marx Brothers making *A Night in Casablanca* to prevent confusion with its own *Casablanca* classic, Groucho wrote a letter of such scorching ridicule that the studio clearly feared a legal row would make it look silly and it abandoned the threat.

All the same, major companies employ teams of expensive lawyers to protect their reputations and that includes their names and trademarks. Even a tiny resemblance is liable to provoke a broadside of intimidating legal paper which will, at the very least, take much effort and management time to ward off. On balance, it is probably sensible to avoid the trouble by picking names and logos that do not conflict.

As to memorability, it just means you need to be different. If all the companies in the sector are called Tecknosys, Systocrat and so on, then calling yours Mabel would be different. If they are all CNG, RTI, MSD, TLI and so on, Bardolph & Pickwick stands out. And if they are called Hafrington, Fosdycke, Winkleman & Horsenail, or Kline, Verdomt, DuParc & Ivanov, then calling yours Sapphire might be distinctive.

Humour is dangerous. There is nothing funny about being parted from your money. A building contractor called Harry Marks decided to extend the range of his business by setting up a sister company for electrical contracting with a friend called Freddie Burns. They decided to name it after themselves as Marks & Burns Electrical Contractors. It was not universally appreciated. Similarly it may be fun to sell car parts under the name of Clutch Throttle & Choke but whether it would work is a trickier question.

Intellectual property

'*Nam et ipsa scientia potestas est*' said Francis Bacon or, as Hobbes a few years later put it in English, 'Knowledge is power'. It is the intellectual content of a product or service that leads to its success. It is this input of thought and ingenuity that is called intellectual property and, like any property, is protected by law. A wide range of intellectual properties exist, ranging from patents to software.

Patents

You cannot patent an idea, only a mechanism or process. And you cannot patent something that is already known. That means an inventor who has told people all about his brilliant new gadget and how it works, will be refused a patent. That is one of the reasons for getting a well-established patent before contacting people to raise backing. One problem has been that many inventors lack the substantial amounts of money needed to get a patent, especially if they wish to renew it or extend it across several countries, and they need to raise the money first.

Obtaining a patent and holding on to it is a long and expensive process, and getting a European patent through the European Patent Office in Munich is horrendously costly, partly because the text has to be translated into the languages of all the countries where you are seeking protection. It is made even more expensive by using a patent agent, but the chances are that the individual has neither the time nor the expertise to see it through without one.

Enforcing the patent in all those countries is even worse because that depends on the local legislation, which is by no means uniform across the continent.

Trademarks

The three-pointed star of Mercedes, the face of Colonel Sanders for Kentucky Fried Chicken, and the broad tick of Nike are all trademarks. As are the logos of companies. In the words of the Trade Marks Act, it is 'any sign capable of being represented graphically which is capable of distinguishing goods or services of one undertaking from those of other undertakings'. Under the law, trademarks can be words, names, designs, numbers, the shape of the packing or even distinctive colours, smells or tastes.

The problem is not only to devise one that does not infringe existing trademarks and is itself distinctive, attractive and supports the sales of the product, but also to ensure that nobody tries to imitate yours. Although protracted use does give some rights on the grounds that people had come to associate the design with the business and its products, it is still safer to register the looks of it, together with the colours you use. Hints can be found from the Chartered Institute of Patent Agents, the Institute of Trade Mark Attorneys and from the Patent Office itself, including from their websites.

If you have spent time making up a snazzy name for the company, which is different from that of the owners, it may be wise to register it as a trademark, although it costs £300. Even if you do not register others are prevented from creating a similar sounding company and, if they tried to trade under a name (which does not have to be registered at Companies House, oddly enough) that was similar, you might pursue them for 'passing off'. But it would be simpler to register your name.

The right to use a trademark can be lost through lack of use. It can also lose exclusivity of use if it takes on a common name for a product. This is why the lawyers from Rolls-Royce regularly protested to journalists at any phrase such as 'the Leica is the Rolls-Royce of cameras'.

Copyright

Artistic creations such as drawings, writing and music automatically get copyright which lasts for 70 years after the creator's death. That protection is extended to some categories of computer software and industrial designs. Some designs can also be registered if distinctive enough.

Work produced by employees in company time is the property of the employer under the Copyright Designs and Patents Act and, therefore, all copyrights, patents and designs are the company's, unless there is a specific agreement otherwise.

FRANCHISING

Strictly speaking, franchising is not an alternative corporate structure. The main reason for putting the subject here is that the franchise operator will usually supply a complete package to someone coming in to operate an outlet. Although one may still operate as a sole trader or partnership, most franchise operators have a package that takes the worry and decision making out of the initial stages, and sets up the whole business from scratch. Thus, it is a different type of problem and a different type of start.

Think hard about whether franchising suits you. On the one hand, it provides help and safety nets with an established and recognized formula, possibly backed by advertising, and a complete package helping even a novice to get going. The failure rate is tiny compared with the accepted statistic of one-third of start-ups failing within three years.

On the other hand, it limits the range of individual initiative by specifying everything from the way the branch is laid out and painted, to the stationery; the whole procedure has been honed and must be followed. In addition, there are the regular payments of royalties and for supplies to the originator of the system.

As a result, franchising demands a fairly specific temperament. People who want to run their own business, but lack the experience or confidence to strike out without a lifebelt, are probably the most likely candidates for it. Although franchising requires some of the traits needed for an entrepreneur, it is a substantially different approach and needs a mindset suited to the life. For instance:

- The product and service are closely defined so opportunities for individual initiatives are few.
- There is a regular fee – called management fee, royalty, licence fee – payable to the system operator (the franchisor).
- There are limitations on the sale of the business, despite it being an independent operation.
- Often supplies and consumables may be bought only from a system operator who can therefore set the price.
- Outlet operators have little or no influence on overall policy or management.
- If the system operator goes bust, the outlet may be left without a viable independent business.

These are not really major handicaps, but they show the sort of personality that may be happiest with franchising. The first step is to pick the franchise system out of the 700 or so currently available in Britain, and the range is growing continuously. If you think that provides a problem of choice, consider America where there are literally thousands of systems. With such a mass of information and crowds of advisers in the sector, the only problem is where to start. Major banks all have a franchise section with advice and information; several firms of lawyers and accountants have experts on the staff; the British Franchise Association provides guidance; and there are three or four magazines dealing with the subject. There are also three exhibitions a year where the main systems recruit. In addition, two universities have departments keeping an eye on the franchising world: Cranfield and Westminster.

Picking the franchisor

The first step is to choose what sort of trade to be in. The range is bewildering. There are dozens of fast food options, headhunting, banking, garages, hotels, print shops, sex clubs, dancing schools and most lines of retail activity. They include McDonald's hamburgers, Amtrak parcels delivery, Kall Kwik print shops, Autosheen car cleaning, Dominos Pizzas, Dyno-Rod drain clearing, Signs Express, Clarks shoe shops, Appletree Cottage greetings cards, Ventrolla sash windows, Molly Maid home and office cleaning, and EVP Recruitment.

Once you have picked the sector, the aim is to find a system that is agreeable, well run and compatible. You are really looking for not just a good product, but one that has been packaged effectively to make it readily reproducible as a successful and profitable outlet. The important questions to ask include:

- Are these people the sort one could work with, and are the rules and financial demands reasonable?
- Is the system profitable for the outlets and is it getting better?
- Did the franchisor provide the training and initial help as promised and are the products good enough?
- Are supplies from the franchise system operator good value and delivered promptly?
- How strict are the rules on operating the outlet and are demands reasonable or just bureaucratic?

If the way into the business is through buying an existing franchise, it is probably wise to get this sort of information from those with nothing to gain or lose by being honest.

Checking on a franchise company's stability is pretty easy. For a start, it helps if it is a member of the British Franchise Association. Next, talk to the bank. All the big four banks – Royal Bank of Scotland (which also owns NatWest), Barclays, HSBC and Lloyds TSB – have well-established franchise departments with access to histories of all the principal operations. The bank may surreptitiously tip the wink about which of the franchise systems is overly greedy or difficult, or which helps its outlets extensively, and which produces fair profits. If one of these banks is reluctant to provide financial help to start a franchise outlet, there is either something amiss with the financial background of the person asking for the loan, or the franchise itself is flaky.

For a personal assessment, visit a few of the existing outlets and ask the people running them what they think of the organization, terms and methods of working. This is even more important if it is a fairly new system. One must then discover whether the system has been properly established and is stable; whether the system operator has run pilot outlets to check how well the formula can be replicated; and how good the back-up is for individual outlets. Do the people running the operation know what they are doing?

Another filter may be the amount of money required for starting. The money may include the cost of premises and kitting it out, the price of equipment, and the licence down-payment (though beware of systems which demand a lot of money up front).

There is a wide range of other criteria for selecting the favoured system, from the degree of freedom allowed to individual outlets to the geographical area currently available, and from the hours worked to the details of the contract including the bits about buying consumables. Martin Mendelsohn of legal firm Eversheds, estimates there are 52 questions a really conscientious investigator would ask before picking the system to go with.

Franchise systems are not all equally developed – they range from recent ones, which are barely past the experimental stage, to those which are still relatively new but have established a few dozen outlets (it takes about three years to sort the problems out of a system and to get it running smoothly), to a few well-known names which have thousands of franchisees operating the system, possibly all round the world. Another decision to make is whether to be in at the beginning when the formula may still be open to adaptation in the light of experience, with the concomitant danger that the company is less well established and more financially precarious, or to go for a venerable but experienced business that has established its name and sorted out its system.

The contract

Finally, before deciding on which system to opt for, look at the proposed contract very carefully. Among the details, check:

- all the financial details are present: royalties, fees, contribution to advertising, franchisor support
- the length of the contract, what happens at the end of it and what the conditions are for renewing it
- whether you can assign or sell the franchise and, if so, under what conditions
- under what conditions and with what consequences either side can terminate the contract
- how disputes are settled and if there is some arbitration procedure
- what happens in the case of your illness or death
- if there are restrictive covenants on running other businesses during or after the franchise period.

PROFESSIONAL ADVISERS

New businesses are unlikely to get going without taking professional advice, from accountants and lawyers at the very least, probably insurance brokers, and possibly architects and doctors. The trouble with most of these professions is that it is rather like submitting a car or a hi-fi to a repairer: there is no doubt the task needs an expert but how are you to know whether this person is a careful, experienced expert or an incompetent buffoon? One does not know enough about the specific subjects to see wool in front of the eyes. In other words there are two problems inherent in the process of using the professions: finding a good one, and then being sure the advice is right.

Finding the right one

Finding the right professional advisers such as accountants or lawyers for a business is just as difficult as finding the right doctor, dentist, osteopath or architect. There is also the additional problem of finding different ones for different tasks – you would not use an obstetrician for a cardiac operation. In the same way, the accountant who is first rate for preparing the business plan and finding a backer may not be ideal for auditing or tax advice.

Some people stand in awe of professionals, yet the only difference between them and other tradesmen who supply a service is the longer period of study. Professions do have codes of ethics and may be rather proud of their elevated moral status, but fundamentally you are the customer and they provide a service. That service can be variable, and we have all heard horror stories of people's conveyancing, tax affairs, or divorce completely fouled up despite a massive bill for the failed service. This is a warning that it is worthwhile shopping around.

Only a member of the Law Society may be called a solicitor, but anyone may be called an accountant, and that does not mean just turf accountants. It is worth checking that the person offering help is a member of one of the major bodies, preferably one of the five major professional bodies:

- Institute of Chartered Accountants in England & Wales
- Institute of Chartered Accountants of Scotland
- Institute of Chartered Accounts in Ireland
- Association of Chartered Certified Accountants
- Chartered Institute of Management Accountants.

To audit is not enough to be a member of one of these bodies, the accountant also has to be licensed to do the work.

Do not go for the firm just down the road because it happens to be close, nor somebody met socially. Ask around. Friends, relations, other businessmen, members of the golf or Rotary club will probably all have used a professional at some stage, and might have recommendations and warnings. However, it is like asking the way in a strange town. The chances are the first two you ask will almost certainly point in different directions, so go on asking until some consensus seems to be developing.

How to use them

The first problem is how to find a sensible adviser, the second problem is how to judge the advice given. Even when you have found as good a professional as can reasonably be expected, you cannot be certain that on any specific problem the advice is totally right. Like anybody else, even the most distinguished of professionals can be wrong, and frequently what they provide is not a fact but an opinion. Since it is backed by qualifications, extensive learning and experience, it should be respected but not accepted blindly. They are only human as well and can be wrong, prejudiced, ignorant or dim like the rest of us. At the very least ask for reasons, and always test advice against common sense. If the suggestions seem illogical, get a second opinion.

This applies with even greater force to bank managers. They are employed by the bank to supply money transaction services. As part of the service they will listen and give some advice, but that is not their primary job, nor are they qualified to be experts in any aspect of it. Do sound out the bank manager, but bear in mind that the advice is simply a few years of second-hand experience speaking, and the manager is not a financial guru.

Insurance brokers are also fallible. They find the best buy from their computer based on the stated criteria. However, they are not on-line to every insurance company or Lloyd's syndicate, and even if they were they may not know about the whole range of policies on offer. Presumably as Internet links and database software get better so will the brokers but, in the meantime, it is probably best to ask three of them to quote and check on expensive policies by doing a spot of ringing round yourself.

If all of this sounds contrary and hard work, then the message is getting through. The longer you run a business, the more you realize that few things are done one-tenth as well as you can do them, and that half the time most people purporting to give you information are bluffing. Scepticism and boundless curiosity are the safeguards against being taken for an expensive ride, not just by professionals, but by suppliers, customers, financiers and tradesmen. A frustrating and demanding course of action is always to insist on getting good service. As Somerset Maugham put it, 'It is a funny thing about life; if you refuse to accept anything but the best you very often get it.'

Perhaps the wisest position to adopt is that of a four-year-old child: for ever asking why. Never be afraid of asking stupid questions – if something is unclear the fault is not yours but that of the expert who was unable to put his subject into comprehensible language. Always remember you are paying for the service, and ultimately the business depends on your judgment. Professionals can provide help and information, but the decision must come from the manager, so accept nothing blindly.

Choices cannot be subcontracted. The accountant may explain the possible consequences of alternative courses but cannot be expected to subvert management by deciding between them. Sometimes a professional may say a course is dangerous – you might be sued, for example – but the manager may still decide this opinion is based on traditional caution and the dangers are not as great as suggested, or even that the risk is worth running.

Costs

Another consequence of taking responsibility for decisions is to resist fleeing to the lawyer or accountant at every difficulty. This will save you money and time, and will ensure the people in charge of the company really understand what is going on. For instance, when faced with a tortuously written proposed contract, it is worth taking a little time and effort to see if some concentrated attention might unravel the thinking behind the murky clauses without leaning on a lawyer every time.

There is no table of set fees. Professional firms usually charge by the amount of time spent on the customer, and the price depends on whether a partner, a manager or a junior did the work. This is one reason for not rushing to them at every difficulty. It also suggests negotiation of fees is possible. Most professionals take a slightly Robin Hood approach and let their large and rich clients subsidize the new impoverished ones, and if you gently twist their arms they may cut the fee.

A logical extension of this is the need to shop around. Talk to several firms, ask what they are planning to charge and, if you are getting help raising finance, whether they will work on a contingency fee. Nevertheless the lowest-cost professional is not necessarily the best buy.

Insurance brokers are even harder to judge. One may not discover for a very long time that there is cheaper cover available from other sources, or that the insurance company the broker has picked is notoriously sticky about paying for a particular class of claim. Once again, it is merely a question of trying a few and asking among acquaintances. Insurance broking is a paradoxical example of how one pays the piper without calling the tune. The broker is supposed to be the agent of the insured – there are laws governing agency relations, but in essence an agent is an extension of the employer – yet it is paid by the insurance company with which it places the policy. Not only that, but the size of that completely legal kick-back is related to the amount of the premium. This means brokers have to be strong-minded and professional to press for lower premiums for their clients. It is a paradoxical position but hallowed by long practice.

Banks

According to the Competition Commission, there is not much to choose between the four major banking groups, which between them have nearly 90 per cent of the small businesses as customers. The Commission's report said the major banks do not compete awfully hard on price or on anything else much either. Certainly none of them consistently come top in the surveys of small business opinions, but they do have different packages which might appeal. The same probably applies to the tariff of charges – it is rather like trying to chase the best interest rates among the banks, bonds and building societies. One would have to move every few weeks to keep up or down with the latest best rate, and in the medium term it is unlikely to be worth it. But by all means have a look at the latest issue of *Business Moneyfacts* magazine for the array of offers at the moment.

There are also seven other banks struggling to grab a share of this market and they might be worth investigating. The only obvious drawback to using one of the smaller banks is a relative dearth of branches. But if one of them has a branch near you or if there is no continual need for a physical presence (for instance, for you to pay in the cash takings of a shop), it is definitely worth asking the questions because they do try harder. In any case, most experts advise keeping the business and personal accounts at different banks.

One way to separate the banks is to interview the managers and ask about overdraft and loan facilities (assuming the company will need them, at least in the early days). Things like interest rate above base, degree of security required, any promises about not calling in the loan without notice, and criteria for the size of overdraft and loan may help to decide which one to pick.

Do not choose the bank for the expertise of the manager – managers shift around at a fair speed. Chapter 5 also covers how to deal with banks.

4 Business plans

Chapter 2 showed how to construct a cash-flow forecast to indicate whether the business idea was likely to be commercially successful. The forecast shows fairly easily how much money will be needed and when. The accumulated cash-flow gap in the initial stages (or even later) is bridged by some form of external finance, and the spreadsheet shows what the total gap is likely to be by adding up all the negative cash flows. Always raise more, however, because whatever the plans say, it will not be enough. And that applies even if you add a contingency reserve. As with construction contracts, the contingencies and the unexpected are always greater than the provisions for them. It is reminiscent of Hofstadter's Law: it always takes longer than you expect even when you take account of Hofstadter's Law. One of the commonest mistakes of entrepreneurs is to start out underfunded, run into a serious cash shortage about 18 months in and then be forced to go cap in hand to financiers who will unquestionably extort painful terms for the extra funding.

It is not just greed and the entrepreneur's poor bargaining position that prompts financiers to be so demanding. Their assessment of risk changed because the managers are now seen as not astute enough to foresee problems. To offset the more worrying picture they now have, they demand tougher terms. That is yet another reason for getting more than you could possibly need. The other aspect is that if the original amount raised turns out to be more than enough, the entrepreneur gains a gold star – it impresses bankers if you do not draw down all the facilities arranged.

There is also a tendency in the planning to forget the company's managers will still have to eat, buy clothes for their children and pay the mortgage during the starting period when the business is generating little or no income and certainly cannot afford to keep the participants.

That initial cash-flow exercise will prove to have been well worth the effort when it is incorporated in the more elaborate business plan needed for raising backing.

SEEKING ADVICE

Before even thinking about what goes into a business plan, much less before getting as far as drawing one up, the intelligent entrepreneur asks for advice. The best defences against financial disaster are common sense and scepticism. Moreover, the scepticism should stretch to one's own beliefs, assumptions, prejudices and conclusions. The point is that even our most strongly held beliefs, knowledge and theories could be wrong. Since we are none of us infallible, test out ideas on somebody you know whose judgment you trust. Even if you do not, in the event, follow the advice, getting an additional perspective is always valuable. Receivers and liquidators note that one of the commonest mistakes of young businesses, and one of the principal causes of collapse, is the failure to take advice. As confirmation of that finding, many entrepreneurs, both initial failures and struggling successes, have explained that if they were starting from scratch now, the one thing they would change would be to turn to people for advice sooner and more often. This applies from the start of the process in preparing the business plan, but even more so when the business is getting under way. Some people refuse to do so from pride or arrogance and some because they do not know where to turn.

As the Bible reminds us, 'Pride goeth before destruction and an haughty spirit before a fall.' There is nothing to be proud of in ignorance and the only way to learn is to ask. As for finding sources of help – small businesses are spoiled for choice. Most banks now have a small business unit, the Department of Trade has a small business section, there is a Small Business Service, there are Business Links around the country, and associations for small businesses have experts on tap.

There are also courses. The intelligent ones realize somebody just starting out in business has little time for anything other than the work in hand, and so they run them at the weekend. Business Links, the DTI, and local Enterprise Agencies have information on what is available. The drawback of course is that some of it may be obvious or the sort of things one already knows. Yet the advantages are of learning short cuts and techniques, and being able to question the lecturers on more specialized topics. People who have been on these courses also say there is a lot to be learnt from the other people there, simply by swapping experience.

All of this is in addition to the help one can get from setting up a sensible board with experienced non-executive directors (see Chapter 3).

HOW TO WRITE PLANS

There are two reasons for writing business plans. One is to clear the mind about what the company is doing, where it is going, and how it will get there. The other is to present financiers with a convincing outline of what the business is about and why it is worth backing. The first one need be only a simple set of statements attended by an elaborate and highly realistic set of cash-flow forecasts. Any manager hoping to keep control of the business will need one of these with a set of ratios to check how well things are going. That is discussed in Chapter 8. However, this chapter deals more with the sort of plan that opens the cheque books of financiers.

The cash-flow forecast already prepared for the exercise in Chapter 2 may be the core of a business plan, but represents only a small portion of the total. The sample sheet here, gives an indication of a comprehensive breakdown of costs and revenues investors like to have and managers need. The one in Chapter 2 derived from an actual business plan, with the figures and headings only slightly altered. The reason for showing both is to show what may be needed and what, in some cases, can be presented to potential backers. As it happens, subsequent additional information changed the projections of Newco (an actual attempted business launch) and it began to look

2 Sample Balance Plan

Cash-flow forecast outgoings

month	1	2	3
Premises			
capital cost/rent/lease [1]			
repair & maintenance [2]			
service charge [2]			
business rates [3]			
installation costs [4]			
Plant			
bought equipment [5]			
installation [5]			
office equipment [6]			
Stock/raw materials [7]			
Staffing			
wages [8]			
commission/bonuses [8]			
Travel/entertaining [9]			
Tax			
corporation tax [10]			
National Insurance [11]			
PAYE [12]			
VAT [13]			

month	1	2	3
Marketing			
advertising [14]			
public relations [14]			
market research [14]			
sales [15]			
Professional fees			
lawyers [16]			
accountants [17]			
Insurance [18]			
building			
employer's liability			
public/product liability			
other			
Electricity [19]			
Telephone [20]			
Postage [21]			
Stationery [21]			
Loan interest [22]			
Dividends [23]			
Administration [24]			
Other/misc [25]			
TOTAL OUTGOINGS			

Cash-flow forecast income

month	1	2	3
Cash from sales [26]			
VAT net receipts [27]			
Sale of assets [28]			
Interest received [29]			
Owners' capital introduced [30]			

month	1	2	3
External capital introduced [30]			
Loans [31]			
TOTAL INCOME			
Cash flow			
Opening bank balance			
Closing bank balance			

* Superscript figures refer to notes

less happy as a prospect, especially in view of the return backers demanded. The project was abandoned, but it still provides a useful, real life illustration. Better to discontinue at this stage than a year into the deal when all the money has been spent and the people involved are out of work and out of pocket.

As well as the summary spreadsheet of the cash flow (see p.18–21), it is useful to provide supplementary sheets showing how the figures were derived – more detailed projections than can comfortably be included in the main table. These might, for instance, show how the costs of raw materials were made up or how the sales would move through the various outlets (see pp.70–1 and 72–3).

Investors prefer the cash-flow spreadsheets to be supplemented by projected profit and loss accounts, and even balance sheets. In many cases that can be unrealistic and one can tell them so, but sometimes there is enough information, or at least sufficiently good projections, to provide plausible figures (see pp.74–5). The final document is likely to be 30 or 40 pages thick in addition to the section showing the figures.

You would not lend a used 10p stamp to most new businesses on the basis of the plans they present to potential financiers. At least if you were sane. These would-be managers seem to imagine that it is enough to say they have a brilliant idea for making a fortune, and anyone who does not immediately acclaim them must be an ill-bred swine for doubting their word or a complete buffoon not to see the obvious. The inability to put oneself in the shoes of the buyer – in this case the financier who is the buyer of the idea – does not augur well for business success. The failure to check whether there really is a business at all is a good sign that the person is unsuited for running a business.

Imagining what the other side needs is paramount in preparing a plan. What you imagine or know is beside the point; what matters is how potential investors see it. If this is a document for raising money, you have to remember who will be reading it. Financiers know about managing money, but you need to fill them in on your business. The investment will be based in part on what they understand of the plan and in part on an evaluation of the team behind it.

3 Pricing

Grocers Pricing Structure - CORDIALS: Drink 1 - 375ml

	Type 1	**Type 2**	**Type 3**	**Type 4**
Retail price £	2.59	2.59	2.59	2.59
VAT £	0.39	0.39	0.39	0.39
Ex VAT £	2.20	2.20	2.20	2.20
Retail Gross Margin - 43% £	0.95	0.95	0.95	0.95
Trade Price £	1.26	1.26	1.26	1.26
Trade Price per case £	**15.08**	**15.08**	**15.08**	**15.08**
Syrup per litre £	2.76	1.53	1.62	2.06
Syrup per bottle £	0.52	0.29	0.30	0.39
Pasteurising £	0.09	0.09	0.09	0.09
Bottle £	0.18	0.18	0.18	0.18
Labels £	0.10	0.10	0.10	0.10
Tray/Shrink £	0.01	0.01	0.01	0.01
Delivery Charge £1.50/.13per bottle £	0.13	0.13	0.13	0.13
Total Cost per bottle £	1.03	0.79	0.81	0.89
Total Cost per case £	**12.30**	**9.53**	**9.74**	**10.72**
Our Margin per bottle £	0.23	0.46	0.44	0.36
Our Margin per case £	**2.78**	**5.55**	**5.34**	**4.36**
Our % margin	18	37	35	29

Wholesale Pricing Structure - CORDIALS: Drink 1 - 375ml

	Type 1	**Type 2**	**Type 3**	**Type 4**
Retail price £	2.99	2.99	2.99	2.99
VAT £	0.45	0.45	0.45	0.45
Ex VAT £	2.54	2.54	2.54	2.54
Retailer Margin - 35% £	0.89	0.89	0.89	0.89
Trade Price £	1.65	1.65	1.65	1.65
Wholesaler Margin @ 15% £	0.25	0.25	0.25	0.25
Wholesale Price £	1.41	1.41	1.41	1.41
W/S Price per case £	**16.95**	**16.95**	**16.95**	**16.95**
Syrup per litre £	2.76	1.53	1.62	2.06
Syrup per bottle £	0.52	0.29	0.30	0.39
Pasteurising £	0.09	0.09	0.09	0.09
Bottle £	0.18	0.18	0.18	0.18
Labels £	0.10	0.10	0.10	0.10
Tray/Shrink £	0.01	0.01	0.01	0.01
Delivery Charge £1.50/.13per bottle £	0.13	0.13	0.13	0.13
Total Cost per bottle £	1.03	0.79	0.81	0.89
Total Cost per case £	**12.30**	**9.53**	**9.74**	**10.72**
Our Margin per bottle £	0.38	0.61	0.59	0.51
Our Margin per case £	**4.57**	**7.34**	**7.13**	**6.15**
Our % margin	23	37	36	31

* plus 15% on syrup for organic sugar throughout.

Grocers Pricing Structure - CORDIALS: Drink 2 - 750ml

	Type 1	Type 2	Type 3	Type 4
Retail price £	1.99	1.99	1.99	1.99
VAT £	0.30	0.30	0.30	0.30
Ex VAT £	1.69	1.69	1.69	1.69
Retail Gross Margin - 43% £	0.73	0.73	0.73	0.73
Trade Price £	0.97	0.97	0.97	0.97
Trade Price per case £	**11.58**	**11.58**	**11.58**	**11.58**
Syrup per litre £	0.20	0.11	0.12	0.15
Syrup per bottle £	0.15	0.08	0.09	0.11
Pasteurising £	0.09	0.09	0.09	0.09
Bottle £	0.18	0.18	0.18	0.18
Labels £	0.10	0.10	0.10	0.10
Tray/Shrink £	0.01	0.01	0.01	0.01
Delivery Charge £1.50/.13per bottle £	0.13	0.13	0.13	0.13
Total Cost per bottle £	0.66	0.59	0.59	0.62
Total Cost per case £	**7.86**	**7.07**	**7.13**	**7.41**
Our Margin per bottle £	0.31	0.38	0.37	0.35
Our Margin per case £	**3.72**	**4.51**	**4.45**	**4.17**
Our % margin	0.32	0.39	0.38	0.36

Wholesale Pricing Structure - CORIDALS: Drink 2 - 750ml

	Type 1	Type 2	Type 3	Type 4
Retail price £	2.05	2.05	2.05	2.05
VAT £	0.31	0.31	0.31	0.31
Ex VAT £	1.74	1.74	1.74	1.74
Retailer Margin - 35% £	0.61	0.61	0.61	0.61
Trade Price £	1.13	1.13	1.13	1.13
Wholesaler Margin @ 15% £	0.17	0.17	0.17	0.17
Wholesale Price £	0.96	0.96	0.96	0.96
W/S Price per case £	**11.57**	**11.57**	**11.57**	**11.57**
Syrup per litre £	0.20	0.11	0.12	0.17
Syrup per bottle £	0.15	0.08	0.09	0.13
Pasteurising £	0.09	0.09	0.09	0.09
Bottle £	0.18	0.18	0.18	0.18
Labels £	0.10	0.10	0.10	0.10
Tray/Shrink £	0.01	0.01	0.01	0.01
Delivery Charge £1.50/.13per bottle £	0.13	0.13	0.13	0.13
Total Cost per bottle £	0.66	0.59	0.59	0.64
Total Cost/case £	**7.86**	**7.07**	**7.13**	**7.63**
Our Margin per bottle £	0.31	0.37	0.37	0.33
Our Margin per case £	**3.70**	**4.49**	**4.43**	**3.93**
Our % margin	0.27	0.33	0.33	0.29

4 Sales Projections

2001	Jan	Feb	Mar	Apr	May	June
Product 1						
New Outlets					40	40
Outlet Build					40	80
Attrition Rate – 3%					–	–
Total Outlets					40	80
ROS					–	–
Total Vol					–	–
Assumptions						
Waitrose for Xmas (Nov)						

2002	Jan	Feb	Mar	Apr	May	June
Product 1						
New Outlets	16	40	40	40	40	70
Outlet Build	171	211	251	291	331	401
Attrition Rate – 3%	5	6	8	9	10	12
Total Outlets	166	205	243	282	321	389
ROS	5.3	5	5	5	5	5
Total Vol	906	1,055	1,255	1,455	1,655	2,005
Product 2						
New Outlets					40	70
Outlet Build					40	110
Attrition Rate - 3%					-	-
Total Outlets					40	110
ROS					4	6
Total Vol					160	660
Assumptions						
Intro of Prod 2 - 4/02						
Waitrose expansion - 4/02						
Grow alternative channels						

July	Aug	Sept	Oct	Nov	Dec	Total
16	16	16	16	46	16	206
96	112	128	144	190	206	206
–	3	4	4	6	6	–
96	109	124	140	184	200	200
4	4	4	4	5.3	5.3	27
384	448	512	576	1,007	1,092	4,019

July	Aug	Sept	Oct	Nov	Dec	Total
100	30	30	30	30	30	360
501	531	561	591	621	651	651
15	16	17	18	19	20	–
486	515	544	573	602	631	631
6	6	6	6	5.3	5.3	44.62
3,006	3,186	3,366	3,546	3,291	3,450	28,177
40	40	40	40	40	40	350
150	190	230	270	310	350	350
–	6	7	8	9	11	–
150	184	223	262	301	340	340
6	6	6	6	6	6	–
384	1,140	1,380	1,620	1,860	2,100	9,304

5 Five-year profit and loss statement original

	2001	2002	2003	2004	2005
Product 1					
Volume in Cases	4,019	28,177	40,000	50,000	60,000
Sales Revenue £	68,119	437,655	639,935	823,916	1,018,360
Cost of Goods £	42,197	295,857	432,600	556,973	688,418
Gross Profit £	**25,921**	**141,797**	**207,335**	**266,944**	**329,942**
%	38	32	32	32	32
Product 2					
Volume in Cases	0	9,304	68,000	118,000	151,000
Sales Revenue £	0	110,973	811,063	1,449,656	1,910,721
Cost of Goods £	0	73,129	534,480	955,304	1,259,140
Gross Profit £	**0**	**37,843**	**276,583**	**494,352**	**651,581**
%		34	34	34	34
Total Volume in Cases	4,019	37,481	108,000	168,000	211,000
Total Sales Revenue £	68,119	548,627	1,450,998	2,273,572	2,929,081
Total Cost of Goods £	42,197	368,987	967,080	1,512,277	1,947,558
Total Gross Profit £	25,921	179,641	483,918	761,295	981,523
% of sales	38	33	33	33	34
Marketing £	33,610	56,221	162,000	252,000	316,500
% of sales	49	10	11	11	11
Overheads £	184,025	239,233	251,194	313,754	359,442
% of sales	270	44	17	14	12
Operating Profit £	**–191,714**	**–115,813**	**70,724**	**195,542**	**305,582**
Total Avg Outlets	147	500	1,200	1,400	1,500
ROS per annum	28	70	90	120	144
Total Vol	4,116	35,000	108,000	168,000	216,000

Five-year profit and loss statement – Brand A only

	2001	2002	2003	2004	2005
Product 1					
Volume in Cases	4,019	28,177	35,000	40,000	50,000
Sales Revenue £	68,122	437,655	559,943	659,133	848,634
Cost of Goods £	42,200	295,857	378,525	445,578	573,682
Gross Profit £	**25,923**	**141,797**	**181,418**	**213,555**	**274,952**
%	38	32	32	32	32
Product 2					
Volume in Cases	0	9,304	37,000	80,000	127,800
Sales Revenue £	0	110,877	440,933	981,969	1,615,756
Cost of Goods £	0	73,129	290,820	647,664	1,065,683
Gross Profit £	**0**	**37,747**	**150,113**	**334,305**	**550,074**
%		34	34	34	34
Total Volume in Cases	4,019	37,481	72,000	120,000	177,800
Total Sales Revenue £	68,122	548,532	1,000,876	1,641,102	2,464,390
Total Cost of Goods £	42,200	368,987	669,345	1,093,242	1,639,364
Total Gross Profit £	25,923	179,545	331,531	547,860	825,026
% of sales	38	33	33	33	33
Marketing £	33,610	56,221	82,800	138,000	204,470
% of sales	49	10	8	8	8
Overheads £	184,025	239,233	246,409	258,730	271,666
% of sales	270	44	25	16	11
Operating Profit £	**–191,712**	**–115,909**	**2,321**	**151,130**	**348,889**
Total Avg Outlets	147	500	800	1,000	1,200
ROS per annum	28	70	90	120	144
Total Vol	4,116	35,000	72,000	120,000	172,800

Consequently, the plan has to be in language that means something to the financiers. They will not know about specialist products or services, although they will almost certainly take advice from experts in the sector to see if the assertions and assumptions in the plan sound plausible. In the first instance, you have to engage their attention to make sure the document is one of the 15 per cent of business plans that are not immediately rejected as unworthy of serious study.

Here is the first real test of whether a person has the stuff of which rich capitalists are made: effective selling skills. The first sales task is persuading people with money to put it into a questionable nascent business – since a third of new companies fail in the first three years, to an investor they are all questionable or at the very least, suspect.

What sort of reassurance is needed to get a person to part with precious cash? The answer is, lots. They are not short of money, but they are insecure and worry about losing it. Large numbers of their previous investments have failed and if they make too many mistakes the fund managers are out of a job. They would have turned down 12 propositions that morning because they were not absolutely certain the money would be safe.

Content

Business plans do not all have to follow a predetermined pattern in approach or content, nor are they all laid out identically. You can even be innovative in the presentation, but only for a good reason. There is little point in trying to be different to gain attention. If the managers of the business have flair, energy, imagination and drive, it should come through in the conversations – flashy presentations for their own sakes can make staid money handlers nervous. Financiers will look to see if you are trying to distract them from a lack of substance.

Yes, that sounds like a contradiction of the earlier advice about being effective salespeople and getting the message across – almost an instruction to be boring – but managers of investment funds are conservative, careful people. On the other hand, this rule can also be broken, but only for a good reason. If you opt for a touch of theatre, it is best to be aware of the dangers.

By the same token, this section indicates what sort of plans financiers are used to seeing. It enables them to compare the good ones with the duffers more easily. That does not mean it has to be slavishly followed. Logic, selling skill and business demands are more important than absolute conformity.

Until they have evidence to the contrary, financiers assume entrepreneurs are unrealistic dreamers, perhaps with a good idea, but without much contact with the real world of money. The managers of the business, however, may find many of the money men have an absence of understanding about commerce or the realities of the market. The fund managers know the theory perfectly well, have read the textbooks and passed the exams, but the practicalities of small business running are alien to them. Even if you have a good business plan, so well tested you can answer any question immediately, reasonable prospects, and so on, raising the necessary cash is a test of the entrepreneur's mental resilience. It takes patience, tact and a readiness to explain what may seem obvious. It will not help the case to call the financiers ignorant, dim and crassly unable to pay attention. They may come from a different background and so need to have your world explained. They have to explain the world of finance to you, and in return you explain the world of your small business to them.

Executive summary

Business plans should start with an executive summary (though not necessarily labelled so). This sums up, in a few concise paragraphs, what the product or service is, who it is aimed at, why they will buy it, and what the result will be. Either within that or as a separate sheet there should be a summary of the business concept: what it is you are trying to do in general terms. If the product is a new one, explain what it does and how it works, and especially what its benefits are compared with existing solutions. In some cases the readers may have to sign a confidentiality agreement to see that section.

There is much talk in textbooks about SWOT analysis in business plans: strengths, weaknesses, opportunities and threats. This is certainly a valuable way of looking at the challenges the young business will encounter, but it is rather limited and a cliché; the summary is probably better off looking at the commercial environment from a common sense perspective rather than merely applying a formula from a book.

An executive summary should seldom exceed two pages, three at the outside.

Senior staff

Usually after the executive summary, comes a list of people who will make it happen. In some ways this is the vital part of the plan. Brilliant managers can make money in a slump, and incompetents cannot sell a glass of water in the Sahara. More than anything else the backers are deciding on the people – can these managers do what they promise and react swiftly and sensibly when things go sour?

That is why the document contains a list of directors, including non-executives, and senior managers, with a potted CV on each bringing out the relevant experience for their posts, spelling out precisely what they have done and where. The idea is to present a team that is competent, keen and experienced, and also complementary in covering all the important areas of management. A balanced team is needed with expertise in all the key areas such as finance and marketing, although greater specialist expertise is sometimes needed at a later stage.

Some people include a tentative organization chart showing who is at the head of which stream of expertise, but this is needed only in businesses planning to start with large numbers of staff.

If there are still gaps in the structure, or extra people will have to be brought on board as the project progresses, say so, and preferably indicate where the people are coming from. That includes potential recruits to be non-executive directors.

The market

The next section of the document is usually an assessment of the market. This analyses who sells what to whom, at what price and why, where the gap in the market is assumed to be and what the competition is doing. If feasible, there can be a table showing what the competition has in the way of alternative products. There should also be some indication of the prices and characteristics of the alternative products. A word of warning: do not say in the plan that the product or service has no competition. That makes financiers very nervous about the realism of the managers; they well know there is no product or service without competition. If they see a claim like that, they discount all the other statements by a hefty margin on the assumption that they are equally exaggerated and unrealistic.

From the market analysis will derive the strategy for the new business and why its unique selling point is expected to appeal. In other words, you have to be able to say why people will want to buy.

There are several approaches to this. One is to say the new product is a marked improvement on the ones currently available, for the following list of reasons. ('Product' here is used to refer to a service as well as a tangible manufactured item.) Another is to suggest that the product is a replacement or alternative to the existing products. Another approach may be market segmentation.

In each case, the plan will need to spell out why the competition will not merely react with a similar or even better product to cut short the newcomer's market entry, or what the new business plans to do when the established companies start fighting back.

If the product or service is a new one, there has to be a thorough explanation of why competition will not emulate it. If it is a technological advance, this requires all sorts of protection, with design and copyright registration, patents and other forms of legal protection. You will have already hinted at this in the executive summary at the start, but here the point has to be discussed in detail. Being first is not enough; there must be reassurance a major corporation with huge resources cannot move in and grab the market the fledgling business has explored.

Production

Now you start getting down to the detail of how it will be done. This is where the production details are spelt out for manufacturers, or the organization for services. You spell out the equipment needed, where it is to come from and how much it costs, plus the source of raw materials or other inputs, with details like quality control.

Distribution/Marketing

Backers like to see some evidence of the systems for reaching the customer. So, for instance, if the product is being distributed through shops, mention any discussions that have already started with Tesco, Sainsbury, Waitrose, Safeway, Asda, and Morrisons and the rest, and what the reactions or promises have been. If sales are going through agents or independent resellers, indicate how many there are and where, what terms they have demanded, and how many of them are likely to be prepared to act.

Cash-flow spreadsheets

The centrepiece of the financial section is the cash-flow forecasts. If you can construct profit and loss accounts and balance sheets all the better, but despite what some people say, they are not vital. The contents of the spreadsheets need a certain negotiator's cunning. It is best to do the initial explanatory work on three assumptions – happy, gloomy and realistic.

The pessimistic assumptions will assume interest rates rise, inflation gets worse, sales are initially very low and rise only very slowly after large expenditure on marketing. It will show people paying later than you could possibly imagine, and the economy becoming sluggish.

The second set shows reasoned optimism. If everything goes your way, and without being foolishly euphoric about the market, the economy and customers, this is how things might progress.

Thirdly, somewhere in between the two, is a conservative but reasonable outcome. All three pictures, however, will evolve only very slowly because this whole process is an iterative mechanism: if that number of people advertise in the magazine, the selling cost can be this, and that will suggest a certain level of circulation or vice versa. But what if it is only half that? What will that do to advertising revenue, paper costs and postage? If it is a soft drink, how will sales change if a major competitor brings out something similar, if the weather turns cold, if the EU produces more directives on ingredients?

There are other factors to take into account, such as a probable seasonal element to which many businesses are subject.

Exactly the same sort of process is possible for most products or services. You simply have to decide who will buy it, which depends on the potential customers, the methods of reaching them, the competition – including alternative products – and the price.

The spreadsheet presented in the document for backers should not be the realistic one but something tending a little towards the happy, but without being silly about it. This is because investors always expect the promoters of a business to be optimistic and will therefore discount the figures presented. Make sure they discount from goodish figures rather than from poor ones.

Financial notes to tables

Even the spreadsheets are merely a jumping off point: they will be viewed with enormous scepticism and the sound of 'prove it' will be almost audible from the financiers' thoughts. Before they even begin to examine the actual numbers, the potential investors will scrutinize the back-up notes and explanations linked to each line of the spreadsheets, to explain in detail how the figures were derived. Since they assume the actual figures in the spreadsheets are over-optimistic, financiers want to look at the basis or assumptions from which they can make their own calculations based on their experience and personal feel for the specific market.

As the headings in the illustration show (p.82), there are likely to be at least 31 notes to the table to explain how the figures in the spreadsheet were arrived at. You do not have to seem omniscient with these. It is perfectly permissible to explain, for instance in Note 1, that

6 Balance Plan

Cash-flow forecast outgoings

month	1	2	3
Premises			
capital cost/rent/lease [1*]			
repair & maintenance [2]			
service charge [2]			
business rates [3]			
business installation costs [4]			
Plant			
bought equipment [5]			
installation [5]			
office equipment [6]			
Stock/raw materials [7]			
Staffing			
wages [8]			
commission/bonuses [8]			
Travel/entertaining [9]			
Tax			
corporation tax [10]			
National Insurance [11]			
PAYE [12]			
VAT [13]			

month	1	2	3
Marketing			
advertising [14]			
public relations [14]			
market research [14]			
sales [15]			
Professional fees			
lawyers [16]			
accountants [17]			
Insurance [18]			
building			
employer's liability			
public/product liability			
other			
Electricity [19]			
Telephone [20]			
Postage [21]			
Stationery [21]			
Loan interest [22]			
Dividends [23]			
Administration [24]			
Other/misc [25]			
TOTAL OUTGOINGS			

Cash-flow forecast income

month	1	2	3
Cash from sales [26]			
VAT net receipts [27]			
Sale of assets [28]			
Interest received [29]			
Owners' capital introduced [30]			

month	1	2	3
External capital introduced [30]			
Loans [31]			
TOTAL INCOME			
Cash flow			
Opening bank balance			
Closing bank balance			

* Superscript figures refer to notes

there are four sites under consideration at a specified variety of rents, lease costs and purchase prices. If you can, give specific details, including the address, state of the premises and reasons for suitability. Circumstantial detail always adds a sense of verisimilitude. You can then go on to explain that some of the premises may not be available by the time the business is ready, so the costs are indicative only.

In Note 3 on the business rates payable, it is logical to set out the amounts related to the various places listed in Note 1, while pointing out the actual amount will depend on the premises chosen. The figure used in the table is, therefore, the most likely, or the average.

By explaining in this way how all the figures were derived and why they are reasonable, one can guide the reader to a better feel for the accuracy of the overall numbers. Do not let entrepreneurial enthusiasm and optimism show in the tables, but be reasonably optimistic nonetheless.

In the cost of sales, and even more in the attached notes, the plan sets out exactly what is needed. For instance, if this is a national market, how customers will be contacted in Cornwall and Cumbria, what is needed in the way of salespeople, warehouse space, advertising, market research, public relations, and direct mail costs. There will be recurring and some continuous figures.

The revenues have to be explained in even greater detail. If the investors are at all interested in the venture, they may grill the managers for hours on every single figure. You have to spell out in painful detail just where the original information came from, how it was tested for accuracy, and what assumptions were made and why. For instance, if the plan says the size of the market for this type of product is £380 million a year in Britain, with a further £3,000 million in the rest of the EU, you have to specify the government or trade association documents that provided the figures, and perhaps even comment on how accurate they are likely to be.

If the document goes on to claim that you expect to get £2 million of the UK figure by the end of the third year, you need to justify that with a list of signed commitments from potential buyers or something as convincing. In other words, it is not enough to pick a modest percentage of the market as your target achievable by a specified date, you have to explain in detail why that percentage and not half or double was picked. That applies not just to the amount but also to the timing: 'What makes you think the orders by month seven will be that high?' is the sort of question to anticipate.

When commenting on the sales predictions, the preliminary work on elasticity of demand (see Chapter 2) will provide ammunition. Potential backers are impressed by someone sophisticated enough to know the concept, and thorough enough to research the optimum level. They will be much more comfortable that the sales projections are achievable – a common lacuna in untutored business presentations.

Risk assessment

In effect, the main part of the risk assessment work has already been done; it is part of the initial calculations when the cash-flow forecasts were tested to destruction. Quite apart from checking whether the scheme is as viable as it first seemed, this is a salutary mind-clearing exercise to think through what to do when things do not go to plan. Finance people cite the absence of focused thinking on this as one of the commonest failings of the business plans they see.

This exercise is called risk assessment because it looks at what could sink the business. It is also a sensitivity assessment that examines the factors that make the greatest impact on the success. The backers will look principally at the former, but will be impressed if the plan can spell out the alternative outcomes on different assumptions, and hence what second-stage funding might be needed if some of the circumstances turn nasty.

There are several aspects to these assessments:

- finances, such as what happens with changes in economic growth, interest rates, exchange rates, etc.
- deriving from the economic changes, how vulnerable are the assumptions to changes in costs
- variability of markets, in particular things like seasonality and changes of fashion

- technology, including what happens if someone comes along with something more sophisticated yet cheaper
- competition, such as what other companies may do in response to the market entry
- management, for example, what the alternatives are if some of the projected staff are not available
- what happens if a supplier goes bust or runs out of capacity
- how vital are any of the major customers and what happens if one of them goes out of business.

A company dependent on its technical leadership must fear somebody coming up with even better products. By definition you cannot know about these (or you would have used them yourself), but there are precautions one can take. Keep in touch with what is happening by watching the Internet, having a network of contacts including universities, and reading technical journals – all help. So does having your own research organization.

There is no point in hiding any of this information, since investors will do many of the calculations themselves if the information is available. If the figures are not in the plan, they will probably seek them elsewhere (their sources may not be as good as yours) and will be suspicious that the details have not been disclosed. They will almost certainly ask questions on the topic at any presentation.

The plan may well admit that one of the major dangers lies in the possibility of, say, raw material costs rising by over 10 per cent within the first 18 months. The note should also go on to explain what could be done about that. For instance, prices would have to rise by 12 per cent which is likely to encounter sales resistance, but all competitors will be similarly affected, and the real danger lies more in substitution goods and those are limited for the following reasons, and so on.

Funding

Deriving from the previous calculations, the funding requirements already alluded to briefly in the earlier section are here spelled out. Some people put this section further to the front, before the cash-flow forecasts – it is simply a decision about how the tale can be told more easily and logically.

This section explains how much equity and how much loan money the business will need now and at various stages over the next three to five years. You can extend that to more distant plans, including perhaps flotation at some vague time in the future. This is a section venture capitalists look at with greater attention than other types of investors do. That is because they are looking for two things: the longer term growth prospects and their exit when they can recover their invested cash with a huge profit, preferably within five years. Other types of investor, including business angels (see p.97), are more relaxed about this aspect, being more prepared to get involved with a new business that takes many years to get off the ground, especially if they need to reinvest for a longer term future. All the same, all business plans show proposals for the continued development of the business and the exit opportunity for investors.

PRESENTATION

There are two schools of thought about presentation. Some venture capitalists will scarcely look at amateur efforts, on the grounds that the managers have not been tested rigorously to see whether their concept is practical and the document lacks the imprimatur of a reliable firm of specialist accountants. The contrary view by other fund managers is that accountants produce such glossy identical presentations that it is hard for an investor to sort the winners from the duds, whereas the managers' own plans may have rough edges but carry the authenticity of the people who actually make the business work. On the whole, unless the managers are experienced

City people and know how such documents should be prepared, it is probably worth getting professional help.

Even if the plan has been prepared with the obvious help of an adviser, such as a firm of accountants, there is no need to present it with fancy, multi-coloured graphics, lavish illustrations, glossy printing and snazzy covers. Financiers are not easy people to impress and, in any case, that is not the way to do it. Indeed, with very rare exceptions, such as an absolutely huge project requiring tens of millions of pounds, such luxurious presentations are more likely to arouse wariness than approval.

Clarity is the main aim of the document. Any obscurity will arouse the suspicion that something is being hidden or that the managers do not quite understand the situation. If the business is in a highly specialized corner of technology or a recondite trade with its own impenetrable jargon, explain all specialized words as you go along, and also provide a glossary at the back.

5 How to fund a new business

FINDING BACKERS

Raising capital is a sort of Darwinian filter which strains out the entrepreneurs unfit to survive. There is little point in complaining that it is an impossibly difficult process; it is meant to be. The process of raising finance tests the very qualities managers need to make their business prosper. It requires an elaborate forward plan and comprehensive market research, as well as brilliant selling skills to understand the other side's point of view and to anticipate both questions and objections. The entrepreneur has to be devious without appearing to be, and look authoritative even when ignorant, without getting found out. Finally, it demands superior negotiating skills. These are all characteristics and activities that will come in very handy later on.

It can almost be said that people who fail to raise the finance have demonstrated they lack some of the qualities needed for survival. That does not mean the entrepreneurs have to like it, but it does mean they have to master it.

Raising capital away from London is even harder. Most of the venture capital companies, financiers and venture capital trusts are based in London, so are most of the advisers such as accountants, lawyers and consultants, and the other sources of information and advice. Even business angels, who generally prefer to invest in companies within easy travelling distance, tend to congregate in the south-east of England. One solution for businesses away from the capital is to set up a structured programme of visits to London.

SOURCES OF FINANCE

There is no golden rule about where the cash should come from. Businesses need a wide variety of financial sources, depending on what the money is for. There is long-term finance for buying factories, plant and licences, and sometimes for working capital; there is short-term cash to bridge short-term needs. As any financier will tell you, the trick is to match the supply to the need.

Among the sources for finding a backer are:

- the British Venture Capital Association and its booklet of members
- the National Business Angels Network
- the Small Business Service
- the Department of Trade
- Business Links
- UK Business Incubation
- venture capital trusts
- university science parks such as those at (not an exclusive list): Aberdeen, Aston, Cambridge, Salford, Stirling, Warwick and York
- university researchers in the subject, e.g. at Bristol and Southampton.

The most common long-term finance comes from issuing shares. The major problem has been the almost paranoid reluctance by some entrepreneurs to let a single share out of their hot little hands. 'I made this company; it's mine,' they say, hugging it all to themselves. Which is fair enough, but that means they have to choose between having 100 per cent of very little, or 60 per cent of very much more.

One of the factors backers and lenders look at is the gearing – the ratio of share capital to borrowings. In fact, for a new business the ratio is only of academic interest and depends on the availability and cost of cash, but the financial world is stuck in its accustomed ways and can be inflexible even when the result is nonsense. So financiers like gearing to be about one for one.

Another factor to bear in mind is that financing is flexible. What was right and necessary for a new business is very unlikely to be suitable two or three years down the road.

For businesses seeking external equity finance, the important fact to remember is not to pursue one source after another. Parallel approaches are vital, or the process could drag on for years. If the plan is to approach venture capital funds, for instance, make sure you get in touch with every single one that has a potential interest in the type of investment, even if that involves contacting three dozen. Not only does it mean a shorter search, but if several people show an interest one can get them to bid against each other to get the best terms.

That does not mean flooding the market with copies of the plan. A certain amount of research is still advisable to find the organizations that do have an interest in that sector or type of investment.

Raising money is an expensive business, and the capital being raised should also include the costs of finding the funds. It can come to 10–15 per cent of the total amount raised by the time you have counted the fees of all the expensive professionals involved.

The main problem is perseverance. You need the patient persistence of a Jehovah's Witness. After 25 doors have been slammed in your face, you must still muster the enthusiasm and courtesy to approach the 26th with the glow of optimism that might just get them to respond.

Terms for structuring equity

If the business is trying to raise more than around £100,000, the founders of the business will very likely have to give away some of the equity to get the funding. Up to that amount, you might be able to raise on a bank loan with a little help from factoring (see pp.102 and

176), leasing and such ploys, but anything higher will almost certainly involve shares.

The crucial question is how many shares for how much. Investors will naturally want the maximum they can get at the lowest price, without losing the incentive for the managers, but entrepreneurs argue against reducing the incentives of big shareholdings for the managers. The larger the amount raised, the more equity will have to be given up. One suggestion is for two classes of share, with the external investors having a preferential issue, and so getting paid before the managers. In practice, it is hardly worth arguing about since any business going bust in the first three to five years is unlikely to have money left over from repaying ordinary creditors to pay shareholders and, if the business survives longer than that, it would be foolish not to restructure the paper it has issued.

It is not only the initial tranche of shares that is at question here. The managers should always include terms for bonus issues or options for themselves if the business does well. There are many ways of structuring this. Some investors insist on a negative version called financial covenants: if the business fails to meet the quality and timing targets in the agreement, they get a larger share of the company. Some of these terms are so onerous and the targets so demanding that the entrepreneurs might find themselves with practically nothing after three years. The obvious response is to laugh and suggest that if you wanted to be the funder's employee you would have applied for a job.

Negotiating is a specialist skill. There are several aspects to it and to get what you want means elaborate preparation. First of all you need to work out what the other side is likely to want, and what its minimum requirements are likely to be. Second, one's own position is articulated: what are the absolutely essential ingredients of any agreement, what are desirable, and what would be nice? Third is the chess-like calculation of how it could be played: if he demands that, what would my reaction be and how is he likely to react? Fourth, one decides what could be traded for what. This last aspect is to ensure you never allow the negotiations to run into the blank wall of an impasse. If there seems to be a fundamental difference on the basic requirements of the two sides, never concede the position is lost, but look for a different way of approaching the problem, and perhaps swap a little here for something over there. If you have chosen the advising firm well, its people will be experienced in all this and will help with the prolonged haggling.

As the company grows and requires further injections of growth capital, the founders' share of the total will be diluted still further. After flotation, it will be unlikely that the managers or the initial entrepreneurs will own more than 25 per cent of the total. However, by that time it will be a quarter of rather a large amount.

WHERE TO RAISE THE MONEY

The sources that follow are not mutually exclusive. On the contrary, the chances are a new business would want to tap into them all. This creates a larger number of potential investors, and it diversifies the providers to enable managers to get the best construction of different types of capital, enabling them to draw on the widest range of expertise.

Personal resources

If you do not believe in your company, why should anyone else? If the owner and promoter of a business is not prepared to hazard his own savings and sometimes even remortgage his house to provide the first injection of money, external investors will probably consider the venture enormously risky or the manager uncommitted or untrustworthy. So, although it may go against the grain to endanger the roof over one's children's heads, it may have to be done. If the managers have put all their eggs in one basket, you can be sure they are going to watch that basket. This is where the cooperation and backing of a spouse are vital. It is not a good idea to be so dedicated to a commercial notion that it breaks up the marriage. If it is likely to be a serious problem, think again.

Savings

Most people have some savings and investments. It may be the amount accumulating for a new drawing-room suite, for a holiday or a new car, that is earning interest in a building society, or the occasional shares from privatizations or demutualized insurance companies and building societies. Cashing in unmatured life assurance policies is a mug's game – they seldom generate as much cash as was put in to start with. It is usually better to use them as security for a loan.

The founders may have to rein back on all sorts of personal spending in the initial years. For instance, in a big town such as London, a car is a major liability. It is not just a capital asset with a depreciating value, it costs far more than most people care to calculate in insurance, petrol, tyres, parking, tow-away charges, repairs, oil, washing and service. Taking taxis and hiring a car for excursions generally works out cheaper.

Even private savings money has a cost, it is called the opportunity cost and is measured by the return the money could have earned if invested elsewhere. As good a measure as any is the yield currently available on gilt-edged securities.

Second mortgage

More dependable in the long run than any stock market investment has been the property market, although like all capitalist markets it gives the occasional sickening lurch. Mark Twain advised, buy land, they are not making any more of it. As a result one's home is likely to be worth a substantial amount of money, the appreciation being dependent on where you live. Most people can realize some of this by a second mortgage or by selling and moving to something smaller.

Family and friends

If you spend long enough asking round family and friends and suggest they also talk to their friends, you will be surprised how many are prepared to put up a few thousand here and there, if the idea is anything like reasonable.

It can be embarrassing to endanger the savings of family members, no matter how confident managers are about the success of the new venture. There can also be tension when relatives feel entitled by their investment to meddle in the running of the business. Those are the main reasons many entrepreneurs approach only family members who have spare investment cash, and understand the investment is on an arm's length basis.

Banks

Banks see themselves as providing loans, not as investors buying shares. Their chosen business is borrowing and lending short term. There is little point arguing about this – if that is the business they want to be in, that is up to them. The corollary is that they will provide an overdraft for any short-term business needs, or a longer term loan for a specific need, but one must seek long-term equity capital elsewhere.

The problem for a start-up is lack of security to back an overdraft or loan; it cannot even provide comfort to the lender by showing a record of achieving the cash flow to pay the interest. Hence, not unreasonably, banks ask for other forms of security, and this usually means the resources of the people running the new venture. That results in having to give a personal guarantee, usually with the security of assets such as the home. In effect, that negates the whole point of corporate structure and returns to unlimited personal liability, but there is probably no cure for that. With luck, it will be only temporary.

Small Firms Loan Guarantee Scheme

Under the Small Firms Loan Guarantee Scheme, the Department of Trade provides insurance for 70–85 per cent of a loan in return for payment from the borrower. That encourages banks to lend to small businesses without the normal requirement for security. The banks seem curiously unenthusiastic about the scheme and seldom bring it to the attention of businesses trying to borrow. One reason may be that the loans are used only for ventures that would not otherwise have gained bank backing, which of course means they are the questionable prospects. As a result, almost half of them go bad, and though three-quarters may be insured, the banks still have to write off the rest.

As it is still a debt, the money must be repaid, but over a period of up to seven years.

How to deal with banks

You do have to watch banks carefully, as with any other tradesmen or suppliers you deal with. Just as it is a good idea to count one's change at a shop, so it is wise to check bank statements. Banks make a surprisingly large number of mistakes – according to one survey, up to a fifth of the companies found a mistake in the previous 12 months. Everybody can of course make mistakes, but it was curious that most of them were in favour of the banks, and included things like the wrong rate of interest.

The banks also impose penalties for unauthorized overdrafts, which can be at absurdly high rates. However, any business manager keeping an eye on the company has no excuse for failing to spot a potential gap, and acting in advance to find resources to supply the cash.

Small businesses chronically complain about their banks, although the tales often bear an uncanny resemblance to husbands petulantly exclaiming their wives do not understand them. The point is banks are not benevolent organizations. They exist to make money, from you as from others, in return for a service. There is no onus on them to help or even to keep a business afloat. That is the first rule to remember when dealing with the banks.

The second rule is that bankers are simple men who are easy to deal with provided that you bear in mind seven rules about the arrangement between you. These rules apply to all transactions, whether it is the first encounter opening an account, or the hundredth asking for an overdraft:

1 Banks are tradesmen like plumbers or greengrocers; they trade in money. They are middlemen between depositors and borrowers (Disraeli commented as long ago as 1845, 'It is well known what a middleman is: he is a man who bamboozles one party and plunders the other'); they are not endowed with supernatural wisdom enabling them to foresee future interest rates, stock market movements, or the currency exchanges, and they have neither power nor control.

2 As with other tradesmen, bankers are open to negotiation and haggling; when they say the overdraft rate is set at 4 or 5 per cent over base, they mean that is their opening position; they need you at least as much as you need them because without somebody paying interest on borrowings they are out of business. Make a counteroffer of 1 per cent over base and so on until you reach a reasonable balance. Paradoxically, a really rough drag-out battle over the terms goes down as a good mark on your file since it shows you are knowledgeable and care about money details. If the manager is intransigent, one can always go elsewhere since there are at least 11 substantial banks in Britain offering business accounts according to the Competition Commission (see also *Business Money£acts*).

3 Bankers are cautious people who need reassurance that the money will come back, so one has to see all the arguments from their side and make them as comforting and reasonable as any nervous lender is likely to want. They are not reluctant to lend because they hate entrepreneurs or because they are stupid, constitutionally weak-kneed or contrary, it is because the borrower does not sound convincing. It is astonishing how many managers think a simple assertion that the venture is sound will suffice and, when asked to justify this, merely waffle or repeat the assertion. What a banker wants is numbers and justification.

4 Banks hate surprises; it is therefore unwise to dash in and demand an overdraft extension immediately. They are much more likely to be cooperative with managers who warn them that

sometime next July they are likely to need further facilities. If you then turn out not to need them, they should worry about your failure to plan, but in fact are happy about your caution. By the same token, bankers like people who say they need two years to repay a loan and manage it in 20 months, and dislike the ones who after 23 months ask for a further extension. The moral is always to ask for more than you need, and suggest a longer repayment than you could possibly want.

5 Always keep the bank informed and, when going to see the manager, have papers and memory well prepared. It will comfort the bankers and make them feel a manager is on top of the job and controlling the business.

6 If the bank is refractory and uncooperative, move to another; the bank is obliged to make this transition as smooth as possible. It is an immediate pain to set up new relationships, ensure all direct debits and standing orders are in place and so on, but if it produces a sympathetic ear and a helpful attitude, it will be worth it.

7 Do not assume the bank is right, even when its computer prints out the figures – there are several organizations (such as Anglia Business Associates owned by the Consumers' Association) kept permanently busy setting right the banks' mistakes, which range from failing to offset the credit in one account against the debt in another contrary to the agreement, charging the wrong level of interest, and failing to credit some items. Watch them all the time and do not be afraid to ask for clarification if something seems awry.

Business angels

Dealing with individuals is fraught with danger. There are great thickets of protective legislation to ensure that individual investors are not made responsible for their own greed or folly. The Financial Services Act has a large number of provisions which will apply on the sending of a business plan. The Companies Acts require that offers of securities to the public must be accompanied by a prospectus which, in turn, requires armies of lawyers and accountants and costs a major fortune.

All the same, there are ways of avoiding the most onerous parts of the law by dealing with experienced investors and not issuing sweeping invitations to invest. The number of individuals who have made a tidy sum elsewhere and now want to put it to work in a new enterprise, is growing quite quickly. Statistics on this are deeply unreliable because there is no requirement to report such transactions, and most of the deals are done through acquaintances bringing together a compatible set of people, but it is thought that around 20,000 people may now be active private investors in such unquoted securities.

As a result, there has been a corresponding growth in the organizations set up to bring investors into contact with the ventures needing their cash. Probably the largest organization is the National Business Angels Network, but others include Beer & Partners, and several Business Links keep lists of interested people on registers. In general, the angels are ready to invest in chunks of between £25,000 and £1 million. Few are at that top level, but they do sometimes form syndicates, in which case a couple of million would not be out of the question.

Quite a lot of these investors are successful business people themselves. They may have built a company and sold it for a lot of money, and are now getting restless. That means they want to invest their cash and their expertise. The entrepreneur's first idea may be that this would mean having someone breathing down the management's neck the whole time. A few of them may be like that, but most must know something or they would not have the money to invest now. So using them as free management consultants can be useful.

Less usual is the senior manager who has been made redundant with a handsome golden handshake and, in return for the investment, is looking for serious involvement, perhaps even a full-time job. There are also a few investors who want to put the cash in and simply reap the eventual rewards with no further involvement.

Private investors have several advantages. One can draw on the experience and contacts of someone with proven business competence – even if they have not made the money themselves, there is a good chance they will know other rich and successful people and networking always helps. In addition, individuals are less restrictive about their requirements of returns than funds are. They are much freer to decide that a venture would be better advised reinvesting its profits for six or seven years at least, rather than paying dividends. Similarly, they are more relaxed about when the investment fructifies: if a public listing of the shares is delayed for ten years, that is likely to be acceptable. A wise precaution is to set up a system from the start for buying out the investors who turn out to need their money back sooner. This will mean setting a price formula for the deal right from the start.

Corporate venturers

There are few corporate venturers in the UK, but this is a well-established route for finding money in America, especially for high-tech businesses. In the US, many major electronics companies such as Hewlett-Packard, when faced with enterprising employees signing off to start their own company, offer to put in money in return for a share of the equity, and the prospect of working together.

It may be possible to get a large company with an interest in a sector to back a complementary product in the UK, but it is likely to be a long and frustrating pursuit. The government has tried to encourage the process with tax advantages: the corporation gets 20 per cent of the amount invested allowed against tax for at least three years, and can defer tax on gains if the money is reinvested within the scheme.

The investing company must not own more than 30 per cent of the shares, and individual investors must hold at least 20 per cent.

Venture capitalists

Britain has pro rata the largest venture capital industry in the world, even ahead of the US. These are funds run by professional managers that raise money from financial institutions, including pension funds, and invest it in private equity (i.e. shares that are not quoted on a stock exchange). Their original aim was to back private companies, but they are becoming increasingly enterprising on their own behalf – buying companies and installing their own managers. This is alongside their continued investments for which they have a rolling programme of raising billions of pounds. The problem therefore is not shortage of available cash, but whether it is available to you.

Venture capital funds proclaim their eagerness to invest in start-ups, but put only 2 per cent of their money into them. They profess to be interested in advanced technology yet find excuses to avoid it. They claim to be short of propositions in which to invest, but turn away most of the people who come to them direct. In sum, they are risk averse.

To be fair, venture capitalists are under pressure from their own investors, who are said to want to see performance indicators on the shortest of terms. It is a combination of factors, but the net result is that most members of the British Venture Capital Association (BVCA), which includes most of the major funds in Britain, will not invest in a start-up, or even in a relatively young company, unless it provides copper-bottomed and gold-plated underwritten guarantees of doubling the money in three years.

Venture capitalists also dislike investing small amounts of money. Sums below about £3 million and preferably £10 million are more trouble than they are worth. That is because it takes as much investigation (the 'due diligence' enquiry) to invest £100,000 as £100 million, and as much supervision and probably more management attention. Due diligence, incidentally, encompasses the individuals, their records, the basis of all the numbers, the assertions about market and competition and so on.

As a result of all these factors, the biggest proportion of venture capital money goes into large management buyouts because they are large, safe and predictable, and will probably go public in a few years, allowing the funds to recover their money with a handsome profit.

The BVCA publishes an annual booklet of members' sectors of interest. It is useful mainly for the names and phone numbers since many funds tick a variety of boxes for areas claimed to be of interest but in which they have never invested, for which they have no expertise and in which they are unlikely to put any money in the future. To compound the problem, some of the smaller or more restricted funds that make small investments may not be members of the association and hence are not in the booklet.

There is no easy answer to this, excepting gossip or contacts. If one of the bigger and more experienced accountancy firms has helped with the preparation of the business plan, it may also have a section with some idea of which funds are likely to show an interest. The firm may also effect an introduction that will open far more doors than an unknown individual off the street can manage.

Britain's venture capital industry totally overshadows the rest of Europe. So much so that the UK fund managers are increasingly moving into the Continent to open up a relatively unexploited market. However, there are major banks and substantial funds in the rest of Europe and many of those can be found on the website of the European Venture Capital Association (see Appendix A).

Venture capitalists in general demand annual returns of 30–60 per cent and, if it is an early stage investment, perhaps higher still. This, in turn, may be another reason why they do not get involved in start-up finance, since scarcely one new company in ten thousand could achieve anything like that. It is also the reason they like management buyouts.

The funds need the high returns and to roll their investments over – they are not long-term investors in the main – they will probably seek an exit in about five years. That means the business, the directors, or another fund must buy their shares, the company needs to be floated or the business acquired.

Alongside these national funds are smaller local and specialized outfits and venture capital trusts. All of these will invest in suitable young businesses.

Venture capital trust (VCTs)

VCTs are companies listed on the stock market set up specifically to invest in small businesses – a type of specialist investment trust.

They invest in unquoted companies with assets of under £16 million even after the investment.

Other

Stockbrokers

It is possible but difficult to get stockbrokers to mention to private clients that an investment opportunity has arisen. They are unlikely to recommend it, but if you can get them to bring it to the attention of their richer clients there is a chance one of them will be interested.

Factoring and invoice discounting

Strictly speaking, this is not much help to a new company since the business will have issued no invoices on which to collect early, but it is a useful device for young businesses. It accelerates cash flow which, in the early days of a business, can be the difference between survival and an early death. In addition, factoring companies, most of which are subsidiaries of the larger banks, have become more creative in the way they are prepared to structure their financial help, and their funds can be cheaper than alternative sources of capital. For details of how factoring works see Chapter 8.

CONFIDENTIALITY AGREEMENTS

There is a fundamental conflict in this process of raising money. The conflict is between the business ambitions of launching something new into the market and wanting to keep the project a secret as long as possible to prevent an early reaction from the competition, or perhaps even a pre-emptive strike; and the need to distribute the plans proclaiming precisely this aim. Benjamin Franklin said three may keep a secret if two of them are dead, so there is a danger your ideas leak out.

One way to reduce the danger is by including a confidentiality clause in the business plan. Such a non-disclosure agreement restricts the use of the information in it, and readers are checked for conflicts of interest. In practice, some funds refuse to sign on the pretence their professionalism would preclude such practices in any case. The clause is extraordinarily difficult to enforce and even harder to get redress if one suspects a breach, but it does put people on warning.

The action you can take practically is limited and therefore other precautions may be in order. Market-sensitive information, designs, and details of products should probably be omitted from the plan, and the gap explained. Once you have picked the backer, who may well put someone on the board, and everything is more or less agreed, disclosure may be necessary and, by that time, harmless.

GRANTS, LOANS AND ASSISTANCE SCHEMES

There are literally hundreds of support schemes available from the EU, and local and central government amounting to some £5 billion a year. Some of these are for new businesses, some for specific industrial sectors, some to attract business to impoverished areas, some to promote employment, and some to encourage technical innovation. Finding out about the schemes and meeting the esoteric requirements can be a challenge, however. The Department of Trade is in the process of simplifying the system to eliminate all but the extremely successful and put the rest into a £1 billion pot, but that still leaves another 400 schemes from other sources.

There used to be a spate of organizations offering to find grants for small businesses. Some of them were wholly bogus and asked for an upfront search fee of £150 to £350 to dig through their database and said it was almost certain they would find something suitable. It was difficult to prove the touts were dishonest because they could merely say their best efforts proved fruitless in that specific case. After action by the authorities against the most widespread and flagrant con artists, the scams seem to have abated. There are some honest companies helping with this sort of work, yet they are becoming scarce as small businesses turn increasingly to more readily available sources of information. A business approached with an offer to unearth a grant should not automatically turn it away – it could be genuine. The sensible course of action is to accept, but suggest that if the agency is so confident of finding a subsidy, it can take its fee out of the money raised. Most will swiftly retire.

The schemes are in such a continuous state of flux, with government rearranging them to draw attention to the facilities and to try putting money where the current success seems to lie, reducing and amalgamating them, and relaunching them under new names, that there is little point in listing them here. Information is available from a range of quangos including the government's Small Business Service, Learning & Skills Council, Business Links, Scottish Business Shop Network, Business Connect in Wales, regional development agencies and the Department of Trade, economic development units at local authorities, small business associations, and major banks. The websites for j4b and the Enterprise Zone also provide information on grants. For details about the various areas of assistance (rural development areas, assisted areas, regional selective assistance areas) try the Department of Environment Transport & the Regions at www.detr.gov.uk and www.scotland.gov.uk. The EU's own website also carries information (see Appendix A).

In addition to government money for grants, there are over 100 competitions for small businesses with prizes that may be computer hardware or free consultancy, but can be several thousand pounds. Some of them may also provide a little welcome publicity for the business. Unfortunately nobody keeps a register of these prizes or some companies could raise decent amounts of capital through them.

There may be numerous sources of such help, but it is wise to be careful about all the handouts. There is a price for everything. Some of the grants and loans run to thousands of pounds, but it takes time to track them down. There is a fair amount of administrative complexity in checking for eligibility and applying, and if they are worth having the competition is likely to be intense. The conditions for some of the grants are demanding, including, in some cases, that the project has not started prior to receiving the public funds. In addition, the subvention is to induce companies to set up in unattractive areas – there would be no need for the bribes if the location or business were desirable and profitable. Before getting involved, check whether the cost is worth it. As Thackeray said, we often buy money very much too dear.

6 Spending the money

PREMISES

Beware of clichés – they may embody some truth but not necessarily the one most people assume. That applies to the saying that the three most important things about property are location, location and location. The implication is that it is always preferable to be in the best location. If best means most obvious, showy and expensive, the old saying is plainly wrong. However, interpret it as the most suitable location and the saying may turn from vacuous to a truism, and truisms are at least true.

Where?

Many new businesses start in a back bedroom as a part-time occupation. Many others can be run from a study at home. Despite malicious rumours to the contrary, consultancy is not invariably the middle-class word for unemployment – sometimes it is the label for a highly profitable enterprise operated by independent and highly qualified advisers. Freelance work of many sorts from market research to journalism, and data analysis to garden design can all be operated from the end of a telephone and a computer connected to the Internet. This sort of working does, however, demand discipline and organization.

If the enterprise is to be something more than a lifestyle occupation that only manages to pay the bills, it will almost certainly need additional staff and its own premises. Choosing those is not so difficult; it is a simple compromise between what you would ideally like and what you can realistically afford. One sure sign of a new business heading for the liquidator is the shining new premises in a prestige site.

It was never vital for everybody to be in posh premises in the City or the West End of London. Most businesses could work just as effectively from Yorkshire or Devon, but the boards of directors have usually wanted access to the fun and are solid metropolitan urbanites. Even when a London office is genuinely useful, it can be small and poky without handicapping the efficiency of the business. The British General Electric under Lord Weinstock was one of the biggest industrial combines in Europe and yet was run from tiny cramped offices containing only the couple of dozen people who had to be in London. When it was renamed Marconi and moved to trendy offices and technologies, it teetered on the verge of insolvency. Major publishers have traditionally run their businesses from offices of Dickensian cramped squalor and still attracted people to work there.

The avoidance of expensive premises and high rates has been reinforced since the much-heralded virtual office – and indeed virtual company – has made a shy appearance. It really is possible for people on the Isle of Lewis and in Lewes to work together via computers linked to the Internet. And they can add video conferencing if absolutely necessary. It is also easy to have specialist outsourcing companies working seamlessly with the business itself, by similar routes. A customer need never know that the person answering your telephone is at a call-centre contractor nor that it is not in Britain but in Bangalore.

There is a range of schemes to attract business to areas of poverty. Enterprise zones exist in the East Midlands, Dearne valley, South Yorkshire, East Durham, along the River Tyne and in Lanarkshire. The benefits include an absence of business rates, enhanced capital allowances and an accelerated planning regime. In addition, there are assisted areas covering poor areas including some derelict city centres. These attract grants for fixed costs such as property and machinery, and for creating high-skill jobs. There is a baffling array of various categories of assistance, which trimmings and simplifications have reduced only slightly. These include regional selective assistance, enterprise grants and some regeneration grants. Information is available from Business Links and Regional Development Agencies.

For manufacturers there are specific constraints on where the premises should be. The plant has to be where there are qualified workers, where supplies of raw material and part-assemblies can be conveniently delivered, and from where the finished product can be distributed cheaply to the market. Communications and access are therefore important. On the other hand, if it is a small, high-value product, that becomes less of a problem.

Food outlets, from sandwich bars to restaurants, have different requirements. The majority of their business will be from passing trade so they have to be on busy streets. If they cannot get access to an economic site of this sort, restaurants have to be 'destination' sites – places to which customers will drive for quite a long time – in Michelin guide language *vaux le voyage* (worth the journey) or at least *vaux le detour* (worth a detour).

Similar criteria apply to other sorts of retailers, with their locations geared to both the customers and the surrounding traders.

When the business is reliant on impulse custom walking in off the pavement, there are other decisions to make. One is to decide who the likely customers are. A very different set of buyers is available in a massive shopping mall like Metro or Bluewater, from Knightsbridge in London or the outskirts of Oldham. Another decision is whether to site where there are lots of other retailers in the same sector or to fill a gap. There is the joke about two friends meeting after a long time. One says he found a long shopping street without a single restaurant so he opened one and is making a fortune. The other says how odd. He was walking down a busy street and noted there were 11 restaurants. 'So I said to myself, if there is trade enough for 11 restaurants, there is trade enough for 12. I opened a restaurant and I am making a bomb.' Jokes apart, it is not an easy decision.

Tradesmen, such as builders, can be located almost anywhere. The same applies to food outlets concentrating on deliveries (provided they are in reach of their customers), publishers, or mini-cab companies – their customers do not need to visit their business premises.

There is a website for finding out about a location. Enter the postcode on www.upmystreet.com and up come details of house prices, crime, schools, council tax, ambulance response times and so on.

It is not enough to pick the area – there are dozens of other decisions to be taken. For instance:

- how many square metres/feet for the office? (Do not guess, work it out from the number of employees, desks, filing cabinets etc.)
- how much manufacturing space? (Similarly, work this out on a careful basis)
- how much warehouse or storage space?

Everybody wants to encourage high-technology manufacturers, whether of software or hardware, and there are public sector specialist funds to sponsor particular sectors or to lure business into areas of high unemployment. Both the British government and the EU have schemes for assisted areas or enterprise zones (see www.dti.gov.uk/assistedareas). They can pay for setting up, buying machinery and training. There are also business parks, science parks and business incubation sites beckoning promising young businesses with offers of low rents and free advice. The incubators are business parks but with small premises where a young enterprise gets cheap premises and advice from a resident consultant, plus the ability to talk to others who are in the same boat.

It is always nice to be given money or to have the price reduced, but it is dangerous to get seduced by such low-cost incentives. Just as with other financial incentives, the main reason for doing something should be its existing financial logic and the taxpayer money should be a bonus. Going for something simply because of an incentive is a recipe for disaster. Only if two potential sites are equally balanced with nothing to separate them should the question of government assistance be a factor.

How big?

Size of premises is always a problem for a beginner. It is a question of whether to go for the maximum obtainable, constrained only by finances, to allow for expansion, or whether to limit the financial exposure by starting modestly. There is no right answer to this, but the initial premises should be suitable for at least the first three years, and the cash-flow forecast will disclose how much that period is likely to require.

In offices, about 9.3m^2 (100 sq. ft) per employee is a fair allocation.

Buy, rent or lease?

Few new businesses would start by buying premises. They have neither the money nor the expertise. Similarly, they are unlikely to have the willingness, cash or experience for a ground lease that provides the site while the tenant builds the property. Far more likely is leasing premises. Under the Landlord and Tenant Act, when the lease ends you can stay on under a new lease.

Finally, a raft of legislation on pollution and other obligations makes ownership of commercial premises a bit of a gamble. To prevent an astronomical clean-up bill, even after leaving the site and moving somewhere else, it might be a good idea to form a separate company to own the property or its lease and, when selling, sell the whole lot including the company. That should leave the main part of the business with no residual obligations.

Finding the place

The evaluation process should have produced the measures for judging the premises:

- Where, not only in terms of where in the country, but where in the town and on what sort of road?
- How big in ground area and, where necessary, head clearance?

- What sort, i.e. how much office, factory, storage, retail, parking and other space is needed?
- What type of occupation, such as buy, build, lease, rent?
- Any requirement for amenities such as near railway or airport, on a bus route?
- What needs to be there or has to be installed, such as multiple phone lines, ADSL, heating and ventilation, partitions?
- Will it need specialist facilities like catering and reinforcement for heavy plant?
- Cost?

This is the preliminary thinking. Next comes the action: finding something to meet the criteria, including the cost.

Estate agents are the obvious start, and one can find them by going to the area, looking at the boards outside premises and noting the agents dealing in the sort of place that could be interesting. Another source is the local press, which will provide potential sites and the names of more estate agents. A third source is the Internet – always worth trying for whatever you are looking for. For instance, there are Business Sale On-Line, Start in Business and Nationwide Business (see Appendix A). Some local authorities have registers of vacant commercial properties, and some know about 'brownfield' sites for sale – these old industrial properties may have derelict property already there but with planning permission to replace it with something new, and there may be money to help with that redevelopment.

When a reasonably suitable site has been found, there are still all the checks and formalities surrounding any change of property ownership. For instance, you have to be sure the property can be used for the purpose planned, how long the lease is and whether it is renewable, if there is any difficulty with changing looks or layout (e.g. it is listed), whether it is possible to sublet, who repairs and decorates, whether there are any local changes in the pipeline, such as road widening, which might affect the building, and if the premises can be made to conform to fire and safety requirements for the purpose it will be used for.

Obligations

These are the obvious safety requirements that anyone coming on to the premises should not be harmed and should be warned of any residual dangers.

OFFICE FURNITURE ETC.

Furniture

It is important for new companies to conserve cash, so good management suggests not just modest premises at first but also restraint in buying office furniture. Even companies having to meet customers on the premises can restrict the new or stylish parts to reception and meeting rooms, and keep the back office less lavish.

Computers

The warnings against overspending apply with even greater force to computers. It is tempting when setting up to go for the latest and most powerful machine, which can practically read your mind and design a nuclear submarine in one-hundredth of a second. For almost all the uses in a business, it is like using a Ferrari to nip down the road for the shopping. Most computers are used for word processing and spreadsheets, and the most sluggish machine of ten years ago will do just as well for those, much less a computer a year or so old. Specialist shops like Morgan Computers deal in discontinued models for a fraction of the price the successor would cost. Something that would have been selling at £1,500 at the start of the year might be down to £250 by August.

Only processor-intensive and memory-hungry applications like graphics need a powerful computer, and even then it is at least as important to have the maximum amount of RAM (random-access memory) as the beast with the highest number of gigahertz in its processor. If graphics and computer-aided design are involved, talk to a professional – instead of the usual Intel-based systems sitting on 90 per cent of office desks, you may need a Mac. Or perhaps something more powerful.

In addition, getting involved with the Internet will demand equipment of a different order – the standard desk-tops even if networked, will no longer do. A server is needed and that begins to get expensive.

Programming is a costly business and best avoided. Most young businesses should be able to start with package software. The desktop computer generally comes with a word processor, spreadsheet, database and diary program already installed – generally speaking this will be some version of the Microsoft Office package. It may be labelled free, which usually means you have already paid for it somewhere else, in this case in the cost of the hardware. Unless there is an extremely good reason for jettisoning all of that, you might as well use what you have paid for.

On top of that there is a wide variety of accountancy programs. These range in price from about £20 to over £100,000 depending on the level of sophistication, the number and power of the computers being used, and the degree of customization involved. With such an enormous number and range available, it is hard to give specific advice except on how to buy.

A sole trader may not need an accounting program at all; a spreadsheet may do what is needed. A company probably will, especially as it needs a reliable audit trail for the end of year accounts. Sit down with an accountant, perhaps the probable auditor, and work out precisely what it is the accountancy program needs to do and how. Even the cheapest version of Sage, Dosh or Intuit (to take a few random examples of big-selling programs) can do the standard minimal things, including monthly management reports and multi-currency accounting (they can handle the euro). If there is need for a more sophisticated management reporting system with the likelihood of more required later, it might be necessary to move up a grade or two. Make sure the program used when starting out is seamlessly upgradable – in other words, the more powerful versions of accountancy programs in the software company's range will accept the data from a cheaper version without the need for alteration. Companies with ambitions to grow and sprout new departments, subsidiaries and more product lines, need to check whether the upgrade programs have the facilities to cope with the sophistication of the big time. Transferring all the data into a different program, and completely changing procedures to fit, are not jobs you would wish upon your worst enemy.

Whatever other provisions are made for the computer equipment, one is essential: facilities for backing up all data. The kit must be there, whether for sending down the line to another machine, transferring to a variety of discs (e.g. removable hard drive, CD, DVD, Zip, or even floppies), or to a tape streamer. The backing up must be comprehensive, frequent and doubly safe. That means, for instance, rotating the back-up medium so there are always several examples, just in case the most recent back-up was already corrupted or infected by a virus. Finally, to ensure they really are useful back-ups, the medium should be kept in a fireproof safe or, better still, off the premises.

Equipment

The company will probably need a photocopier, preferably one that can enlarge and reduce, but whether A4 is large enough or if it needs to cope with A3 will depend on the business. Similarly, how big and powerful – in other words what sort of printing capacity it is made for – will be dictated by a reasonable assessment of the sort of likely use.

For a sole trader working from home without a need for huge amounts of copying, it is worth considering the combined machines. These contain a photocopier, fax, printer and scanner all in a single box. For a long time the unreliability of the equipment rightly made people wary because a fault in one function can incapacitate the whole machine. However, it looks as if the kit is now pretty reliable, and there is a wide range available at reasonable prices.

At the other end of the scale is the business with a steady demand on a copier, and then it is a mistake to get a cheap lightweight machine that will give up the ghost. Overworked photocopiers can be temperamental and it is worth doing some research to get one that does not turn up its toes on Friday evening when you need desperately to get a quotation to an important customer. The second consideration is cost; not just capital cost but toner and whatever needs to be replaced regularly to keep it happy.

Telephones

A business needs several lines, quite apart from any being used for connection to the Internet. Broadband availability is still pretty patchy. One advantage of broadband is the ability of the system to carry more than one set of signals. Thus you have a phone and an Internet line on the same wire. Another boon is a much faster connection to the Internet. The disadvantage is cost – there is a higher regular subscription. The main options are via optical cable, although NTL and Telewest have not been down every street in the country, or via the existing wires installed by British Telecom, but the exchange needs to have the spare capacity and the business's premises have to be close to it.

STATIONERY

Printing letterheads, invoices and all the other official documents a business sends out used to be a huge upfront expense. It can be safely ignored. Unless you opt for something really expensive looking, like raised lettering on heavy-gauge expensive company writing paper, the computer can be programmed to print it all on the document as it is produced. A decent colour printer, which need not cost the earth, can reproduce your logo and heading details in full colour, if that is your fancy.

Visiting cards should, however, be bought in from specialist printers. The logo and design will be consonant with the company's other stationery to keep a professional-looking cohesion of concept. If the company owns any commercial vehicles, those will have the same design emblazoned in the same colours.

Whatever the choice of colours or designs, the first priority is the paper. The sort of paper used for internal documents is beside the point and there is nothing to be gained in buying anything but the cheapest for that, but what goes to clients has to look professional, expensive and be of good quality to inspire confidence.

Design

Entrepreneurs seem to go for one of two extremes. Either extreme conservatism with plain white paper and simple black lettering at the top, or lurid colours of paper with computer-generated 'watermark' as background and vibrant jazzy designs for the heading. The sensible choice lies with not what you like, but what will impress customers and suit your market.

As with the company's logo and brochures, etc., it is worth hiring a decent designer. There are so many different ways of laying things out, so many typefaces to choose from, so many lines, rows of dots and so on to add to the layout that it takes someone knowledgeable to know the options. Amateur design is all too obvious and makes the business seem less substantial and reliable.

STAFF

Hiring staff scares most managers witless and many stay sole traders merely to avoid the ever-rising pile of legislation, legal decisions and miles of red tape. They are right to be frightened (see Chapter 7), but if the enterprise is to become a business, staff are needed. The technical aspects of hiring, from defining what you want to meeting the regulatory requirements, are also in Chapter 7, and this section merely covers the procedural parts of where and how to look.

Sources

Where you look for staff depends on what you want. The government's Jobcentres are scattered around the country, and are useful for filling clerical and manual jobs; there is a huge range of employment agencies from national and international chains such as Adecco, Reed, Brook Street and Office Angels, to small local and specialized businesses (the Recruitment & Employment Confederation is their trade association and can give advice on the one to use for a specialist application); there are a couple of dozen reasonably sized headhunters, and a variety of places to advertise. Advertising provides a huge choice – the ad can go into just the local paper if you are looking for a delivery boy, a specialist journal for a technical job, or a national newspaper like the *Daily Telegraph* for reasonably paid jobs such as engineer, accountant or manager. A large number of web-based recruitment systems have sprung up in the past year or two, yet the most satisfactory ones are linked to another type of recruitment, such as an agency or journal.

Framing the advertisement is another selling job, and like all such it has to consider the other side's needs. People look for interesting, creative work with good pay and the chance of promotion. They would prefer to work for a company that was ethical and had congenial premises, and was financially sound enough to provide security. These details have to be in the advertisement, and those reassurances need to be stressed.

INSURANCE

With the accumulation of safeguards and protection funds, the danger of one's insurance company going bust, even when its reinsurance underwriter has folded, are much reduced, which is one less worry. Even if it did, there are safety nets to prevent the insureds being totally without cover.

Insurance contracts are on the basis of *uberrimae fidei* – the Latin legal jargon for 'utmost good faith'. In other words, the insured is under an obligation to disclose anything that may affect the underwriter or the policy terms, even if they are adverse and unfortunate. A mistake, an omission or a misrepresentation that changes the evaluation of risk can invalidate the policy.

After any serious claim, the insurer may send in a loss adjuster to see to what extent the claim is valid and if it should be adjusted downwards to offset excess claims. In theory, the insured company can appoint its own loss assessor to produce an alternative calculation of what the claim should be, but it hardly ever does. If the adjuster reckons the insured goods have been undervalued to minimize the premium, he will reduce the value of the claim by the same proportion. For reasons best known to the insurance industry, this is known as averaging.

There is nothing to stop an individual from buying insurance direct from the underwriting company, except time. There may be dozens of underwriters in the sector to be covered, some of them Lloyd's syndicates to which an outsider does not have access, and getting comparable quotes from them all may produce a useful and comprehensive picture of the market, but could take weeks. Insurance brokers exist as personal shoppers. They are supposed to trawl the market to find the best value policy for the customer. In practice they are human, the market is large, and judgment about value is subjective. One broker may not find the best every time. A shrewd buyer will talk to several, but once you have experience of the market and the brokers' performance, that will probably come down to three. It is not enough however that brokers are good buyers, they must also be good payers. That means the broker itself, as the agent of the insured, should be a tough negotiator with the underwriter when buying the policy, but even more so when making a claim. And a good broker will point out that one policy may be cheaper but the company has a practice of never paying, and even when obviously liable dragging out the time, while the other, although slightly steeper in initial cost, will work out better if a claim is ever made. The choice is then still up to the buyer.

From time to time the underwriter will send notifications of changes in the conditions or levels of cover. Scrutinize these carefully and it is probably also worth checking every three or four years whether the underwriter and broker are still giving the best value. It is tedious, but it may be worth going through the whole process from the start again. It is certainly important that the level of cover being bought is always up to date.

There are many more possibilities for insurance than are listed here, but some are specialized, some uneconomic and some are bought in a different form of market. For instance, buying currency forward is a form of insurance against exchange rate fluctuations.

Insurance premiums are allowable against tax.

Employers' liability

Cover for £5 million is compulsory, even if the employees are temporary or part-time. This type of insurance is extremely expensive. The sharp increase in litigation, encouraged by ambulance-chasing solicitors and the government's increase in award ceilings, has made underwriters nervous. Premium rates have rocketed and some employers have difficulty buying a policy at all. Extensive shopping around – possibly using several brokers – is the only answer. Even then negotiations may be tough, but one ploy is for the company to explain it will install extensive conflict-resolution mechanisms and careful personnel policies to reduce the risk of claims.

Lifting tackle and pressure vessels also have to be insured by law.

Vehicle

This is compulsory for third-party cover. How far you extend cover beyond that depends on an individual decision on risk, and the sort of deal the insurance broker can extract from underwriters.

Public liability

Britain is rapidly becoming as litigious as the US. Somebody slips on the shiny stairs to your office and damages their back, a tile slips off the roof and hits someone's head, and you can be taken for thousands. Public liability would be necessary even if many large customers did not demand it of their suppliers. Ensure the cover extends to subcontractors and temporary staff.

Product liability

Nobody accepts there are such things as accidents. If there is damage, somebody must be to blame. People are quick to sue, although in theory Britain does not yet have strict product liability (that is the expression for the manufacturer being to blame even if at the time of the manufacture all possible care and attention was paid to making the product safe).

Two widely quoted cases in this context are from America. One concerns the owner of a poodle who used to dry her pooch after a bath by putting it by the warm oven. When she got a microwave, the consequence was a very dead hot dog and she sued the makers for not warning that it was unsafe for such purposes. She won millions of dollars. The other case concerns a man cutting a high hedge with an electric hover mower which inevitably fell, severed the cable and electrocuted the gardener, producing millions of dollars for the widow. Urban myths. Despite the best efforts of three legal firms in Los Angeles, Chicago and New York to find the sources, absolutely no record has ever been found of either of them.

All the same, a company may still need to pay if someone is hurt, and the cover should extend to recalling products and latent defects.

Business interruption

If something serious were to disrupt the company's operations, such as fire or flood, resulting in the destruction of records (although see p.114 about computers), the loss of stocks or the production facilities, the business could well fold. Customers would go elsewhere and might not return, and the company may not be able to pay for all the replacement from its own resources. Insurance for this eventuality is important, but even more vital is contingency planning. When creating the policy, bear in mind the company may also be susceptible to failures at suppliers, including utilities such as electricity, water and telephone services. Part of the policy is for replacement of assets.

Contingency planning is vital since not even the most cooperative insurance company will pay a comprehensive cost. A range of facilities from computer back-ups, power generators and knowledge of alternative premises to buffer stocks stored away from the main building may mitigate the damage.

Premises

As with the contents of the premises and the stock insurance (see below), this category should include 'consequential loss' cover. In other words, the cost of the disruption and loss of business while things are restored to normal.

It is probably worth including cover for goods in transit either under this or the stock policy.

Contents

This will cover records as well as usual contents because the consequential loss from losing these could be catastrophic. Imagine losing all the accounts or the names and addresses of customers. Theft cover is also likely to be needed, especially by retailers.

Stock

Consequential damage for loss of stock could be substantial. The customers may not be prepared to wait for your products to be made all over again, and could take their business to a competitor, never to return. It might also be that with a clothing company, say, by the time the stock was recreated the fashion will have changed. So insurance is vital. It should cover not just fire and flood but also theft.

Directors and officers

Legislation imposes ever stricter requirements of conduct and competence – the range is wide, from the Insolvency Act to the Data Protection Act, from Companies Acts to health and safety regulations, and all demand appropriate and systematic action, with penalties for failure. Directors under these laws include the executives, the non-executive and part-time directors, and even 'shadow' directors who are defined as people whose advice and influence can change the conduct of the board. Breach of duty by one of the directors could be expensive for the person and the company, but usually only in fairly substantial companies. It may be worth taking a chance on this and going uninsured while the company is still tiny, but it soon becomes important – the costs of defence against claims are ruinously expensive even if you win.

Fidelity guarantee

In the catering business, 'shrinkage' can rise to 11 per cent. In plain English this is theft by staff. It is not just the bottles of whisky they may walk off with, in trades where staff handle cash some of it finds its way into their pockets. Tight controls and rigorous recruitment procedures control the problem, but insurance may also help. The two are not alternatives – most policies insist on some form of recruitment screening plus precautions against fraud and theft.

Professional indemnity

Most of the professions insist on member firms taking out insurance to enable them to pay claims from clients. Since they will not license the firms to practise without the cover, this is the equivalent of a legal requirement. In other cases, the customers themselves might demand such cover. Similarly, travel agents have to have ABTA cover to protect customers' money in case the business fails.

Key man

This is increasingly called key person insurance. The premise is that a range of employees, directors or sales staff, may be vital for the continuing health of the business. If a key technician or production manager died or contracted a long-term illness, things could look bleak for the business, at least in the short term until alternative arrangements are in place. Whether this insurance is bought and for how much depends on a realistic assessment of the risks to the business from the prolonged absence of some staff members.

Credit

The need for insurance against bad debts will depend on the trade – some are reasonably reliable – and on the degree of other protection taken, such as factoring, prior investigation, vulnerability of the business to customer failure, and so on.

Computer

There is a variety of risks, especially if the company is on-line to the Internet. There are dangers from malicious damage through viruses, Trojan horses, hacking, degradation of data and the like, in addition to possible consequential claims if you inadvertently pass a virus on to someone. There are potential but overstated dangers from copyright infringement, allowing access to data which should have been confidential, and breaches of the financial security protection. Whether this is covered by insurance also depends on a realistic assessment of the risks, both of occurrence and the degree of pain felt by the business if the worst happens.

Legal

You will at some stage almost certainly face a legal action. It may come from a disgruntled employee claiming unfair dismissal, a VAT tribunal or prosecution under health and safety directives. It will be an expensive distraction, but a legal policy covers costs.

Environment

The range of legislation is growing to insist on the safe disposal of hazardous waste and the recycling of much else. Penalties for infringing some of the laws are heavy. This sort of insurance is advisable for manufacturers and chemical businesses with toxic or unpleasant by-products.

Personal

The entrepreneur is vital for the survival of the business in the early stages, and prolonged illness could be a serious setback with unpleasant financial consequences. This can be partially offset by insurance.

In addition, employer's liability covers only cases where an accident was the legal fault of the business. If there are some hazardous tasks involved, or as a benevolent gesture to valued employees, the company can take out personal accident cover for them.

PENSIONS

Pensions have recently changed from being considered the most tedious subject (except for people on the verge of retirement), to provoking inflamed debate and argument, threats of strikes and political embarrassment. The cause has been partly the economy and partly the government taking billions of pounds from pensions and making it increasingly unattractive to save, while at the same time making it clear the state would not be paying the old much in future.

In 'occupational pensions' – those organized and partly paid for by employers – final salary schemes (where the pension is dependent on the pay received in the years immediately before retirement) are reckoned to be almost defunct. As fast as the trust deeds and their employees permit, companies are closing them down, at least to new entrants, and instead substituting defined contributions. These are also called money purchase schemes – the pensions are dependent on the money accumulated in the fund at the time of retirement.

The Inland Revenue has to approve all these schemes to ensure they meet various requirements, including the maximum pension payable. Staff may pay up to 15 per cent of earnings and the company must contribute something. There are Small Self-Administered Schemes for family companies with up to 11 members, which have a fair amount of freedom, including buying the company's own shares or commercial property (including the business's premises), and making loans to the employer. On retirement, the pension is paid from the income up to the age of 75 and then an annuity is bought.

Personal pension schemes are available to people who are not in an employer's scheme and contributions are on a sliding scale from 17.5 per cent up to the age of 35, to 40 per cent for those aged 61 and over.

Stakeholder

The employer designates an acceptable scheme (this does not count as a recommendation), usually run by an insurance company, and offers to make regular payroll deductions for employees but need not contribute any extra money. The employees can opt for a different scheme from the one recommended if they prefer. The scheme has the advantages of being simple and the government sets a low ceiling on the fees the funds may charge for administration, but experts reckon that it is most suitable for low-income employees.

Employers that do not have to provide the facilities for stakeholder pensions include those with a suitable group pensions scheme, those with fewer than five employees, and those with occupational schemes open to all employees.

7 Staff

Some businesses need employees from the outset – the sort of work or commercial structure demands it. Such companies have to be prepared for the complications and administration from the start. Others set out as sole traders and then grow to the point of needing people. The prospect of hiring people terrifies many who do not want to be bosses, have heard the reports of incessant problems and endless tangles of red tape, do not want the administration or responsibility or do not think they are good at managing people. For them there are four alternatives.

The first is to turn surplus work away. Explain to clients that you cannot cope, you are fully booked, and if they want you they will have to take a slot in September when the schedule permits it. This may appear to solve the problem, but could make a sole trader extremely uncomfortable. Valuable clients may get offended or disinclined to wait and defect to the competition. It may work if you are unique or have some quality for which you can charge inordinately, and for which clients are prepared to wait.

A second course is to realize you are doing something right and have come into great demand because you are valuable. The answer then is to raise the charges. All small businesses hate doing this and the vast majority of them undercharge for their goods and services; raising fees goes against the grain. But try it. If it fights the instincts so fiercely that it is worrying, try raising them by only 10 per cent and see what happens. In reality, if work is coming in substantially faster than you can cope with it, the chances are a rise of 25 per cent will not make the slightest difference. But by all means try it gently. If it does not make much difference, you can go on increasing fees until it does, and demand and supply come into balance.

A third option for those opposed to hiring staff is to take on a self-employed person on a temporary basis or on a contract for a specific task. Interim staff can be brought in to cope even with highly specialized work, or portions of the task can be subcontracted to an expert in the field. That expert could even be a fairly large company, yet there is no reason why a sole trader cannot employ someone larger. Be careful of the IR35 income tax rules which may decide the person on contract is actually an employee and has to be taxed as such, including National Insurance contributions.

The final choice for those with a deeply entrenched hatred of employing staff is a variation on a franchise operation, something like the outsourcing or interim contract but on a more formal long-term basis. This can work for specialist consultancies. If you find people who are as good as you are and are ready to take on work, then, when a customer offers a task for which you are too busy, explain you have somebody lined up to do the work on your system. Obviously you take a cut of their fees, and recruit only people you can trust not to go behind your back and steal customers after they have been introduced. It works best when there is a system or approach individual to you.

These are all ploys to get round the headaches of complying with proliferating employment regulation and the much-publicized and soaring number of applications to employment tribunals, and the even greater rise in the amounts being awarded against companies. The publicity for those cases suggests widespread insanity, but this is in fact only represented by a small number of cases – the tribunals are in the main level-headed and do not usually support a try-on.

It does take care and concentrated attention not to fall foul of some of the legislation, yet much good practice is actually the sort of thing that any good employer with a fair and generous spirit would probably do in any case. The trouble is the company might not be doing it in precisely the form outlined in the pile of legislation.

The volume of employment law is horrendously thick and growing, and its more remote thickets are impenetrable to the lay person, but so is all law. Most of the employment problems can be avoided by treating staff in a sensible, courteous and compassionate way.

By taking a sensible and methodical approach, including careful records of the care and consideration employed, not every sacking will inevitably result in massive legal comebacks. That does however mean care and observance of the formalities to provide a defence if it does come to a row. This applies with even greater force for cases of sexual harassment where the existing legislation turns traditional English law on its head and the company is guilty until it can prove itself innocent.

There is no shortage of advice and guidance from the Advisory Conciliation and Arbitration Service (ACAS), the Equal Opportunities Commission, the Commission for Racial Equality, the Race Relations Advisory Service and the Disability Rights Commission (see Appendix A for contact details and Appendix C for examples of the material they produce).

EMPLOYEE OBLIGATIONS

In return for the mountain of legislation protecting employees (the examples mentioned in Appendix D are a long way from exhausting the list), there is little enforcing compensating employee obligations to the employer. The key obligation is the duty of good faith and loyalty. These embrace the common sense requirements one would expect. In the main an employer can expect employees:

- to be at the workplace regularly and promptly
- to spend working hours at the job rather than on some private occupation
- not to operate a spare-time job in competition with the employer
- not to make private profit during working hours or at the employer's expense
- not to reveal confidential information about the business (a breach can lead to uncompensated dismissal or even claim for compensation)

- to tell the employer about inventions, discoveries and creations produced during working hours
- to do the job properly and without negligence
- to be honest, which goes beyond simple avoidance of fraud or theft
- to obey reasonable instructions.

MOTIVATION: INDUSTRIAL PSYCHOLOGY, COMMUNICATIONS

It should go without saying that what distinguishes a good company from a dud is the people working in it. You can have the most wonderful device the world has ever seen, but if disgruntled employees make little of it, and that badly, if the salespeople are slovenly and untrustworthy, and the financial control is slack and incompetent, the business will fail. Many managers repeat the mantra that people are the most valuable resource and make the company a success, and yet their actions can make them liars – either they do not understand what is involved or they are trying to kid people.

Several things follow. The first is that finding and keeping the right people is key. Then, having got the right people, the way to retain them is to keep them happy, and the way to get full benefit from them is to motivate them properly.

The American psychologist B. F. Skinner spent a lifetime finding out how to train animals, like pigeons and rats. He invented the Skinner box to test various simple training techniques. By pecking or pressing the correct disc the animals got a reward, such as some tasty food. Sometimes, if they pressed the wrong one, they got a mild but unpleasant electric shock. Among the things he discovered was that 'positive reinforcement' (reward) acted as a better stimulant to fast, accurate and lasting learning than 'negative reinforcement' (punishment).

That applies to humans too. People respond to a pat on the back, a word of praise, a congratulatory note. They feel appreciated and cared about (see the Hawthorne Effect described on p.230), and they respond by working harder. It is possible to rule by terror, to shout at every mistake, to lacerate employees regularly, and to fire the worst ones on a regular basis *pour encourager les autres*. It may even work. In fact, although the current fashion is for a gentle, inclusive, empowering type of management, nobody has yet shown that the tyrannical system is less effective. Common sense indicates, however, that the best staff members will soon get tired of it and quit, leaving only the unemployables to suffer, and that morale will be low enough to damage effectiveness.

Incidentally, Skinner discovered not only that rewarding was the more effective way to encourage preferred behaviour, but that the most effective of all was intermittent reward. If the animal did not get the food every time it did the right thing, but only the majority of times, then it learned even faster and retained the lesson longer.

Staff contentment

It takes two aspects to make the business attractive. The first is what industrial psychologist Frederick Herzberg called hygiene factors. These are characteristics of the workplace which do not in themselves give us satisfaction or make us happy, but if they are not there people become grumpy and dissatisfied. In other words, they are the minimal requirements and part of a sensible set-up. This includes a physical environment that goes beyond the minimal demands of the Offices Shops and Railway Premises Act or the Factories Act. It also covers considerate treatment that accords staff dignity, including such basics as praising in public, and blaming in private. In addition, it has been shown time and again that workers are more committed when they are kept informed. That does not mean a glossy company newspaper, but just letting them know what is going on and why.

The second aspect is providing recognition and incentives. One of the failings of many entrepreneurs is the reluctance to release any of the equity in their new creation (see Chapter 5). Yet not only managers but other employees work with more of a will when they feel they own part of the business. The shares can be provided on some form of performance-related incentive basis, but they do help motivation and retention of staff.

DISCRIMINATION

It is illegal to discriminate against somebody on the grounds of gender, their race, age (from 2006), sexual orientation, disability, marital status, trade union membership, if they have a 'spent' conviction, or because they are part-timers. At the moment there is no legislation to prevent discrimination on the grounds of religion, though if it occurred a legal action by the employee may be possible under the Human Rights Act. It is also legal to refuse employment to someone if you are unhappy about the state of their health.

That applies to all conditions of employment from selection, through pay and holidays, to sacking, although there are exemptions for small companies. Positive discrimination – favouring any of those categories – is similarly illegal. There are few exceptions to this, and they are mainly when there is a genuine requirement for a person of a specific gender to do the work; for instance, an actor in a play, or, for public decency, a changing-room attendant. The requirement for strength or stamina are not considered acceptable grounds for discrimination.

Indirect discrimination covers selection by criteria that make life difficult for one class of employee without actually excluding them explicitly. For instance, the requirement that all workers must be full-time and work the standard hours has been taken to discriminate against women because they are more likely to want to work part-time and flexible hours.

Harassment

The feeling of being picked on, harassed or discriminated against is subjective. That is the conclusion of the case law only, since sexual harassment does not appear in the legislation. It can be verbal or physical abuse on the grounds of sex, ethnic origin or disability, and if a person reckons to be on the receiving end, a claim may be made against the employer. The company is liable if one of its employees has harassed another, even if that is in clear breach of corporate rules – the law believes it ought to have ensured better supervision and enforcement of the rules. One defence that has proved acceptable is that an employee has gone 'on a frolic of his own'. Believe it or not that is a legal phrase and it indicates some wholly unexpected and uncontrollable action by a worker. There are not many other defences and the case of Chief Constable of Lincolnshire v Stubbs established that an employer is liable for harassment even at staff entertainment off the organization's premises and outside office hours. There is no ceiling on compensation, and large awards have been made to soothe hurt feelings.

There are few objective criteria, and it is enough to feel hard done by to have grounds for complaint. The employer then has to prove innocence. Since it is tricky proving a negative, the best defence to this sort of allegation is to have proper procedure, ensure all the staff know the rules, and show the policy of fairness is properly policed. Moreover, demonstrate that the complaint was properly and promptly dealt with.

Whether the allegation is upheld or rejected, there are strong rules against victimization. This also applies to 'whistleblowers' – workers who inform against the employer under the Public Interest Disclosure Act. The grounds for disclosure are:

- a criminal act has been or is about to be committed
- the employer is not fulfilling legal obligations
- there has been a miscarriage of justice
- an individual's health or safety is in danger
- the environment is likely to be damaged
- the information on any of these is being concealed.

HIRING

There are three ways of reducing the chances of an expensive transgression of the employment legislation: careful recruitment, treating people with courtesy and understanding, and having the proper legal procedures in place.

Selection

It may seem absurd, or even condescending, to spell this out, but before hiring somebody you have to know what you want them for. It is odd how seldom this is thought through in the hiring process. As a result, people are taken on without a proper job description and without being told fully what they are supposed to be doing. Being more methodical about the process means compiling a detailed description of what the person is to do, and therefore what skills are vital and which additional skills would be useful, and to whom the new person is answerable. The next step is to work out the terms, including pay and holiday. That means the advertisement will be able to specify precisely what is wanted and there will be fewer arguments later.

When setting out these criteria, it pays to be realistic. All employers want paragons, with the brains of a Nobel prize winner, the honesty of a saint, the diligence of a Stakhanov and the enterprise of a Bill Gates. Even if such avatars existed, is it likely they would want to work for you at those wages? So match skills to jobs, remembering that dull repetitive jobs are as ill done by really bright people as intellectual jobs by dullards.

If people claim qualifications, show a record of previous employment, and list references, follow them up. Few employers do, which is why so many bogus people with totally spurious CVs manage to continue finding employment. Under the Rehabilitation of Offenders Act you may not discriminate against anyone who has been sentenced to under 30 months in jail or has received a suspended sentence, or against ex-prisoners on longer sentences who have been rehabilitated (which is anything from five to ten years, depending on the sentence). Applicants who have 'spent' convictions – the jail sentence was long enough ago that they are considered rehabilitated – do not have to disclose the fact they were convicted and are even allowed to deny they have ever been convicted after their sentence is spent. If the employer does find out about the criminal record, it is illegal to discriminate against a person on those grounds.

Staying clear of all the anti-discrimination regulations requires a lot of effort and care. For instance, the advertisements must exclude terms which suggest only one sex could be eligible, such as foreman. Do not use the word he or she on its own.

Interviewing

People we have known for decades – including husbands and wives – still manage to surprise us quite often. Yet most people are hired, even for sensitive and senior jobs on which the health of the business depends, after a half-hour casual chat. The interviewer usually does not even have a formal list of the subjects to be discussed, the questions to ask, or the criteria for scoring the applicants. Perhaps this is because of the astonishingly large number of people who fool themselves into thinking they are good judges of character. To show the fallacy of this, turn it round the other way. How much of yourself do you show to a complete stranger within the first half hour of acquaintanceship? How well do you think your colleagues know you? It is even harder talking to a prospective employer, because obviously we would all be on our best behaviour, keep faults and fears hidden, and show off the characteristics likely to win approval.

Even allowing for all this, interviews are necessary. They are more useful with careful homework. Show good manners by having read the applicant's CV and application letter before the person appears, and ask only questions that arise from that or to fill in the gaps. Unless the job involves working under personal attack and being intimidated by other people, the discussion will be more fruitful if relaxed and friendly. It is more constructive to let the candidates explain themselves than to try trapping them into some damaging admission. Also in the interests of getting the maximum information, ask open questions requiring an extended answer rather than closed ones which can be despatched with a single yes or no.

Some experts recommend a list of useful interview questions, for example, 'What do you consider to be your greatest failure and why?' Or, 'When were you last angry at work, what caused it and what did you do about it?' Or 'What are your greatest strengths?' These may be quite handy for recruiting salespeople, but not every job is best filled by plausible, glib people who know how to deal with easy lobs like that. Any candidate with an experience of interviews and a high degree of articulacy can turn such questions to show themselves to advantage for the panel they are meeting. Even when discussing failures the obvious tactic is to praise oneself with faint damns. It is more important to discover whether the candidate has the specialist capabilities suited to the job.

In general it is best to move the discussion in a way that shows personality, rather than mechanically rehearsing the previous experience record.

During the interview some subjects are taboo. It is still permissible to ask a man about his wife, but asking a woman about her husband, family responsibilities or if she plans to have children soon are definitely inadvisable.

When somebody has been hired, ask for a P45 and let the tax office know.

Terms and administration

The employment contract may be assumed to include anything in the original advertisement, anything said at the interview, and any other written communication between the employer and the worker. That is in addition to the written statement of terms which the employee is entitled to receive within eight weeks of starting work, unless terms were set out at the start. This has to include job title, conditions, pay, pension, holidays, sick pay, notice period, disciplinary and grievance procedures and, if fixed, the length of employment. A wealth of helpful leaflets is available from the Inland Revenue, the Equal Opportunities Commission, the Commission for Racial Equality, the Department of Trade and ACAS (see Appendix C).

Pay and hours

Staff pay slips must show how the pay is made up, including tax and other deductions. Fines or any docking from the pay have to be notified and agreed at the time, and not merely noted in the slip. However, employers are entitled to withhold pay for the period staff are on strike.

Under the working time regulations, the maximum hours permissible, averaged over 17 weeks, is 48 hours a week and 13 hours a day, unless the employee gives written consent to waiving that right. This includes a 20-minute rest break after six hours of work. Night workers have restrictions on the hours worked, and access to free health assessment.

The minimum wage legislation sets the amount payable. This depends on whether the worker is under or over 21, and on the latest revision of the rate.

The company acts as administrator for the government for:

- collecting taxes (PAYE and National Insurance)
- collecting money to repay student loans
- organizing stakeholder pensions deductions
- payment of tax credits to the worker
- enforcing court orders to pay the Child Support Agency.

Sick pay

Employees earning over £67 a week are entitled under the Social Security Contributions and Benefit Act to sick pay for up to 28 weeks a year. This is subject to all the normal taxes of National Insurance and PAYE, but the employer can claim back money if it is more than

13 per cent of the National Insurance payments that month from employer and employee.

The contractual sick pay established in the terms of employment can be better than this, and generally is. In that case, the employer is free to ask for a sickness certificate for any absence, although they may be forced to pay the doctor to supply it.

When there is no addition to the statutory requirements, the first seven days of sickness absence self-certification is enough under the Statutory Sick Pay (Medical Evidence) Regulations, and an employer may not demand more.

If an independent doctor is asked to examine the employee, the company pays for that cost. Employees who are persistently sick and/or absent on the grounds of ill health are entitled to refuse the employer access to their doctor or medical records under Access to Medical Reports Act. However, if they do refuse both an independent check and the employer having a word with their own doctor, they are likely to face an unsympathetic employment tribunal when dismissed.

Holidays

After 13 weeks with the company, an employee gains entitlement to paid holidays with a minimum of four weeks a year. The entitlement to holidays continues to accrue even if the worker is absent through sickness. Bank holidays can be counted as part of that entitlement.

Parental leave

You may not dismiss employees for becoming pregnant, married or not, and they must be allowed time off for ante-natal care. Staff are entitled to maternity leave and statutory maternity pay, and the job must be held open for one year minus 11 weeks after the child is born. In addition, before the child reaches five, parents are allowed 13 weeks' leave taken in chunks of one week to four weeks a year.

Stakeholder pension

Every business with more than four employees is obliged to offer the administration of a stakeholder pension scheme, unless its own company scheme allows it to be exempt. In practice, this is not too onerous, although if the employees are indecisive or awkward it can be a nuisance, because it is administered through the payroll programme. In any case, the take-up has been small, partly because employees understand that pensions funds of all sorts are invested in the stock market and they have grown nervous of the oscillations of the share prices.

The company nominates an administrator of the fund from the list held by the Occupational Pensions Regulatory Authority, which does not amount to a recommendation, and invites the company – generally speaking one of the larger insurance companies – to come and explain the scheme to employees. The workers can then elect to have the premiums deducted from their pay.

The Department of Work and Pensions has a website and a phone line explaining details.

Health insurance

Some employers provide a group scheme health insurance that employees can then top up if they want better cover. It counts as a taxable benefit, and so it will have to be declared on their P11D. There are four main types of cover:

1 Medical cover for fast treatment of short-term conditions in the private sector.

2 Permanent health insurance, which is the opposite of what it says – it is in fact income replacement to provide income (usually about half the salary) for people so unhealthy they can work no longer.

3 Critical illness policies provide a tax-free lump sum to somebody who is seriously ill.

4 Long-term care is just what it says.

Trade unions

If the majority of the workforce wants it, the employer must recognize a trade union under the Employment Relations Act 1999.

Illegal immigrants

Under the Asylum and Immigration Act, an employer may legally hire only people who have a right to work in Britain. Giving work to an illegal immigrant or to someone legally in the country but without a work permit can result in a fine of £5,000. This applies to casual staff, for example, in catering or building trades. The company is expected to demand some certification, such as something from a government office bearing the National Insurance number, a P45, P60, work permit, or passport to show that the person comes from the European Economic Area.

The Race Relations Act makes it illegal to discriminate on the basis of race or ethnic origin, and so the same process of screening must be applied to all applicants.

HEALTH AND SAFETY

As soon as somebody is employed, the business must notify the authority supervising the health and safety legislation for that sector. This will be either the local authority's environmental health department for businesses such as restaurants and shops, or the Health and Safety executive through its local office. The compulsory employer's liability insurance is demonstrated with a certificate pinned to the wall, together with a poster on the law. Moreover, the premises must be assessed for potential hazard, including fire risk, and employees must be told the safety code of the company.

Further to making the place safe for workers and visitors, the law requires fire exits and extinguishers, training for the workers, testing of electrical equipment, hygiene, provision of first aid kits, and explaining and displaying safety rules. With over nine workers, there must also be an accident book. There are extra provisions in the Controls of Substances Hazardous to Health regulations.

The Health and Safety at Work Act demands protection 'so far as is reasonably practicable'. This legal phrase is interpreted on the merits of each case. However, if a company is prosecuted for failing to implement some safety measure adequately, it is considered guilty unless it can prove the measure was not practicable. According to a 1949 legal decision (in Edwards v National Coal Board), practicable in this context means balancing a degree of risk against the money, time and trouble necessary to reduce it.

Given the overall responsibility and that proviso, the Act lists five responsibilities:

1 To make sure equipment does not damage health.

2 To make sure the goods on the premises are safe.

3 To inform, train and supervise employees.

4 To make sure the premises are safe and have emergency exits.

5 To make sure the environment is safe and has necessary facilities.

If one of the workers is known to be clumsy and somebody gets injured as a result, the employer is liable. A worker who breaks the well-publicised safety rule, and was told this was a disciplinary offence, can be sacked.

To be fair, difficult though the legislation may be, it is obviously the duty of an employer, not in law but in common humanity, to protect workers from harm. Fortunately ethics is well buttressed by economics in this instance – it is probably less expensive to look after staff than to suffer the cost of replacing an injured or sick worker and training the new one, plus the sick pay and bad reputation from neglecting employees' welfare.

A serious accident caused by failure to follow the rules could close a business almost overnight, and the senior people could be sent to prison. Directors are expected to create a safe environment, instigate safe practices, and ensure they are obeyed.

Repetitive strain injury

Repetitive strain injury (RSI) is sometimes made more portentous by being called work-related upper limb disorder, mainly because arms are the usual case of the problem. It is caused by performing the same movement too often or an awkward movement regularly, and causes pain, problems with the tendons, swelling of the hands and the loss of strength and mobility. Typing can set it off. Some people are more prone to it than others for reasons still disputed, but tension, an awkward workplace layout, and heavy workload are probably contributory factors. When workers have brought claims against their employers for damaged health, the courts have not been unanimous – some have said RSI does not exist, while others have made awards.

The trend seems to be acceptance of the fact and the requirement for employers to avoid the dangers. This means good chairs, ergonomic layouts for computers (foot-rests for people under 1.7m (5ft 8in), hand-rests in front of keyboards, correct height of keyboard and screen, etc.), and regular breaks from working in front of a screen. Similar measures may be needed for other types of occupation that can produce the symptoms.

A few years ago there were reports of damage caused by cathode ray tube computer screens, ranging from cataract and cancer to miscarriage of pregnant women. Research suggested that was unlikely and the displays themselves have improved. They are now increasingly replaced by flat LCD screens which have produced no scare stories so far.

Stress

Since the 1980s, there has been a steadily growing volume of cases and studies attributing many of the ills suffered by people to stress. Even backache and colds, two of the commonest causes of illness absence, have been blamed on stress. Stress is such a common complaint, so widely discussed and so difficult to prove, and it has become a growing source of claims against employers.

The classic case was a local authority employee who had been off work because he had asked for help with his workload but had not received it and had been made unwell. When he came back the load was at least as great, and he suffered a nervous breakdown for which he received substantial compensation. This exemplified the criteria by which an award is decided: whether the danger was foreseeable (his illness and request for less work indicated that), and whether the employer was the cause (giving him a pile of work on return from illness).

Employers are expected not only to react to cries for help, but to watch for signs of debilitating stress and act before things get worse. The symptoms include:

- feelings of fear and panic
- unpredictable mood swings
- anger and irritability
- poor concentration
- inability to sleep.

Stress is not suffered most by people with the heaviest responsibilities. On the contrary, for them it is frequently a source of adrenaline and excitement. The most affected are people in humble, repetitive jobs over which they have no control, having to work long hours, and with the fear of reprimand at the slightest mistake.

CONSULTATION

Employees have to be consulted about a range of health and safety measures, especially if something is going to affect the degree of risk. In addition, if independent trade union members are included in redundancy or other sackings, representatives of the union have to be consulted. Trade unions must also be told if the business is to be sold or another bought.

GRIEVANCE

Under the Employment Rights Act, the terms of employment have to include mention of grievance procedure. This procedure sets out to whom a grievance should be notified and how and what will happen. If the immediate supervisor cannot deal with the problem, the statement specifies what happens next. If it has to go to a second stage, employees should realize they may be accompanied by a union representative. If the dispute is sufficiently entrenched, it may have to go before the Advisory Conciliation and Arbitration Service whose decision is final and binding on both sides.

Employees often counter a disciplinary action by raising a grievance. Even if the employer realizes this is merely a ploy to avoid the consequences of some infringement of the rules, the complaint is heard fairly and, as far as possible, independently of the other action.

It is probably a good idea to treat complaints about harassment separately from other grievances.

REVIEWS

Regular performance reviews help both the individual and the employer. They help employees to discover how well they are doing and whether some aspect of their jobs could be improved, and it helps the company by ensuring the employees realize where problems lie and allows them to improve. Reviews also protect the corporation from claims for unfair dismissals. In any case, it is only fair to tell people when they are doing well, and to encourage them to do something about their weaknesses. Not many of us are perfect.

DISCIPLINE

Employers specify the required standards of work and behaviour and, if there are more than 20 employees, the written statement of employment includes some reference to the disciplinary procedures, such as who is subject, who enforces, and what appeals routes exist. Quite apart from what the government and Brussels demand in the way of rules and procedures, setting it all out from the start prevents argument later, even in a small company. Managers of small concerns say there is no need because everybody is on first-name terms with everyone else, and so the rules and consequences are known and accepted. The whole point is that if it turns out you employ people who endanger others, incompetents who cannot cope, or idle or malevolent staff whom you need to discipline or sack, they are unlikely to be friendly and cooperative.

The disciplinary rules should contain provision for:

- absence
- use of facilities
- discrimination
- bullying
- harassment
- theft
- fraud
- drunkenness at work
- drug taking
- unruly behaviour, including fighting
- breaches of health and safety rules
- serious insubordination
- serious breaches of confidentiality
- misuse or personal use of the Internet.

At the end of any list, add that this is merely an indication of the type of misconduct that will not be tolerated, and it is not intended to be an exhaustive list. Unfortunately, there is no useful civilian phrase that can act as a catch-all equivalent to the army's 'contrary to good order and military discipline', but that is what the document should imply.

The Internet has grown to be a serious and complex problem. The safest way to contain it is to set out from the start what is acceptable. The employer can say in the employment contract that no private use is permissible, even the sending or receipt of personal e-mail, and that to police that rule the system is continuously monitored, including incoming and outgoing messages and what is stored on the company's machines. By stating this from the start you may prevent repercussions under the Human Rights Act and the Data Protection Act.

Procedure

The Advisory Conciliation and Arbitration Service has a code of practice that can be lifted wholesale into the document given to employees. Among its provisions are the requirement that the procedure is in writing, prompt, and confidential, entails proper investigation, provides a chance to respond to charges, and includes a right of appeal. Workers should not be dismissed for a first offence except for dire misconduct, and they can have a union representative accompany them at hearings. The employer keeps records of disciplinary action, including the cause, action taken, and whether there was an appeal and, if so, with what result.

Warnings

If somebody is not up to the mark, the regular reviews will already have told them so. Employees do of course need to know what performance is expected and should have been given any necessary training. If their work is unsatisfactory, it is wise to give them a written statement of what is amiss and why. They can then come back to explain the reasons, dispute the assessment, or they can improve. If there is no improvement, the formal course is to give a second written warning, explaining what happens if they continue to fall short, including reminders of the terms of the contract of employment.

If there is a disciplinary procedure for some other, but not too serious, reason and the complaint on investigation is upheld, the employee normally first receives an oral warning. If there is no improvement in the conduct or the misdemeanour is repeated and confirmed, there is a written warning. Continued failure can result in a second written warning, and only if the problem persists after that can the employer sack someone with impunity.

Sacking

The surest way of reducing the problems of sackings is to hire the right people in the first place. The second surest is to behave well. Combining the two should help to steer clear of the most painful aspects of the law.

Behaving well means at the very least following the rules set out in the multiplicity of legislative regulations but, more to the point – and this is presumably what those bureaucrats are trying to induce, and this chapter keeps emphasizing – treat people with courtesy and consideration. This is important not just because it is the right thing to do, but because an employer can be sued for unfair or wrongful dismissal without having sacked the employee. For instance, putting employees in an impossible or humiliating position, or making their working conditions seriously worse can be defined under current law as a technical or constructive dismissal, and called unfair or wrongful even if they resign. This can include leaving a senior executive with a previous title but in a tiny branch office with only menial jobs to do. The same provision applies with a change of business ownership that makes the situation worse.

A criminal conviction for action outside work for some reason unconnected with the person's business capacity is not necessarily grounds for dismissal.

On the other hand, following the rules can protect employers against the most recalcitrant barrack-room lawyer. Companies can even sack workers on strike provided the workers receive a written notice stating that if they do not get back to work within a stated time they will be dismissed. There are some obvious situations where it is safe to get rid of someone such as a lorry driver who has had his licence taken away or an employee who has set up in competition on a part-time basis.

In the cases of genuine redundancy, the safest course is to dismiss on the basis of last in, first out.

Instant dismissal

Gross breaches of the contract of employment do permit instant dismissal. An example is a substantial theft.

Employees, including senior managers, found with their hands in the till are often allowed to leave and are hardly ever prosecuted. Companies claim they do not want to advertise their vulnerability or their lack of security for fear of losing customers. In fact, they do not want to expose the incompetence of their total lack of precautions which would show the absence of professional management and, in any case, cannot be bothered to spend the management time needed. Perhaps they think there is little chance of recovering the money and so the quicker they get rid of the crook the better. The consequence is that such fraudsters rob one company after another until they finally encounter somebody with enough backbone to prosecute.

Other reasons for summary dismissal are serious insubordination, thumping another employee or taking drugs at work.

Fair dismissal

The law allows only five reasons for sacking someone, but even then the procedure has to go through the pre-set rules to be fair and the grounds reasonable:

1 **Capability** – skill and physical and mental ability, which can also encompass ill health if the company can show prolonged and persistent absences caused serious disruption to the business. Competence is likely to lead to disagreements; the employer

should already have notified the worker that all was not well and either offered to retrain or find alternative tasks. A largish company is obliged to find a task more suited to the person's capabilities, but tribunals accept that this is less possible in a small one; that also means a sick employee should be found more suitable, perhaps sedentary, work if possible, but there is no obligation to create a new sort of job for the person.

2 **Conduct** – the disciplinary procedure will already have been spelled out in the contract of employment, and employment tribunals usually inspect them to check they are comprehensive and reasonable; handling this sensibly and sensitively not only reduces claims for unfair dismissal, but probably reduces dismissals altogether. If there really is a need for action, the company must swiftly gather all the facts, decide on the appropriate action and, if necessary, have a formal disciplinary interview with the worker. The worker has a right to be accompanied by a trade union representative and to answer the charges. Warnings are oral, and two written, and can be appealed. Gross misconduct is reckoned to cover persistent lateness, although the worker has to be warned in writing to mend his ways.

3 **Legal bar on work** – the Employment Rights Act 1996 is notably vague on this, but a potential example may be contravening the Asylum and Immigration Act 1986 which makes it illegal to employ a foreigner without a work permit.

4 **Redundancy** – even when the case is sound and the need to cut staff numbers is obvious, the procedure must be fair, and avoid discrimination when choosing the candidates to go.

5 There is also a wonderfully elusive catch-all phrase of '**some other substantial reason**' for dismissing someone.

By contrast, there are some reasons which would make a dismissal automatically unfair and the company liable to pay damages with no legal ceiling. These grounds include:

- sackings connected with maternity (businesses with fewer than five employees are exempt from post-maternity reinstatement)
- those covered by the Transfer of Undertaking (Protection of Employment) Regulations 1981, which is mainly about staff having the rights of continued employment after their company has been taken over
- being a union member
- being an informer (or whistle-blower), which is protected by the Public Interest Disclosure Act 1998, though only if the informing was in the public interest
- having a statutory right under minimum wages working time or other employment right
- tipping off the health and safety regulators.

Failing to follow the required procedures would also make a dismissal unfair. If the terms of the employment contract itself are broken, however, the employee has been wrongfully dismissed and can put in a claim for far more compensation than would be awarded under an unfair dismissal claim. Damages are awarded on the basis of what a person has lost and would expect to continue losing as a result of losing the job. Either way, the company cannot be forced to take a person back if it would rather pay compensation.

Employees come under the unfair dismissal provisions after one year in the job.

Anybody being dismissed has to receive a written reason with one week's notice if they have been there for at least four weeks, after two years a week's notice is needed for every year of continuous employment, or payment in lieu.

Tax notification

The tax people need to know when someone leaves.

REFERENCES

Employers are not obliged to give a reference to departing employees (except for jobs regulated by some law such as the Financial Services Act), but if they do it has to be fair.

Sometimes this can be difficult, especially if the employee has been a real headache. The reference has to steer between the Scylla of defamation of the person (who can sue), and the Charybdis of misleading the next employer (who can also sue). The only sure course is to write it very carefully and make sure the reference is both true, and cannot be said to be malicious. The safest one is merely a job description and avoids all subjective judgments about the individual's performance or personality.

EMPLOYMENT TRIBUNALS

The number of cases going to employment tribunals is soaring out of sight, with every indication that the additional rules and higher awards will accelerate the rate of growth, despite the government's stated aim of trying to mitigate this problem. Although the tribunals have the power to require someone making a wholly unjustified claim to pay the other side's costs, they seldom exercise this. As a result, with the potential for receiving substantial awards and no penalty for a completely unmerited accusation, employees are prepared to have a go, and may be egged on by lawyers and some trade union officials. The problem for the small employer is that even winning can cost an enormous amount in management time, quite apart from professional costs. The best way to stay out of these frightening statistics is to follow the rules with meticulous and painstaking precision. This will both reduce the incidence of cases and may lead to a quicker dismissal of unjustified try-ons.

Claims

Employees have to notify a tribunal within three months of leaving a job for claims of unfair dismissal or discrimination, but claims for statutory redundancy payments can be made up to six months after. The tribunal sends the employer details of the claim and asks for details of anti-discrimination policies. A detailed explanation of those policies and their implementation would then form part of the defence. At this stage, ACAS contacts the two sides to see if the dispute can be settled without a hearing.

Tribunals can award reinstatement in the old job and/or a cash compensation. The money can be on the same basis as redundancy; on the basis of compensation for loss of earnings (in 2002 that had a maximum of £52,600); a higher gift for discrimination on the grounds of sex, race, or disability, or for whistle-blowing or health and safety reasons; or a penalty for refusing to employ that person again.

Employers generally settle such cases even when they are fairly clearly unjustified because the cost in management time and legal fees could well be greater than the claim. Some employers' organizations have tried to dissuade them on the grounds that paying such Danegeld only invites mischievous claims. However, unless there is a major point of principle involved, most employers opt for the cheapest course and one that will get rid of both the troublesome employee and the irritating case.

8 Watching the money

The point of going into business is to make money. Even if the venture is little more than the extension of a hobby, it should at least 'wash its face', or it is not a business. The only way to tell whether it meets that aim is to watch very closely. You cannot take your eyes off the money for a minute without something going wrong.

This chapter spells out some of the aspects that need watching and some of the ratios to show whether the business is on the right lines. There is no substitute for this. Businesses go bust because of bad management – that is so great a truism it is almost a tautology. The most common aspect of bad management is slapdash financial control. Every survey of insolvencies shows companies going under because they priced too low, did not chase debtors effectively enough, and failed to plan ahead.

Setting up a company creates a separate legal entity, with its own rights and obligations. Its finances have to be kept separate from the managers' and proprietors' even if in practice the people are very much intertwined with the business. It is not just the tax man who will get nasty if the finances are mingled, the law can step in as well.

STATUTORY ACCOUNTS

This will be the sole mention in this book of the black economy. We have all come across it – tradespeople who will do a job cheaper for cash, no questions asked. There is no VAT, and they presumably pay no income tax. Anybody reading this book is trying to set up a business and not preparing to be a fly-by-night fugitive from the law. Not paying taxes is illegal and, more to the point, it is wrong.

The legal requirements for a business are that it keeps accurate records, has suitable financial and management controls in place, and its financial statements provide a true and fair view of the state of the business.

Keeping books

There is a threshold below which companies need to be audited only if the shareholders insist. In reality, creditors might require an audit in any case, well below the legal threshold. Nevertheless, presumably the business will soon burst through that ceiling and it makes sense to create the systems from scratch because trying to synthesize the complete set of figures a couple of years down the line is a real pain. Even a partnership or small private company needs decent books if only to reassure the participants that the business is as the managers say. Finally, there is always the danger of a tax investigation by either the Inland Revenue or Customs and Excise and, in the absence of accurate and comprehensive records, tax inspectors will act on the assumption you are attempting a massive tax fraud and will dare you to prove them wrong. They will be even tougher with any business that deals in cash – tax authorities assume they are all on the fiddle. Without records, that proof is unavailable, which could prove jolly expensive.

For a related reason, good details of employee pay and hours are needed for taxes such as PAYE and National Insurance. A record of fixed assets will help to work out depreciation and tax allowances.

The law requires some records be kept; auditors like rather more information. Common sense dictates managers need as much as they can get. Banks believe an absence of financial control causes over 80 per cent of business failures, and the biggest contributor is lack of financial records. This is a cause/effect problem because good managers keep extensive records, which helps them to be better. (However, see 'Management accounts', p.157.) Unfortunately, the entrepreneurial temperament of getting out and doing the business seldom coincides with the dogged clerical patience of sitting late into the night at a desk feeding data into the computer and tallying the figures.

Here is another example of the need for self-knowledge, emphasized since Chapter 1. If you recognize the impatience and lack of aptitude in yourself, then for heaven's sake get somebody else to do it. It could be a spouse or somebody local who will pop in on a part-time basis, but even the smallest enterprises need to keep records if they are to survive. This is less of a problem for someone starting off big because, as Chapter 5 pointed out, any investor demands a balanced team and that means somebody preparing to watch the finances, but it is frequently a hazard for the micro-business.

At the very least every business, no matter how small, should keep a cash book to record payments and receipts; a petty cash book to know where all that money dribbles away to in stamps, pencils and tea bags; customer accounts for sales on credit; and purchase lists for items larger than the petty cash. This must be kept separately from any records of the owner's money. There are still some stationers that sell books for entering all this, but only a masochist would resort to paper and pencil. Computers are available costing only a couple of hundred pounds if you are prepared to buy from one of the dealers selling discontinued models. Quite often they come with loaded software, which will probably not include an accounting program but will probably have a spreadsheet package, and this is adequate for maintaining a minimum level of financial records.

The additional beauty of the spreadsheet is that it can be made to do all the calculations automatically whenever any new figure is entered, avoiding the problem of mistakes in additions and subtractions by hand. It can also be used to compare actuals with cash flow forecasts, and can produce sophisticated mathematical calculations from the figures.

If the business is audited, the accountant may comment on how the records have been kept, and when you haggle about the cost – as everyone should – will point out that quite a lot of money can be saved by presenting the auditor with neat well-prepared accounts that require a minimum of preparation work.

Among the records that should be kept for law or tax are:

7 Spreadsheet

Calculation: Revenue £m	**Year 1**	**Year 2**	**Year 3**	**Year 4**	**Year 5**
Retail Sales: Type 1	0.22	0.30	0.41	0.57	0.78
Retail Sales: Type 2	0.22	0.30	0.41	0.57	0.78
Retail Sales: Type 3	0.22	0.30	0.41	0.57	0.78
Retail Sales: Type 4	0.22	0.30	0.41	0.57	0.78
Total Retail Sales (exc VAT)	**0.86**	**1.19**	**1.64**	**2.26**	**3.12**
Retailer Gross Margin @ 35%	0.30	0.42	0.57	0.79	1.09
Value of Total Sales at Wholesale Prices	0.56	0.77	1.07	1.47	2.03
% of Sales via Wholesaler 50%					
Wholesaler Gross Margin @ 15%	0.04	0.06	0.08	0.11	0.15
Net Value of Sales to WRS	**0.52**	**0.71**	**0.99**	**1.36**	**1.88**
Newco Projections	**0.07**	**0.60**	**1.07**	**1.72**	**2.57**
Cumulative Sales	0.52	1.23	2.22	3.58	5.46
Newco Cumulative Sales	**0.07**	**0.67**	**1.74**	**3.46**	**6.03**

- name, address and National Insurance number of each employee
- PAYE reference number for each employee
- salary, showing basic, bonus, commission etc., and net pay
- deductions from pay, including pension
- total pay and taxable pay in the year
- tax due and tax paid in the year
- National Insurance paid by employer and employee
- VAT paid on purchases and recovered on sales.

Annual report and accounts

The information really small companies need to file at Companies House is so rudimentary most people could compile it in an hour or two, and it provides little guidance for inquisitive people wanting to discover something about the status of the business.

The accounts filed at Company House – sole traders and partnerships need file nothing at all – may be much abbreviated, but the real annual accounts need to show a number of factors. There are massive accountancy manuals to explain all this, for instance, the GAAP tome (*Generally Accepted Accountancy Practices*). The section here is, of necessity, merely skimming the surface for a small and new business.

Audits

The purpose of audit is to check that the managers are not playing fast and loose with the business, not running some private scam, and not letting circumstances run away with them. For accountants that means the annual financial statement shows a true and fair picture of the business, and has been prepared in compliance with the rules. The auditor is supposed to be an independent outsider appointed by the shareholders to ensure this is the case by checking that the figures tally with the records, the formulae have been followed, and taking a sample of tests to see if there is anything physically present behind the numbers.

From the point of view of the company, the value of audits is open to debate. Really small companies are excused the procedure. That means they have a turnover of under £1 million, assets of under £1.4 million and fewer than 50 employees. The medium-sized ones sometimes find it a useful discipline for ensuring the shoe boxes full of invoices and records are transferred into a sensible format that tells the owners whether the business really is solvent. The well-run concerns often find it an unnecessary expense since they already have monthly management figures (see p.157). In large companies the value depends on the management and the auditor.

Accountants always proclaim themselves to be watchdogs and not bloodhounds, which means they are there to see order and spot obvious lapses into questionable practices, rather than to try to uncover every fraudster. However, as a series of scandals in recent years from Maxwell to Enron has shown, the watchdogs sometimes fail to bark.

MANAGEMENT ACCOUNTS

The minimal way of keeping a check on what the business is doing is through the cash flow. Companies commonly predict profits over the next three to six months as they slide into receivership. It has become a cliché to say cash is king. But clichés are merely truths repeated too often, and that is certainly so in this case.

By the time a company has started trading, it has learned about the value of cash-flow forecasts (see Chapter 2). That, however, is not a one-off job for raising finance. There is little point in producing the forecasts to show financiers and then forgetting about them. A rolling cash-flow projection for the next six to twelve months is crucial for survival. To make sure it stays in touch with reality, and to improve forecasting, the forecast is then compared with reality. A computer may do much of the actual maths. Duplicate the headings on the forecast on to sheet 2 of the same spreadsheet file, and feed into that the actual out-turn figures under each of the headings.

Then, on sheet 3, the spreadsheet can calculate differences between the two. From the combination of sheets 2 and 3, a picture emerges of what the company is actually doing and how its performance departed from expectations. This in turn will suggest questions to ask and aspects that need closer examination. The questions should be searching. It is not enough to say something unpredictable came up – one has to differentiate between the unpredictable and the unpredicted. Chapter 11 shows that with contingency planning one can learn to expect the unexpected (p.237).

How frequently figures are needed depends on the type of business – a restaurant probably needs daily summaries, but most businesses manage with monthly data. At the end of each month, preferably within 48 hours, a manager should have details of trading. These will contain total purchases and total payments, total sales and total cash received. In addition, there will be a breakdown of sales by product (or type of activity or group of product, as appropriate for the business) and, depending on the sort of company, there may be other useful indicators such as biggest customers, outstanding debts, cash position, stock levels, etc.

Some of this information will then be put into a cash-flow statement. That is to show, in a quick and readily apparent way, what is happening and what the totals are, and how performance tallies with what the managers expected.

By looking at the cash-flow results, and comparing with the continuously updated forecasts, you will see some interesting discrepancies, and some ominous warnings. The two will always disagree – that is fair enough – the question is why. If sales have been lower than forecast, is that because there is something wrong with the forecasts, the product or the salesmen? If costs have risen more than they should, is that because there has been unexpected inflation (why was it not expected?) or because management has taken its eyes off the ball?

This sort of post-mortem helps improve the next effort at forecasting and cash-flow projections.

The cash-flow statements are good for other comparisons. For instance, checking the change in overhead costs. The one certain thing is that these will rise inexorably. The moment you take your eye off any class of expenditure it grows. There is always a huge range of justifications for adding more staff, more entertaining and stay-over expenses, higher stationery spending, and all the other rising tide of outflows. Do not believe them – demand a cut. When that has been achieved, demand another.

A series of ratios and calculations evolved over the years by managers and financiers can provide a quick and constant guide for a manager to his company's state of health. In addition, they can show how ready the bank and development capital organizations will be to supply additional capital when needed since they will be using these same ratios. The following section details some of these ratios.

Figures to watch

So many indicators have been found over the years that if a manager were to watch all of them there would be no time for eating and sleeping, much less for running a business. All the same, several are indispensable and others useful. A sensible manager picks the ones most likely to provide an indication of the health of the business, and programmes them into the computer. Every month the figures are routinely entered into the table and the comparisons leap out to provide reassurance or warning. Here are some to choose from:

- monthly sales compared with the cash-flow tables' predictions, and with the same month a year ago
- monthly sales for each salesman
- monthly sales per product line
- customers exceeding credit limits
- unfilled orders (with reasons)
- stock levels related to sales
- the spread of time from order to delivery
- time for invoices to be paid
- debtors, by time and size
- debts as ratio of sales
- returns: complaints, claims, refunds.

Service companies, where clients are charged for the work done, need a rigorous system of recording the time spent on the work to various clients. The management then needs to keep an eye on the percentage of total staff time that is being charged out.

FINANCIAL RATIOS

If this business is going to become something more than a hobby, something more substantial than a 'lifestyle' company, you really do need to be methodical. Start out as you mean to go on. In other words, have a large company, publicly quoted business mentality from the off. It is harder work at the outset, but more than repays the effort. You not only have the comforting feel that you are in charge of the business, rather than constantly running to pursue events, but there is far less trauma reorganizing as the company grows.

Management accounts are tools for the managers to feel the pulse of the continuing business. Beyond those figures come the retrospective, and hence less urgent, calculations. These are used mainly to check the company is on the right lines, that pricing and efficiency are up to the mark, and that you are not giving hostages to fortune by borrowing more than you can safely afford. In other words, they are intermittent checks to verify stability. Retrospective figures are also useful indicators of long-term viability. Some of them are needed with the monthly management accounts and some can safely be left for an annual check. They are the calculations the big businesses use, and so do the analysts watching them.

The reason those ratios are omitted from practically all manuals on running your own business is that a small company will certainly not need them all. Indeed, at the outset the chances are you will probably need very few, if any. Nevertheless, some may come in handy from time to time as a double-check that everything is on the right lines. The following selection covers the more commonly used and helpful indicators.

Gross margin

Gross margin should probably be the first calculation, and most accountants will provide it in the annual accounts. This is the sales figure minus the direct cost to the company of manufacturing those goods or services (i.e. excluding overheads such as administration and interest payments) as a percentage of total turnover. In other words, the gross profit as a percentage of turnover. It is sometimes also called return on sales; it shows the profit margin.

$$\text{Gross margin} = \frac{\text{turnover} - \text{purchases} + \text{direct costs} + \text{change in stock} \times 100}{\text{turnover}}$$

For each industry there will be a satisfactory level depending on risk, costs of research and capital expenditure. It can vary from 15 to 60 per cent. Manufacturing industry should probably aim for at least 40 per cent. Professional research organizations collect data for industries that provide the average for a particular trade. It is worth taking a little trouble to find that out and aiming to top it by at least 10 per cent since the average will include a large number of deadbeats in any industry. Not only that, but if anybody is getting a better return, find out why and how, and aim to beat the best.

It is not enough merely to establish the absolute level; one needs to know the trend. For instance, if the number is falling, a rapid investigation is necessary to discover just why the margins are being squeezed.

Break even

There are several ways to calculate a break-even point – the level of sales you need to beat to start making a profit (see p.168). It can be done on a product by product basis to determine in advance how many have to be sold before the product is paying its way, or on a company basis.

For a product, one can start with direct costs assessment – for example, if we have manufactured 10,000 stepladders, how many must we sell at £45 before recovering the cost of manufacture? (An extra sophistication of this is called discounted cash flow, see p.169.)

For the business as a whole, the calculation is slightly different because it has to consider the fixed overheads such as premises, employee wages, heating, lighting, telephone, etc. The calculation is:

$$\text{Break-even point} = \frac{\text{overheads} \times 100}{\text{price of product} - \text{direct cost of product}}$$

The denominator in that equation is the gross profit margin, and the answer provides the number of items to be sold before that product line starts contributing to the cost of the overheads.

Another way is to draw a graph. Take as base the cost of equipment, such as a lorry. If it cost £30,000, that is the fixed cost incurred before it starts rolling. Once it is used, the cost is, say, 30p a mile.

Stock turnover

It is worth discovering what the normal rate of stock turnover is for an industry from one of the surveys of corporate performance, then check how it compares with one's own figures. Clearly one must beat the industry average by a comfortable margin to survive, much less to prosper.

Current ratio

A widely used measure of a company's underlying financial stability is the ability to pay its immediate bills. One way of gauging that is the amount of current assets compared with current liabilities. In other words, is the amount of cash and near-cash in hand enough to pay the short-term bills such as suppliers, bank interest and wages, in time? If not, the bank may call in the receiver, suppliers may sue or petition for bankruptcy, and the staff will be distinctly unhappy.

Current assets include stock, debtors (i.e. the invoices sent out that customers have yet to pay), plus any cash in the bank. Current liabilities include the overdraft and creditors (i.e. bills received but not yet paid). Divide the assets by the liabilities and you have the current ratio. The result should be at least 1, which means if push comes to shove the company can just pay its bills. For comfort, a ratio of 2 of assets to 1 of liability is thought reasonably safe, and financiers sometimes ask for something around a current ratio of 3.

The problem is that it is impossible to compare the ratios in different industries. A shop that buys in finished goods and has 30 days to pay, but sells them pretty quickly for cash, can run pretty close to a 1:1 ratio. Anything substantially more than that could mean the wrong sort of goods are being traded, and slow-moving items are accumulating in stock. By contrast, a manufacturer with the need to keep a stock of raw materials, semi-finished products plus financing the work in progress may need a ratio of 2 or even 3 to be safe. It is therefore a good idea to get an indication of the acceptable limits for your specific sector.

Return on capital

There is little point in putting money into a business that does not yield more than alternative investments. All businesses use a fair amount of capital. If that cash were not in the business it could be in gilts, a building society, a bank deposit account, other companies' shares and so on, and the money would be earning a return. One needs to know whether the decision to put money into a small company was financially worth it by comparing the returns. It should certainly be producing more than the return from a deposit account in a building society or the yield on gilts. The calculation should also be compared with the rate of inflation – there is little point in making a 5 per cent return when inflation is 7 per cent because you are slipping back by 2 per cent. There is also a risk premium – the return has to be higher than depositing the money in a major bank to offset the greater risk. On top of that is the need for a substantial enough return to fund the company's future reinvestment.

The figure is determined by taking profits as a percentage of the capital employed, or for the sake of simplicity, the net assets.

$$\text{Return on capital} = \frac{\text{pre-tax profit} \times 100}{\text{net assets}}$$

It is not quite that straightforward since some managers when they do their calculating use pre-interest and pre-tax profits to check how efficiently the company is working its money (the tax paid is an extraneous factor in that), while others prefer after tax, which is probably the one to use when assessing whether to put the money on deposit instead. In addition, assets can be either the book value or current value. Companies have two classes of assets: fixed and current. Fixed assets are the factories, leases, equipment and furniture, etc.; current assets are things like stock, work in progress, finished products at the warehouse, and the like. Total up these two as shown in the balance sheet, deduct current liabilities (overdraft, unpaid bills, etc.), and you have the net assets – the amount of capital employed in the business.

The next step is all in the profit and loss account of a company. Deduct from the turnover figure the cost of sales, miscellaneous expenses, financing charges, and tax to produce the net profit. This figure as a percentage of the capital employed is the figure you are after. Or rather it is one that financiers look at. It is worth checking that all these factors are in accord with usual practice when making comparisons with other similar companies, and this is another purpose of the exercise.

The point is that there is no absolute ideal value – some capital-intensive industries will inevitably have low percentages, while service companies with practically no assets beyond the people can even top 100 per cent. The aim is to get an absolute value – is it worth putting the cash in the business in the first place? And a relative value – is the company doing at least as well as the best of its competitors?

Quick ratio/acid test

A tighter version of the current ratio excludes stock because it can take too long to turn into cash. This is a measure of financial soundness, or at least the ability to pay creditors if they turn nasty, and measures whether foreseeable bills can be met from readily available short-term assets. It really is a very tight and conservative criterion. The ratio takes a narrower view of resources, concentrating on what can be mustered in three months or so, such as cash and debtors (on the assumption you will extract what is owing within 90 days), and divides them by current liabilities – i.e. bills to be paid within the next 12 months. A preferred ratio is at least 0.65 of cash to 1 of debt, and 1:1 indicates a safe position.

$$\text{Quick ratio (acid test)} = \frac{\text{cash (and cash equivalent) + debtors}}{\text{current liabilities}}$$

Gearing

The ratio of borrowings (overdraft plus debentures and preference shares) to ordinary shares is called gearing in Britain and leverage in America. Loans have to be serviced first while dividends on shares are optional. At times of low profits, paying the bank interest can absorb all the cash and shareholders get little or nothing. Being highly geared – high borrowing in relation to equity – is dangerous for two reasons. One, the company is vulnerable to increases in the rate of interest; and two, overdrafts can be called in at the bank's whim. If the latter happens when things are already precarious (which is when banks get nervous), the company would probably become insolvent.

This is not a theoretical danger. It happens regularly, and during the economic downturn in the early 1990s, thousands of small businesses succumbed for precisely these reasons. This has left a lingering wariness of banks in the small business community.

Current assets and quick ratios are, as the names suggest, tests of immediate survival. As well as providing a gauge of the riskiness of the immediate financial position, gearing is also a guide to how easily the business will be able to finance expansion. The money for that comes from internally generated cash, borrowing and issuing shares. How much is available of each and at what price can depend on this debt-to-equity ratio. For instance, bank managers would be happy to lend more than £1 for every £2 of share capital in a new business – i.e. a debt-equity ratio of 1:2, although a longer-established business might get 1:1.

Equity to long-term debt

A good general rule is to match borrowing to the use to which the money is put. Short-term borrowing finances current uses such as working capital, but long-term borrowing pays for the acquisition of stable long-term assets such as land, buildings and manufacturing equipment. Predictably, lenders have a ratio to check suitability to borrow long term. They like companies' net worth (total assets minus total liabilities) to be at least double their long-term debt (i.e. 2 of net worth to 1 of long-term debt), and preferably more.

$$\text{Equity to long-term debt} = \frac{\text{net worth}}{\text{total debt} - \text{current liabilities}}$$

Debt to worth

Another way to test how deeply a company is in debt is by working out the debt-to-worth ratio. This is the proportion of total debt to tangible net worth (tangible assets minus total liabilities). If this is much higher than, say, 3:1 lenders get nervous; but if it is down to ½:1, growth could be compromised through reluctance to borrow even up to safe limits, i.e. the managers are being too conservative.

$$\text{Debt to worth} = \frac{\text{total debt}}{\text{tangible net worth}}$$

Credit control

To find out how much the company is owed, and when it is likely to be paid, produce an aged debtors/creditor list – i.e. a list of debts owing and owed, by date. For debtors who have been supplied with goods and have not yet paid, this is a table with the horizontal axis showing how much is due per month. The table will also show how good the company is at collecting the money it is owed.

An indicator of cash management is the number of days of average outstanding debtors. This is the amount unpaid at any moment, divided by the turnover of the previous 12 months, multiplied by 365. If a company is owed £720,000 at the moment of calculation, and total turnover for the 12 months to that time was £8 million (having grossed up the figure to include VAT for the sake of a fair comparison), it is taking 33 days on average to collect its cash. That is fairly well in line for Britain, but it is too long for comfort in a small business that is always strapped for cash. The aim is to keep it under 30 days if possible, and if it ever tops 60, the chances are someone is not doing a good job of pursuing customers.

INVESTMENT APPRAISAL

Any company not dying on its feet will have several alternatives for capital spending. These will include plant renewal; expanding capacity (by factory, equipment, staff); the company may want to launch a new product; it may want to bring work in-house that is currently subcontracted; there may be a desire for new facilities, such as research and development; and so on. The question is whether any of these are sound investments; to find out place them in a league table. This will enable the company to invest in the most profitable and go on down the list until the money runs out.

As with all other accounting figures, there are alternative ways of assessment; how the figures are produced will depend on the purpose.

Return on investment

At its simplest, you should check to see what dividends the investment will pay.

$$\text{Return on investment} = \frac{\text{profit} \times 100}{\text{capital outlay}}$$

Payback

This is a simple (and rather simplistic) addition of future revenues to discover how long it will take before the cost of the original investment can be paid back. However, this ignores the effect of depreciation on future cash amounts.

Discounted cash flow

Money is not free. If borrowed it has an interest cost; if it is your own cash it could be earning something. So, £1,000 today is worth more than £1,000 received a year hence. Returns from a capital investment will go on flowing in for years ahead, and so one should offset this time factor, which affects the value of inflows, to make income comparable to the expenditure that is all in today's value.

For example, if you can lend out money at 10 per cent interest, £1,000 received in a year's time will have lost that potential revenue. If you got it now it would be worth £1,100 within 12 months. Or to put it another way, if you invested £909.09 now at that rate of interest you would have £1,000 in a year's time. In the phrasing of management accounts, at the level of interest, the £909.09 has a net present value of £1,000. Discount factor is the term used for the number by which you multiply the income a year away to get today's value (sometimes this is also called present value factor).

The formula for calculating the future value is to multiply the sum of money invested by:

$$(1 + \text{interest rate}^{\text{the time in years}})$$

where the interest rate is expressed as a decimal, which means 10 per cent comes out as 0.1. So, still sticking with the figures in the paragraph above, if £1,000 were invested at 10 per cent at the end of three years the equation is £1,000 x $(1.1)^3$, which is the same as £1,000 x (1.1 x 1.1 x 1.1), and the return would be £1,331.

For one example of how this works in practice, see p.169.

Figures thrown up by this sort of calculation of future cash flow are

8 Discounted cash flow

Brand A only – Net Present Value of Investments

Assumptions and Inputs

Equity Stake	Equity	NPV of Investment		IRR
Supplier	17.0%	£19,143	33%	22.9%
Management Team	83.0%	£38,487	67%	22.9%
	100.0%	**£57,630**	**100%**	

Valuation on Sale		
Multiple of Operating Profit		4.0
Discount Rate	20%	
Annual Management Salary Foregone	£135,000	

	2001	**2002**	**2003**	**2004**	**2005**
Capital Expenditure £	5,700	6,000	6,000	6,000	6,000
Working Capital Requirements £	30,000	40,000	50,000	50,000	60,000
Forecast Profitability £					
Discount Factor	*1.00*	*0.83*	*0.69*	*0.58*	*0.48*
Operating Profit £	(191,712)	(115,909)	2,321	151,130	348,889
Taxation £	–	–	–	–	(58,416)
Operating Profit After Tax £		(191,712)	(115,909)	2,321	151,130
290,474					
Cumulative Retained Earnings £		(191,712)	(307,622)	(305,300)	(154,170)
136,303					

Funding Requirements £

Funding Requirements Outflow/(Inflow)						
Capex		5,700	6,000	6,000	6,000	6,000
Working Capital Movements		30,000	10,000	10,000	–	10,000
Post Tax Operating Cashflow		191,712	115,909	(2,321)	(151,130)	(290,474)
Net Funding Requirement/ (Cash Surplus)		227,412	131,909	13,679	(145,130)	(274,474)
Funded by:						
Ransom	*(250,000)*	(125,000)	(125,000)	–	–	–
Management	*(125,000)*	(100,000)	(10,000)	(15,000)	–	–
Repayment of Funds Invested						
Ransom	*250,000*	–	–	–	100,000	150,000
Management	*125,000*	–	–	–	50,000	75,000
Dividends		–	–	–	–	45,000
Cumulative Cash Outflow/(Inflow)		2,412	(678)	(2,000)	2,870	(1,603)

Net Present Value of Investment £

		2001	2002	2003	2004	2005
Supplier						
Funds Invested	*(250,000)*	(125,000)	(125,000)	–	–	–
Funds Repaid	*250,000*	–	–	–	100,000	150,000
Dividend Income	*7,650*	–	–	–	–	7,650
Sale Proceeds	*237,245*	–	–	–	–	237,245
Net Return	*244,895*	(125,000)	(125,000)	–	100,000	394,895
Net Present Value	19,143	(125,000)	(104,167)	–	57,870	190,439
IRR	23%					
Management Team						
Funds Invested	*(125,000)*	(100,000)	(10,000)	(15,000)	–	–
Salary Foregone	*(675,000)*	(135,000)	(135,000)	(135,000)	(135,000)	(135,000)
Funds Repaid	*125,000*	–	–	–	50,000	75,000
Dividend Income	*37,350*	–	–	–	–	37,350
Sale Proceeds	*1,158,313*	–	–	–	–	1,158,313
Net Return	520,663	(235,000)	(145,000)	(150,000)	(85,000)	1,135,663
Net Present Value	38,487	(235,000)	(120,833)	(104,167)	(49,190)	547,677
IRR	23%					

crucially dependent on the discount rate chosen and, unfortunately, that has to be a guess. Interest rates in the future are not known, even by the Chancellor of the Exchequer. Economic forecasters provide guesses about prospective rates of inflation, and from that it is usually possible to deduce a base rate of some 3 to 6 per cent more. Regrettably, such figuring is vulnerable to the vagaries of international conditions and the decisions of the Bank of England's monetary policy committee about the best way to control inflation without causing damage to the economy.

IMPROVING CASH FLOW

Many a business has gone bust although its accounts showed a profit, because it lost track of cash flow. When the flow of money goes awry, you cannot pay the bills and if the creditors, including the bank, get sufficiently tetchy, they can put the company into the hands of the receiver.

Discounted cash flow

It is not only in investment that the future value of money matters. A pound in the hand is worth more than a pound in the post, and much more than a pound promised. That is because rising prices erode the value and also because if the money were invested it could be earning interest. Clearly this is a less important factor at a time of low inflation and low interest rates but, considering the slim margins tormenting most small businesses, it is still a factor. The moral is obviously to collect the money owed you as soon as possible, while delaying until the last possible ethical date the payment of your debts.

Credit control

Small and new businesses are too busy getting going to have spare time for financial control, which is one reason why they fail. Customers do not pay or turn out to be unable to pay, and that means disaster in a precarious young enterprise without resources to tide it over.

Bad debts

At its most extreme, the problem is not getting paid at all. If a company goes under, trade creditors are usually too far down the list to stand much of a chance of getting paid, and certainly nothing like the full amount will be available from receiver or liquidator.

There is no way to avoid the occasional bad debt; it is part of the cost of doing business and is tax allowable. If a sale is a small one, the best option is to accept that some customers will fail and hope they are not too numerous. If the amount is large, it is worth doing a credit check on the customer.

Before taking on a new customer, especially if the sums are going to make a difference, ask for a bank reference plus a couple of trade references. The question to put to the referees is up to what amount is the business good for, or is a safe risk. If the customer is to be a big one, it is a good idea to make personal contact, and a visit to the premises can also show what sort of an outfit it really is. (Incidentally, this is an inducement to make your own premises look good, not only because it makes for better morale and greater efficiency, but because it might help improve your own credit standing.) There are also credit reference agencies, for example, CCN, Equifax, Experian, Dun & Bradstreet, Instant Search, Standard & Poor's, and Euler Trade Indemnity.

All this research should help in setting the credit terms. How much is it safe to allow that business on 30 days' credit?

Collecting the cash

Small businesses are notoriously inept at collecting the money they are owed. There are two main reasons: the managers are too busy trying to run the business and fighting to get new orders to pursue the paperwork; and they are frightened of antagonizing important customers by being too pressing about payment. The late payment legislation has had practically no effect except to extend payment times still further as big buyers insist on longer payment terms. Small businesses are too frightened to employ the dunning rights because there is little point having a power which you believe is merely financial suicide. A consequence is that these tiddlers are using so much money to fund customers, the sales are producing practically no profit.

Cash with order is pretty rare. For non-retailers, the normal course of work is to send the goods or provide the service, and send the invoice. Some people get payment on account or staged payment through a job (builders, for instance), but the majority of trade is paid after receipt of the invoice. Often long after.

The fear of offending important customers is misplaced. Tough but polite insistence on being paid promptly is taken as a sign of efficiency and usually yields results. Even the most reluctant payers can be induced to pay by suggesting that in future orders may need to be accompanied by full payment in advance, or perhaps even a reminder that under the late payment legislation one can levy interest at 8 per cent over base rate on late payments.

Tight credit control improves finances substantially, and sophisticated and courteous collection of money due is not resented. In any case, in a major corporation there is unlikely to be much contact between the department dealing with payment and the one dealing with ordering.

The Better Payment Practice Group has innumerable tips on how to do all this better, but the essence is straightforward. It seems so obvious once spelled out, but it is often forgotten: it is worth selling only to someone who will pay the bill. It is amazing how often naive businesses will go out and chase every order because they do not stop to think of that vital fact. It is sometimes worth selling only to someone who will pay in reasonable time – expecting them to pay promptly may be too idealistic. While the customer is not paying, that deal costs you money. On £10,000 a small business can be paying 8 per cent for the overdraft which, after a year, comes to £800. Proper credit control can make a lot of difference to the finances.

Check all new customers with one of the credit reference agencies mentioned earlier, to see if they are good enough for the amount of credit they ask for. Even then be cautious about the amount of credit a new customer gets – it is easy enough to lift the ceiling if the customer turns out to be a reliable organization that pays on the dot. Large public companies are supposed to publish payment policies in their annual accounts, but many do not. Check with a couple of trade references and ask the questions you need answered: how long it takes to pay and up to what level is the business a good risk. Have a look at its latest balance sheet, and visit the people at their own premises.

Institute policies for your business that make it easier to collect debts. At the start of a new relationship, explain terms of trade and payment policies to a new customer, and print them on every document, such as acknowledgement of order and invoice. This can include incentives for early payment. For instance, if the payment is received within seven days of delivery, a customer can claim a 1 per cent discount from the bill. The one drawback with that is the large customer who pays late or even on time, but automatically deducts the early payment discount – a common try-on. On no account let them get away with it – the next invoice should show in bold the underpayment which is added to the total. If necessary, add a little form slip explaining the terms again.

In any case, payment is due within 30 days of invoice date. Ensure all products have an attached delivery note with the same details included on them, and the invoice is despatched at the same time with the terms repeated yet again in clear and emphatic terms.

Have someone keep an eye on cash receipts, and if the money is not received on time, somebody rings the accounts department of the customer and asks when it can be expected. Statements go out exactly 28 days after the invoice date. Even the cheapest accounting programme will produce a regular output of debts analysed by time (so-called aged debtors), and this will alert you if a payment is overdue. Pounce on it at once. Send statement and/or reminder, perhaps by fax, for instant receipt with a copy in the post to follow. If that has not generated a payment within seven days, fax another reminder plus a copy by recorded delivery. Some companies pay first the suppliers who are most pressing, irrespective of other factors. It has been known for the tiniest supplier to a big company to get fed up with the treatment, and put on the statement that all future dealings would require cash with order. The debt, some of which had been owing for over ten months, was paid within 48 hours.

If the customer is still recalcitrant, ring and ask for the senior person responsible, which may be the chief executive. At this stage it is useful to remain cool and polite, and simply ask what the problem is. The excuses will be the usual and predictable set of silly quibbles and delaying tactics. The man who signs the cheques is on holiday, they have already paid, the goods did not arrive, they were late, there was no despatch note enclosed, no invoice has been received, the goods were the wrong ones or the wrong number, the goods were faulty.

Treat any such stories with serious concern, no matter how preposterous. With proper procedures at your end, you will be able to knock down each one until the customer runs out of excuses. Complaints about the goods have to be within a short time of receipt, and after that goods are legally deemed to have been accepted. Ask how often cheques are assigned – i.e. weekly or monthly – and when. If the customer claims to have sent the money, ask for cheque number and date of posting. A handy counter-ploy is to say the cheque has not arrived so perhaps it could be cancelled and someone will be round in the morning to collect a replacement. If you do, make sure it is paid in instantly, before anyone has time to put a stop on it.

A common debtor response is to say the person will chase the matter to see what has happened; either offer to hang on for the answer or ring back in an hour to see what was discovered. If nothing is received after three days, ring again. Still polite and puzzled, ask what progress has been made. If the money is still not forthcoming go round in person, ask to see the chief executive, and politely demand a cheque there and then. Examine it carefully for date, recipient, amount and signature and again take it straight to the bank before anyone can stop it.

If all of that has failed, you can start being nasty. That means a letter from a solicitor threatening legal action or even to wind up the company, or placing the debt in the hands of a collection agency. If that produces no action, admit defeat and carry out what you threatened.

An alternative course, if you want to go on doing business but still make a return on the business with a recalcitrant client, is to build the payment delay into the price and charge a fair rate for the cost of cash.

Reservation of title

One way to reduce the dangers of a customer not paying through going bust is by reservation of title. The seller retains ownership of the goods until payment for them has been received. That means if the customer goes into receivership, the goods can be recovered by the seller instead of joining the other assets of the insolvent business.

One of the versions of this is the Romalpa clause, named after a 1976 legal case that said the seller can retain rights not only to the goods but also to anything manufactured from them, and if they are sold it can have rights to the proceeds of the sale. In a more recent case of Clough Mill v Martin (1984), the court ruled that the seller can march into the premises and repossess the goods. These clauses have to be worded very carefully, however, or they will be struck down.

Factoring

There are ways of subcontracting the hassle of credit assessment and chasing invoice payments, and two of them are factoring and invoice discounting. The procedure is fairly similar and is carried out by the same companies. There are about 90 factoring companies in Britain, more than 40 of them are members of the Factors and Discounters Association, and 70–85 per cent (depending on whose statistics you believe) of the business is done by subsidiaries of banks. And a pretty substantial business it is, running at around £90 billion a year and growing.

A factor takes over the whole of the sales ledger and in return pays, say, 80 per cent of the value cash down. The actual percentage depends on the company's record of customer behaviour, the practice in that industry, and the sort of payments concerned. The factor pursues the debtors with professional efficiency and the effectiveness that comes from being a large company and a subsidiary of an even larger bank. It also removes from the supplier both the hard work and the odium of forever badgering an important customer. In addition to the immediate payment, which is a boost to the small company's cash flow, the factor will usually make a supplementary payment depending on how long it takes to collect the money.

An invoice discounter also pays immediately the goods have been invoiced, but the business still has control over its own sales ledger and collects its own debts. When the payment comes in, the company passes it to the discounter. This is normally only for medium-sized businesses with well-established and efficient debt collection systems that are merely trying to accelerate the cash flow.

Just as with a bank, do not be fooled by assertions that the factor's terms are standard. There is always latitude for a haggle, either in the terms or the price, and usually both.

9 Tax

When starting the business you have to notify the Inland Revenue which will send on the details to Customs and Excise and if turnover is more than £56,000 you are also obliged to register for VAT. The Revenue has a number of useful leaflets to guide the novice through the first faltering steps of taxation.

Remember that the safest position is to be able to prove and justify to the tax authorities everything you do and everything you say. That requires meticulous records and keeping every scrap of relevant paper, which is tedious and space-consuming, but in the long run well worth it. Staff in the taxation offices have a jaundiced view of humanity and tend to assume most people are trying to cheat in some way. Only elaborate proof that everything you say has been documented and can be justified will convince them that, in this case, they do not have a proven case of tax evasion.

Beware of amazingly clever and devious schemes evolved by specialist advisers and some ingenious accountants for saving you substantial amounts of tax. The Inland Revenue has been doing its work for a couple of centuries and has got its collective head round most dodges. If the Chancellor's mind-bogglingly lengthy and complex tax changes occasionally open a tiny loophole, it is safe to assume it will not remain open for long. There have even been some rather naughty moves to make some of these remedial measures retrospective. And some loopholes are, in fact, illusory.

There is also precedent (for instance Ramsay v IRC 1981 STC174, Furniss v Dawson 1984 STC153) for the Revenue taking a fairly brutal approach to circuitous tax avoidance schemes, no matter how legal: if the tax payer goes from A to B to C as a way of reducing the tax liability, the Revenue merely acts as if the process had been direct from A to C, and charges tax accordingly. A series of legal decisions over the past 20 years means there is little you can do about it.

Finally, it may turn out that some of the schemes are not tax avoidance (taking advantage of legal benefits), but tax evasion (dodging tax illegally), in which case the penalties include back tax, fines of usually double the tax evaded, and up to seven years in jail. Saying your tax adviser dreamt up the whole thing and you did not know it was illegal is unlikely to carry much weight in court. These are not threats or notional penalties – directors and individual traders are sent to jail all the time.

The tax-gathering authorities, especially Customs, now have terrifyingly broad powers to enter premises, seize documents and interrogate people, without having to justify their actions. They have wider powers than the police and have been known to act fairly high-handedly. In recent years, their actions provoked such antipathy that they are being less aggressive, and will provide advice and even help with the forms. However, no matter how attractive the velvet glove, the mailed fist is still there underneath.

The structure of the business defines the type of tax. Sole traders and partners pay income tax, companies pay corporation tax. There are also different treatments for the increasingly expensive National Insurance, which the government is trying to pretend is not just another tax. Accountancy firms have remained as partnerships to minimize National Insurance. This suggests that in some circumstances it may be worth allowing the corporate structure to be dictated by the need to keep tax payments low. Recent changes in legislation have increased the attraction of incorporation. Small owner-managed companies with low wage costs are in many cases paying less tax than equivalent unincorporated businesses, and it can also minimize the owners' tax because they can keep their wages low and take the rest in dividends.

Everybody has a right to minimize their taxes. That was summed up rather well in a 1929 legal case by the judge, Lord President Clyde:

No man in this country is under the smallest obligation, moral or other, so to arrange his legal relations to his business or to his property as to enable the Inland Revenue to put the largest possible shovel into his stores. The Inland Revenue is not slow – and quite rightly – to take every advantage which is open to it under the taxing statutes for the purpose of depleting the taxpayer's pocket. And the taxpayer is, in like manner, entitled to be astute to prevent, so far as he honestly can, the depletion of his means by the Revenue.

The American judge Learned Hand concurred powerfully:

Over and over again courts have said that there is nothing sinister in so arranging one's affairs as to keep taxes as low as possible. Everybody does so, rich or poor; and all do right, for nobody owes any public duty to pay more than the law demands; taxes are enforced exactions, not voluntary contributions. To demand more in the name of morals is mere cant.

The difficulty is knowing what the loopholes are and how to take advantage of them legally. One place to start is with the UK Taxation Directory. This is an independently compiled website with links to all the taxation bodies, several firms of accountants, and a range of other support services. Tax is, nevertheless, exceedingly complex and constantly shifting, not just because legislation is for ever changing the rules, but because judgments at tribunals and in the courts constantly change the precedents or interpretation. It is a complicated world with its own language, and it is wise to have professional advice. What follows gives only a hint of the important aspects and unfortunately cannot come close to explaining all the ifs and buts.

INSPECTIONS

Quite apart from descending on people and organizations where the Revenue has grounds for suspecting shady dealing, a few people are picked at random for investigation by an inspector. It can be a terrifying prospect even for the extremely honest. The tax-gathering departments have been told to confine their investigative and prosecuting efforts to instances where the rewards in recovered unpaid tax more than cover the cost of the pursuit, but sometimes they may get their teeth into a case they find suspicious, and will not let go. Then the various tax authorities can go to frightening lengths to try to unearth wrongdoing. There was, for instance, the case of the VAT inspector who had several meals at a Thames estuary restaurant because he said he suspected the number of whitebait served in the starter portions did not tally with the quantity claimed in the accounts. In another case, they took apart a small business for three years, at the end of which the traumatized owner was presented with the finding: he did indeed owe back tax, to the tune of 22p. So you can depend on the tax collectors being thorough.

Tax inspectors also check company accounts at Companies House, and have a look at the premises both of the company and its directors/shareholders. Failure to produce the required documents can produce a hefty fine.

The problem is the Revenue and Customs and Excise have sweeping powers including, under the Income and Corporation Taxes Act, the right to demand a wide range of documents. They can also get warrants to search premises and take files away. Long experience of human frailty has schooled them to expect the worst. When they find something wrong – and no matter how scrupulously the accounts are done there is always something that is askew or does not quite match – they will presume you are on the fiddle. Or at least that is how they will come across.

What is even worse, the taxpayer does not really know whether the special compliance officer is there because there is an existing suspicion all is not well, or because the name came out of the computer. It all just starts with a 'Mae West' letter, so called because it does not merely ask for information but promises to come up and see you sometime.

All the figures will be examined sceptically, and every claim or allowance will have to be justified and the amounts proved. There may be a demand for further payment. If you have followed the rules and are honest, it might be wise at this stage to seek the help of an accountant to argue with the inspector.

If it looks like a serious case, it might be best to say nothing beyond a polite good morning before having somebody act as a mouthpiece – you are under no obligation to talk. If you do talk, do not lie, but do not volunteer information – stick strictly and concisely to the question as asked. That approach takes a cool head, self-control and confidence enough to withstand psychological pressure. For instance, an answer may be greeted with a prolonged silence, which provokes nervous people to babble on to fill the vacuum and, in their anxiety, to say things they do not quite mean. This may reveal suspicious-sounding details that are then used to tighten the knot further. Similarly, if the inspectors say something like 'Is there anything else?' or 'Have you left anything out?', it does not necessarily mean they know something; the chances are they are just fishing, so do not start a guilt-ridden chattering.

The following tax rates apply to the 2003/2004 tax year. Although every effort has been made to ensure that this is all up to date and correct, tax is constantly changing because of both the legislation and the case law built up from appeal to commissioners, or the courts.

INCOME TAX

'The hardest thing in the world to understand is income tax,' said Albert Einstein, and if he had problems what are your chances?

William Pitt imposed a temporary income tax in 1799 to fund the war with France. In an era with a greater sense of privacy it was not thought proper for a civil servant to know an individual's full financial status. Instead, they devised a series of schedules allowing a person to pay under different heads to different sections, which could not, therefore, ever know the full state of the person's affairs. That remained when Robert Peel brought the tax back as a permanent part of the fiscal landscape in 1842, and the relics of it are still with us. Income tax continues to come under a range of schedules depending on the source of the money and the organization:

- Schedule A covers income from land and buildings, such as rent.
- Schedule D comes in different flavours:

Case I is for income from self-employed trade
Case II is for income from a self-employed profession or vocation
Case III is mainly interest received gross
Case IV is for income from overseas securities
Case V deals with income from overseas possessions
Case VI is for anything else.

- Schedule E covers the pay received from being in employment
  Case I deals with UK residents
  Case II is income by residents who are not ordinarily resident in Britain
  Case III deals with work done overseas.
- Schedule F is for dividends and the like received from companies.
- Schedules B and C have fallen by the wayside.

Self-assessment was introduced avowedly to make the tax system simpler and accountants have grown fat as the system became so complex few taxpayers could cope on their own. Most people are unaffected since their only source of income is the salary from an employer and tax is deducted automatically on Pay As You Earn (PAYE). A few of those are nevertheless sent the form, which has to be returned by 30 September when the Inland Revenue will do the calculation of tax owed, or by 31 January if you work out your own liability. Sending the form or the payment in late produces penalties.

Self-employed people pay their income tax in three lumps: on 31 January within the tax year, on 31 July after the end of the tax year, and a final equalizing payment on the following 31 January. If you have set up a company, however, and are a director of it, you do not count as self-employed even if you own all of it. You are then an employee and liable to PAYE on salary, though with the option of taking income via dividends instead.

Being self-employed allows the trader to offset expenses for travel against income. Quite often you have to spend money before you start earning it. Everything from stationery and desks to leafleting potential customers can be counted as pre-trading spending and set against the income from the first year's trading. If you are still in employment while the business gets off the ground, the losses of the business in the first three years of trading can be set off against salary to get a tax refund.

A self-employed person making a tax loss in a financial year has the option of setting that off against other income (such as from employment if that is still being continued or dividends from shares) or capital gains, or carrying the loss forward to offset the loss against future profits. If the following year shows another loss, the sum of losses can be carried forward forever until they are used up against eventual profits.

Benefits in kind

People with a salary of over £8,500, including benefits, and directors, have to pay tax on the perks from employers. That includes things like medical insurance, subsidized loans and mortgages, luncheon vouchers of more than 15p a day, and accommodation. The details of all this are sent to the taxman every year on a P11D form supplied by the employer.

Allowable expenses

The phrasing of the Revenue and the legislation is that expenditure 'wholly and exclusively' for the business is allowed against tax, but as you would expect it is not as easy as that. For instance, if some of the work is done from home, it is possible to claim part of the cost – lighting, heating, cleaning, telephone, insurance and security for instance – as a business expense. Even the interest on that part of the mortgage may be offset against tax. There is a downside to this, however, because, as business premises, the place may be subject to business rates, and that room used for commerce is then not part of your home and may be subject to capital gains tax when you sell the place. If you do not confine yourself to any particular place in the house, but explain to the Revenue that you work wherever happens to be clear, which could be the kitchen or the dining room or even the bedroom, then no part of the house is specified as an office and cannot, therefore, be subject to capital gains tax. Some tax experts recommend keeping a sofa bed in the room used as an office to make it a spare bedroom as well.

Similarly, if the car is used sometimes for business, that proportion of the cost of running it can be allowed against tax.

Other expenses deducted from profits before calculating tax include:

- cost of raw materials, part assemblies or goods used in a product
- costs of marketing, including advertising, promotional gifts, public relations
- premises costs: rent, rates, council tax, heating, lighting, cleaning, repairs, maintenance
- administration, including telephone, postage, stationery, printing, delivery charges
- cost of computer and software if the useful life is under two years
- travel, but not between home and work
- miscellany such as membership of professional organizations, books, magazines
- the cost of hiring or leasing capital equipment
- insurance
- professional fees, including accountants, lawyers, patent agents
- bank charges, including interest payments
- bad debts – not as a general provision but specific items
- special clothing, cleaning and repairs
- research and development up to £25,000
- employee pay, including bonuses, contributions to the pensions plan
- pensions paid to retired employees and pensions payments to

previous employees

- training
- the costs of employing a spouse (but only if you can demonstrate to the taxman the work really is being done)
- entertaining your own staff, such as a Christmas party (up to £150 a head)
- business trip expenses.

However, you cannot include the owner's own pay.

If the venture is registered for VAT, the claim should include the VAT content.

Capital costs are a special category of complexity all on their own. The costs of buying capital equipment, such as vehicles and machinery, are not an allowable expense. Nor is the money deducted from taxable profit the same as the amount shown in the accounts as depreciation. There are, however, capital allowances. At this point most novices to tax begin to wonder why it is the UK accountancy profession mocks the Italians for having three different sets of books – one calculation for tax, another to show the real finances as required by management, and a third as prescribed by the Companies Acts.

There are different rates of allowance for different items of plant, and the rate varies from year to year. For instance:

- **cars** – a maximum of £3,000 per car, 25 per cent of the reducing balance
- **machinery** – except for long-life assets, 40 per cent in the first year, and 25 per cent after that
- **buildings** – 4 per cent of cost; 100 per cent in enterprise zones
- **hotels** – if more than ten bedrooms, 4 per cent of cost
- **patent** – 25 per cent
- **research** – all written off in the year

PAYE

PAYE is one of the areas where the government has delegated the work of collecting tax to companies. In addition, the payroll administration involves dealing with statutory sick pay, maternity pay, deductions of student loan repayments, stakeholder pensions and other administrative work for the government.

Pay is subject to Pay As You Earn deductions of income tax. The Inland Revenue sends forms to acquire a long list of information on every employee and provides a code number that sets the level of deductions. That is fed into the payroll system, which should produce the amount payable by the employer for the various taxes: income tax and National Insurance.

NATIONAL INSURANCE

For the sole trader or self-employed there are two classes of National Insurance to pay: Class 2 consists of a flat rate of £2 a week if profits (as shown in the accounts) are more than £4,095 a year; Class 4 takes a rate of 8 per cent of the profits between the figure of £4,615 and £30,940. If the income is too low to make National Insurance compulsory, people can make a voluntary contribution of £6.95 to make them eligible for the state pension.

People in employment earning over £89 a week, pay the Class 1 employee portion and the employer is taxed on the workers by the employers' National Insurance.

VAT

Most people have a rough idea of how income tax works, even if the details perplex them, and again an idea of the similar basis of corporation tax. VAT, however, is a mystery, causes extensive unease, and the accounting for it has most novices pleading for help.

The basis of VAT is that tax is payable on the value added at each stage of the business process. For instance, Arthur sells £100 of timber he has grown to Bertie, and adds VAT at 17.5 per cent to create a bill for £117.50. In due course (probably at the next quarter), Arthur sends the £17.50 to Customs and Excise. This is called output tax.

Bertie makes furniture out of the timber, and charges Charlotte £250 for the products, plus 17.5 per cent VAT, to make the invoice total £293.75. At the same time, Bertie does the calculation of the tax Arthur has already charged him (which in his case is called input tax), and deducts it from the VAT output tax he has charged Charlotte. That is £43.75 charged to Charlotte minus £17.50 paid to Arthur, equals £26.25. This amount Bertie forwards to Customs at his next VAT payment.

Charlotte is a wholesaler who resells the furniture to a retailer, Dottyshop, for £300 plus 17.5 per cent VAT, to make £352.50, and does the same calculation and pays the £8.75 to Customs. Dotty, in her shop, finds a customer prepared to pay £550 for the furniture, plus 17.5 per cent VAT, to make the retail invoice £646.25. She claims back the £52.50 input tax she was charged by Charlotte and sets it off against the £96.25 charged to the shop customer to produce a net VAT liability of £43.75, which she duly forwards to Customs. The consumer cannot claim back any of the VAT.

This is on the assumption each of those traders was registered for VAT. If their business turnover was below the £56,000 threshold they do not have to register, but as that example shows it may be wise all the same if they want to recover the input tax paid. Small companies have a special dispensation to make a flat payment based on turnover to save the hassle of having to work out the input and output tax on all their dealings.

Not everything is subject to VAT. For instance, leases, sales and lettings of land are exempt unless it is car parks or hotel space, and so are several financial dealings, such as providing credit or insurance. Healthcare companies and undertakers, bookmakers and training establishments are also exempt. None of the companies in these sectors charges VAT, but neither can they recover any VAT they have paid to any of their suppliers.

In addition, some items are zero-rated: food and drinks, books and newspapers, children's clothing, public transport, new domestic buildings, prescription medicines. None of the dealings attract VAT and these companies can claim back any VAT paid to their suppliers from Customs.

Some things nobody can recover VAT on include cars, business entertainment, and some of the fittings going into construction.

As this suggests, keeping Customs happy and paying the right amount of VAT requires meticulous and comprehensive record keeping. Indeed, failing to keep proper records invites a penalty from Customs. Another warning – the VAT is payable to Customs on the due date for invoices sent out, whether the customer has in fact paid or not. Paying the tax late can provoke a 2 per cent surcharge, and a second late payment sends that up to 5 per cent. The third late payment is surcharged 10 per cent and the fourth 15 per cent. That is the ceiling, although by that time VAT inspectors may be crawling all over the business and removing its files for a full investigation.

The delay between trade and forwarding the tax to Customs can help a company's cash flow if carefully thought out. If the peak trading period is November and December, as with a toyshop, then ideally the VAT accounting period should end in January. This means the money does not have to be paid until the end of February.

One of the reasons some people buy an accountancy programme is to generate the automatic quarterly return to Customs.

CORPORATION TAX

Self-assessment now covers corporation tax, and it must be sent in within 12 months of the end of the accounting period. If the return is not sent within that period, the fine is up to £3,000 and, if it is fraudulently or negligently wrong, the extra tax due can be doubled. Tax is calculated on the trading profits, capital gains and some investment income.

Allowable expenses

The costs allowable are almost the same as the ones listed under income tax, except that the pay to directors is also deductible from the taxable profit. Losses can be carried forward to set off against future profits.

Rates of tax

The rate of tax is related to the profit on a sliding scale: up to £10,000 profit there is no tax to be paid; over that and up to £50,000 the marginal rate is 23¾ per cent between £50,000 and £300,000 it is 19 per cent; £300,000 to £1.5 million it is 30 per cent.

Paying directors/owners

Although there are tax advantages to being paid in dividends rather than a salary, most advisers recommend enough payment to come just into the National Insurance bracket to build up entitlement to a state pension, statutory sick pay, incapacity benefit and bereavement benefit for a spouse. In 2002/3 that meant over £3,900, but if the pay remains under £4,615 there will be no need to pay either National Insurance or income tax. Go above that and both the individual and the company has to pay National Insurance which rose to 11 per cent in April 2003. Payment in the form of dividends does not attract National Insurance, and the higher rate tax is paid later – dividends are paid net of 10 per cent tax so higher rate payers must then make up the difference in their own tax returns.

Pension contributions and life assurance paid by the company for the directors are not classed as taxable fringe benefits, but most other things are. The tax on company cars is particularly complex, depending as it does on both the cost of the car and the amount of carbon dioxide it is assumed to emit.

CAPITAL GAINS TAX

The main reason this section is included is because it affects not just businesses but individuals. However, there are special provisions to encourage entrepreneurs by reducing the amount of tax payable when they sell the businesses they have built up.

The rules are slightly different depending on whether the asset being sold at a profit was owned on 5 April 1965, 31 March 1982, or 5 April 1998, because those dates are when the tax laws were changed. What follows is for only the latest period.

Above the threshold of £7,900 the individual pays at the highest rate of income tax paid. The tax is payable on the disposal of land, buildings, machinery, or goodwill over £7,500. Normally homes are exempt, but if the home has also been used as business premises, that portion may be liable to tax as well. On the other hand, if any of the business assets are replaced within three years, the capital gains tax can be deferred.

Individuals

To encourage entrepreneurs to set up successful businesses, the tax on selling them after four years is only 25 per cent of the capital gain, with a tapered reduction for shorter periods of ownership.

INHERITANCE TAX

Inheritance tax is payable not only on what one has inherited, but also on any gifts within seven years of the death, and includes any asset. A few exemptions and reductions have been introduced. For example, there is no tax payable on the transfer to a spouse, or on gifts made more than seven years before dying.

The first £265,000 is tax free, and after that it is taxed at 40 per cent.

10 Marketing

CORPORATE IDENTITY

Talk of image seems to bring out the worst in people. The design experts and advertising people can get so convoluted and precious that it transcends parody. Businessmen are generally scornful and dismissive of the notion, partly to undermine the camp chat and partly on the assumption that a good wine needs no bush – the word will get round anyway.

Both are probably wrong. The deep complex significance that consultants impute to logos to explain their designs and justify their fees passes over the heads of 99.9 per cent of the audience, and the other 0.1 per cent probably misconstrue it. The imagery is lost on almost anybody. But the image, if good, remains. Most people can recall the symbol for Shell, ICI, Nike, Coca-Cola, Penguin Books and McDonald's, and not only because of the huge advertising budget behind them. It is worth spending a little time thinking out a logo design that will represent the company, and making sure that the name of the business and the symbol support each other. In the previous list of companies – chosen totally from the first logos that came to mind – all but Nike have a strong link with the name.

Logo

Designing logos is a job for a professional. It had better be good because the logo is what customers will see most and what they will remember the company by, almost as much as the products. A good designer will talk to the managers to get a feel for the image they have and want of the company, and examine what the business does. The main point is that the logo should not fight the product or the name.

For instance, there is little point in producing a stark, minimalist modern design for a business that promotes itself on old-fashioned values and boasts of handmade craft goods. Or vice versa. On the other hand, products change, fashions move on, and priorities vary. Thus, it is probably wise not to marry the style too elaborately to the current lines or you may have to go through the design and promotion costs all over again. The main point is that the design should be appropriate, different, memorable, and instantly linked with the company's name. Examples of the stylized and written out identities are the wavy Ms of Macmillan, which may suggest an open book, and the familiar type of *The Daily Telegraph*, recognisable even in its recently simplified version.

The Daily Telegraph

British Petroleum, for instance, went through a number of changes of logo before deciding it wanted to be seen as ecologically kinder than the other oil companies, and produced a pattern of petals as part of its logo.

Having hired a hot-shot professional at an appropriately impressive cost, it is easy to be browbeaten by the superior knowledge of design. Listen, but not in awe. Accept good advice, but not if it runs counter to your instincts.

Stationery

Stationery means not just the letter heading, invoices and business cards, but all the brochures, compliments slips, order forms and other items that companies send out. Like the logo, which they should obviously show, they should be consonant with the company's intended image, and look professional. It is a one-off cost and makes a great difference in how the company is perceived. Splash out and get someone who understands the current approaches.

Having gone to all that effort, it will repay a little extra effort to ensure the design is well used. All stationery and uses of the company logo and designs should be consistent – do not let departments or individuals do their own thing.

PRODUCT QUALITY

No amount of publicity, whether advertising, public relations, or other means is going to sell a dud product for long. You can certainly fool quite a lot of people for a while, but eventually even the dimmest consumer cottons on to the fact that the product or service is a stinker. Word then gets around surprisingly quickly.

All that means is that a good manager, as the first priority, has to get the product right. Not only must it be what the customer needs, but it must be faultless. Consider the British car and motorcycle industry. Neither was much good at innovation, but far worse than that in the eyes of consumers was the quality. One major reason companies have disappeared and been replaced by Americans, Germans and Japanese is because faulty design and slovenly manufacture produced unsuitable and unreliable products.

Therefore, before starting to advertise, make sure the product or service is not only good, but excellent. Not just the best in your area, but the best in the world. It can be done.

PUBLICITY

Having produced the best product or service, it must be seen to be the best. That entails attention to detail. It means getting the design and packaging right, having the corporate vehicles in company livery and clean, a receptionist (if you have one) who is friendly, helpful and informed, and a telephone that is answered promptly and courteously without eight layers of automatic routing to make it look as if you are a big organization.

Only when that is all in place, is it worth ploughing into publicity. Or at least thinking about it.

It is an easy trap to think there are only two forms of publicity: advertising and public relations. There is much more to it than that. Moreover, even these two areas are generally misunderstood as the later sections in this chapter will show.

Whatever the medium for the message, the first question is: what do you want to say? And that, in turn, depends on what is being sold and to whom. Chapter 2 first posed the question of who will buy your product or service. The answer to that determines both the method and content of any publicity.

The message

Why are you doing all this? The choices are wider than at first you might think. Increasing sales might be one reason. Another could be to make the company seem friendly as a way of creating customer loyalty. You might want to reinforce the benefits of the company and its products. Or you might want to raise the prestige of the product to justify a higher price. And so on.

Thus, the starting point is to decide precisely what you are trying to achieve. That does not mean woolly things like a better image, but the details behind this – what the better image is intended to achieve. It might be higher sales; a school might want more applications; a service business might want a classier set of clients to increase fees; a company might want to attract better salesmen. Setting a target dictates the criterion of success as well as the medium for achieving it. Even if the aim is just to increase sales, the choices can be wide. What route is likely to work best for those people and this product: straight description? information about its facilities and the benefits? and so on.

The answer to the question about the aim of publicity may determine the approach to the means, and help to establish precisely what sort of image and unique character you want to convey. This is separate from the unique selling point of the product. Your approach to publicity is closer to the search for a recognizable identity, a way for the customer to remember something about the company. Avis, for instance, made a virtue out of being smaller than its rival car hire company Hertz with its slogan 'We try harder'. British Airways differentiated itself from the fleets of other airlines by calling itself 'The world's favourite airline'.

The need for differentiation is greatest when the products or services available in the market are most similar. Then you have to search hard for some characteristic of the business that can justifiably be promoted and would gain increasing customer acceptance and recall. The factors could be reliability, high quality, good value, latest technology, trust, honesty, long establishment and stability, and personal touch and helpfulness. This is not a decision to be lightly taken because a mistake can take years to cancel, and a false perception of the business can hold it back without anybody realizing what is amiss. So try it out on as many people as possible.

Advertising

Most forms of advertising are expensive, national newspapers and television exceptionally so. It is usually beyond the reach of a small new company, although there are exceptions of businesses that kick off with piles of cash. This means that most new businesses have to be more canny and company-focused.

Who will buy and why? Even if the product has a general consumer appeal, there must be some sections more likely to be interested – teenagers, working-class people, northerners, farmers, married couples, home-owners, joggers, women. Once you have isolated the primary market, you can start thinking about the medium for advertising that they are most likely to encounter.

To revert to the earlier example of a healthy soft drink. Such products tend to interest women more than men, they sell in the south more than the north, and not just through supermarkets but also specialized health food shops. Now you can start focusing on the best way of reaching these target audiences. What magazines do they read? Would they go to a gym, and so on? Thinking through connections can suggest inexpensive means to reach a target market.

If the business is a small tradesman-based organization like plumber, locksmith or decorator, then leafleting may yield better results than advertising. However, if you are going to advertise in the local paper, there is little point in placing one large ad. Nobody will cut it out. It is far better to have a small and regular advertisement than the occasional big one. Getting into directories like *Yellow Pages* and *Thomson* is also a good idea.

If a business school wanted more student applications, it should advertise in the magazines that go to human resources managers because they send the majority of pupils. A small builder might call on clients directly and pop leaflets through the letterboxes of others. A local newsagent will deliver the advertising sheet with the papers for a small fee.

Major multinational corporations spend money on corporate image advertising because they are trying to appeal to a wide range of non-customers: they need to explain themselves to the environmentally concerned, as well as keep politicians and shareholders happy, and encourage the best people to work for them. Small businesses neither need nor can afford to go in for that sort of approach. Their meagre advertising budget has to produce concrete results in better sales. The budget is therefore directed, precise and tailored in both its message and its medium.

The range of media options is wider than most people realize. For example:

- national daily papers
- national Sunday papers
- local papers
- free sheets/magazines
- professional magazines
- hobby magazines

- women's magazines
- men's magazines
- posters
- national radio
- local radio
- direct mail
- point of sale displays
- brochures and leaflets
- trade directories
- national television
- local television
- cinema
- website.

Even this list does not exhaust the possibilities. You can, for instance, use sandwich boards or give away free balloons, or indeed have a large tethered balloon with a message on its side, etc. A garage may lend a car – with a suitable message on the side – to a local worthy, such as a football player, or a company can sponsor a local team. Some of that may also generate additional coverage in the local press and radio. Only ingenuity, finance and relevance set a limit to the range of ways of publicizing a business.

Types of advertising

Within the general advertising label there is a variety of approaches. There are direct response advertisements, perhaps with a cut-off coupon, an Internet address or a phone number. And there are hard-sell advertisements telling people this is the best and an absolute bargain, and to order now before the chance slips away. A couple of minutes in front of the television set or with a newspaper will quickly show the range of potential styles and messages.

The reason advertising is expensive is not just because most of the media are pretty pricey but also because it takes a professional to devise a successful ad. No matter how much you fancy your talent as a graphic artist, typographer, copywriter, designer or whatever, the result will almost certainly shout amateur, which is probably not the image to present for the business.

Even the professionals need guidance about what you want, and this invariably causes conflicts. The agency, designer et al. have strong ideas about what looks best and what constitutes good presentation; the business manager has strong ideas about the message to get across. Their ideas do not always coincide.

A few general rules may help. Keep the message clear and simple. That means restricting the content to one or two points at most. A concomitant of that is spareness of words, the fewer the better. There is little point in writing sparkling persuasive copy if the sheer volume of words deters anybody reading it. No matter how much one admires another advertisement current or past, do not copy it. The result will be unoriginal, derivative and merely help sell the product that first used the technique. When devising advertisements think like a consumer – customers are not interested in the factory, the chief executive's face, or other extraneous details. What matters is the product and how it will help them solve a problem. Finally, make sure the advertisement is within the law and does not contravene the rules of the Advertising Standards Authority.

Lord Leverhulme, one of the founders of Unilever, notoriously said he knew half the money he spent on advertising was wasted; the trouble was he did not know which half. The aphorism may be funny but does not say much for his systematic approach – modern businessmen need to try harder. It is certainly true that it may be hard to attribute specific sales to specific advertisements, even with return coupons, but it would be silly not even to try. And if you do try, some answers will appear. It is well worth trying to assess effectiveness. This is not easy, and remember there will be a delay between the ad and the effect on sales; there is an enabling effect (salespeople may be received with greater enthusiasm); and repeated advertising has a cumulative effect. Measurement is easier when the advertising campaign has a specific target.

Content

A number of people watch advertisements to ensure they are not misleading or offensive. These include the Advertising Standards Authority, which demands that printed ads be legal, decent, honest and truthful; The Independent Broadcasting Authority and, under the Control of Misleading Advertisement Regulations Act, the Office of Fair Trading. There are also special rules for health and financial products, trades giving credit, companies selling tobacco and selling to children, etc. Beware of advertising in countries outside the UK without extensive local advice; for the most part the rules are more restrictive than in Britain.

Public relations

There is much more to public relations than pouring gin and tonics down the throats of journalists in the hope that they will say nice things in print about your company and its products. It is good to have nice things said about you, but only if the right people notice. There are other ways of reaching customers, actual and potential. The innumerable vehicles for achieving this range from pictorial calendars, to mugs bearing the company's logo, from putting a page on the Internet to distributing leaflets at exhibitions or even in the street.

Press relations

Press relations is just one branch of public relations, and it has three major advantages over advertising: it is nearly free publicity, it is noticed more, and even though people always claim to believe nothing they read in newspapers, they do believe what journalists say more than they do advertisements. It has one major disadvantage however: you are competing for newspaper space and air time with every other company and publicity-hungry individual in the country.

Predictably, it is not easy to get journalists' interest. Most manuals and books of advice make a big thing about sending out press releases, but the prospects of success with that activity are so small as hardly to be worth considering. As with all successful selling – and in essence this is selling on behalf of the company – winning demands seeing the picture from the other side. If you were a journalist on *The Daily Telegraph*, would you really spend time on one of hundreds of thousands of tiny companies claiming to be unique or brilliant? And if that has not made the point and you still rate your chances, think about it this way: how many references to tiny new companies appear in the pages of the national broadsheets on an average day? Why should they make an exception for you?

Like all the other warnings in this book against getting carried away with your own brilliance, this is not a counsel of despair. It merely suggests the second requirement for success in this field (as perhaps elsewhere) is researching the market. Read the papers anyway – it is useful to keep up to date with the economy, with changes in taste and so on – and especially the ones in which you hope to figure. In the process, one can spot opportunities. One paper may have a slot for small businesses, with occasional tales of how they got started or overcame problems. The person who writes or edits this is more likely to be receptive to stories about novel methods of funding or an unusual business success than the news page of the same paper, or than a horde of other journals with no reserved space for that sort of story. Ringing the journalist may yield rewards, if you can explain why your story is an especially interesting one or would at the very least yield a good photograph (a striking picture is a powerful selling factor for you, because newspapers increasingly devote space to photographs). There is a chance you may wedge your story in, but on the whole the local paper is a better bet.

Keeping an eye on the medium – radio or TV station, magazine, newspaper – not only shows what it likes, but avoids fatuous mistakes when you get in touch. It does not endear you to the people you are trying to influence if you blurt out things that clearly demonstrate you have never seen or heard their product. Whenever reading a journal of any sort, be on the alert for ideas. This does not mean the 'me-too' approach. If a journal has recently carried a feature on a maker of left-handed toothbrushes, the last thing it wants is another doing exactly the same. There would soon be few readers left. Think what you as a reader would want from such a feature; certainly not a plain story of setting up and then claiming to do wonderfully well. It needs anecdote, humour, drama, personalities. Something to make it worth reading. Think even harder about what the journalist wants.

For all their reputation for being hard-bitten, cynical and stroppy, most journalists are simple, gullible people like everybody else. And they are not hard to manipulate. What they like in a story is also simple: nice human-interest material, a good yarn, some nicely pungent quotes, and a decent touch of novelty.

When talking to a journalist, say nothing that you would not be happy to see quoted in print the following morning. You have to know a journalist extremely well before straying from the path of safety. You may say something is off the record (not to be used at all), or unattributable (can be used but without revealing the source of the information), but you cannot tell if the journalist is malicious enough to ignore that, or incompetent enough not to have made the warning clear in his notes.

None of this needs a professional PR, either within the company or as an external adviser, but it does need somebody with an alert mind, and sufficient brass neck to try and try again despite frequent rebuffs. External agencies can bring specialist expertise about drafting readable press releases, organizing a press conference or facilities visit, commissioning photographs and even designing brochures. They may have contacts within newspapers and television stations and they know what the media want. The really good ones can bring an external independent view on how the company is perceived and how it can improve.

Good agencies are rare, however, and generally cost a fair amount of money. Whether that money is well spent is hard to tell. A common reaction is that the benefits of PR cannot be measured, but as the physicist Lord Kelvin remarked, anything that exists, exists in some quantity and can therefore be measured. One is tempted to add, if it cannot be measured, perhaps it does not exist. About £12 billion a year is spent on PR in Britain, but hardly anybody knows if this produces value for money. One way to find out is to set clear targets, ask the agency to meet them, and review progress regularly.

Alternatively, an alert person within the company is more likely to have a finger on the pulse of what is novel in the business. Such a person would also be familiar with the company and its people, and would therefore know who is best protected from the media and who would shine. The ones with an ability to talk then need to be promoted ruthlessly. If one of them is an expert on something in the industry, let journalists and broadcasters know. Nothing is more useful for a journalist compiling a story for a radio news bulletin or next day's paper than an expert who can not only explain what the events being covered really mean, but can also supply a good trenchant quote to go with the story.

It is a good idea to start this early on and to develop a relationship with the local media at the very least. This will help sell the company on a continuous basis and it will come in very handy when things go wrong (see 'Contingency planning' in Chapter 11).

Broadcasting

Even without malicious editing, broadcast interviews can be remarkably effective ways of making executives seem shifty, evasive, ignorant, stupid, criminal and inept. Not all interviewers are destructive and not all programmes set out to trip up managers, but it happens often enough that it should make novices wary. In a chat with a print journalist you can retract and say 'No, I am sorry that came out wrong. That is not what I meant. What I mean is . . .' In a broadcast there is neither the time, nor often the opportunity. Take advice and training before venturing into broadcast.

Nevertheless, sometimes that is not possible. If, for instance, you are cornered by a television crew, or a disaster has befallen the company. If you are ambushed, it may be better to pour out a stream of obscenities that will prevent the footage being broadcast than hide, run away, or mutter 'no comment'.

If you are making a broadcast, here are a few elementary rules for beginners:

- Think through why you are there and hence what sort of questions are likely to be asked.
- Ask in advance who else will be on the programme and avoid arguments with experienced broadcasters.
- Ask what the first question will be to prepare an answer – if they ambush you with a different one, ignore the question and give the prepared answer.
- Before the broadcast, work out three things you are going to say, and say them by twisting the question if necessary.
- Rehearse with a colleague before the interview.

Broadcasters try to unbalance you and to shorten the interview by interrupting answers. Be ruthless in interrupting their interruptions, if necessary talk loudly over them or explain that if they want an answer they will have to listen more and talk less. Alternatively, one can pause (remembering while the broadcaster is talking what it was you were planning to say), and when they have finished carry on as if the interruption had not happened.

One of the broadcasters' weasel techniques is to preface an attack with 'Some people might say . . .' Those should seldom be answered. If you feel you must respond, dismiss them with 'Some stupid people will say anything to get attention.'

Other PR

There is an awful lot more to public relations than getting a mention in a newspaper. That is only the means to an end. The end is getting known by potential customers and the people supplying them, and persuading them this new business or product is exactly what they have wanted all these years.

The answer is to get among them. Join every organization that will have you, and go and mingle. For example, there are the local chamber of trade and chamber of commerce, Rotary, Lions, Masons, golf club, political party, trade association, professional bodies and local councils. Join any body that gives you a logo to stick on your letterhead and the shop window to show that you are a recognized expert, deeply qualified and wholly reliable.

One can also try marketing gimmicks. For instance, organize a band to play in the square on a specific day each week, month or year. Create a competition with jolly (but not necessarily expensive) prizes given at a public ceremony by a celebrity – giving something away is always popular. This sort of event gets more interest and coverage than any amount of advertising. Do try to make the gimmicks interesting and fun without being obviously stupid or crass.

Investor relations

This is seen as the prerogative of large quoted companies, yet keeping the backers happy should be important to any size of business. Keep investors informed more than the legal requirement and prepare thoroughly before meeting them so you can answer questions and satisfy their interest in the company.

Telephones

Another aspect of continuous good relations with customers and others is the contact with the public. Telephones and the Internet are key. Guidelines can be summed up as simple good manners, and in particular:

- Answer the telephone promptly, and certainly within three rings.
- Avoid automatic answering systems except as a last resort; they are liable to lose customers. If unavoidable, see if there is a way of logging how many callers ring off without going through or leaving a message.

- Operators should avoid time-wasting greetings like 'Good morning. Bloggins and Snooks customer services division. Sharon speaking. How may I help you?'; they should stick to good morning and the name of the company.
- If there is no response from an extension, ensure the caller is put on to someone else or to a helpful message service.
- Voice-mail messages should be in the voice of the person being called, and should specify when he or she is likely to return.
- During holidays, calls should be automatically diverted to someone who can deal with the caller.
- It is minimal good manners to return calls promptly, certainly within the day.
- That applies to internal messages as well; they may be about an external call.
- If the volume of calls is so great there is no time to return all in the day, delegate some.
- The chief executive should call in occasionally posing as customer or journalist to see how well fielded the calls are – if the voice is too distinctive get a friend to do it and listen in.

Correspondence

Many people who can talk in simple, direct and forceful language to friends and colleagues suddenly slump into some strange alien form of communication when they start writing. They become pompous, obscure and absurd. It is jeans and T-shirt when they speak, but a Victorian frock coat with a shiny top hat when they write. And it does not matter whether they are writing a letter, a press release or an article for a magazine.

Would any sane person start a conversation with something like 'As discussed previously between your good self and the undersigned on the 15th ult, please find enclosed our appropriately signed cheque in full and final consideration . . .'? The person you were talking to would edge away in alarm prior to summoning the men in white coats. It is hard to know why anybody would therefore write such gibberish. But they do. What on earth does 'please find' mean? And what is wrong with 'I enclose'?

Some business letters look as if they ought to end with 'I beg to remain, sir, your humble and obedient servant.' That sort of pomposity was unacceptable but common in 1850, but is a bar to communication now.

Simple declarative sentences with few sub-clauses are needed. Active verbs and short words of Saxon origin get the message over more clearly. There is no surer sign of failing confidence and lack of education than painfully constant use of long Latinate words when there are perfectly good short equivalents. It makes the writer seem sweaty with embarrassment, and the text lame and weary rather than important. So, start is better than commence, try than attempt, end than conclude or terminate, buy rather than purchase or acquire. Epicentre is not the same as centre; sea change is not better than change; showcase is a meaningless extension of show; and a learning curve is not more explicit than learning. Also avoid the makeweights like far and wide, hearts and minds, law and order, by and large, part and parcel, tried and tested, kick start, above and beyond, quantum change, nation state, and so on and on. If in doubt, read it aloud and imagine an audience of friends at the pub.

Trying to be matey and intimate can be just as bad. The sentences clog with isn't and doesn't and won't. The rule is keep it simple and unadorned.

Corporate hospitality

Some people call corporate hospitality customer relations rather than public relations, and an enormous and lucrative trade has grown up in recent years telling people about CRM – customer relationship management. This is a parallel activity to the more direct method of entertaining customers, suppliers and other useful contacts. Corporate hospitality has grown to be an industry costing about £700 million a year. It is, however, trying to lose some of its reputation as merely an excuse for the directors to indulge their hobbies and pastimes, to get free tickets to the best sports events, and get pleasantly sozzled in company with a few friends designated for the day as important clients.

The usual venues are indeed delightful, ranging from sports events like golf, rugby, football, Wimbledon tennis and Royal Ascot, through high culture such as the opera at Covent Garden or Glyndebourne, to activity events like driving a tank or Formula 1 racing car. Some add spice by making it an overseas event like the Le Mans or Monte Carlo Rally, Longchamps racing, or the Vienna opera.

Nevertheless, enjoyment on that scale demands a long pocket, and it is doubtful whether a new company could or should afford it. A pleasant drinks party in an appealing venue, or a dinner around the Christmas period may be more appropriate.

Customer relationship management

CRM is usually defined as establishing a long-term relationship with the people who buy the company's products. As marketed, it is full of wonderful and vague phrases about customer information systems, personalization schemes, data warehousing, and large and expensive computer systems to do precisely what every manager ought to be doing in the first place: keeping customers happy enough for them to buy again. For a small business, the technology is best avoided.

Keeping customers happy means finding out what they buy and why. The first part is easy – it is available from accounting records and can be analysed by several criteria. The second part may mean a chat with the chief executive, principal buyer, supervisor, or whoever buys and uses the product or service. Keeping contact with good customers is, in any case, sensible. They can tell you what is going right and where mistakes are coming from, and suggest new lines or approaches.

Knowing what the customer buys and likes can then suggest what else might appeal. An approach or direct mail shot about the latest developments would be automatic; probably both.

The Data Protection Act has elaborate rules on what records may be kept on individuals. Among the long list of regulations governing the information is the fact that the database must be registered, even if it is on paper only, and the records must be fairly processed, which means the person's permission has to be gained, some negatively some positively. It must all be accurate and used only for the purpose for which it was collected. It must be secure and kept no longer than necessary.

Individuals can enter their name in lists to be protected from receiving mailings, faxes, telephone sales, calls and e-mails, and the law demands that businesses respect their wishes. Companies have no such Preference Service options.

SALES

As with other aspects of publicity and marketing, the first step in successful sales is to know just who it is you are selling to. For instance, in the book trade, publishers are selling not to readers but to journals and the book buyers of shops. If the book is mentioned in the heavyweight press, it will be stocked by the shops – paradoxically, even if it is panned. If the bookshops decide it is going to be a seller, they put it near the door at eye level, and it becomes a self-fulfilling prophecy.

Similarly, if you are selling training courses, the people to target are the ones making the decision – the personnel/human resources managers of major companies, not the finance directors or chief executives.

Unless the business is starting with a tremendous éclat and substantial backing, the first sales will be garnered by the entrepreneur who set up and is driving the company. That is a pity because few of them are good at it. The facility can be improved with training and practice, but it is an innate talent requiring supreme self-confidence, charm and empathy.

Sales representatives

Sole traders are famously bad at selling themselves and their products. Obviously there are exceptions, but they are noted on the whole for being bashful, reluctant to puff themselves, uncomfortable at talking about money, and rotten at haggling about terms. Yet they are generally in the best position to sell – the person who started the business has a comprehensive knowledge of the product/service, which is vital for a convincing selling job.

For all but a lucky few who are in natural demand and, despite not making the slightest effort, customers come flocking to their door, selling is going to make the difference between comfort and starvation. Consequently, it might be best to go on a course. This may also teach the entrepreneur how to accept rejection. With one call in seven reckoned to generate an order – for a good salesman – one has to get used to a lot of 'no' without feeling dejected.

There are ways to reduce the opposition. One is to get appointments. It is possible in some markets to walk in unannounced and talk to the buyer, but they are getting fewer. At this point the ploys start for making a refusal more difficult. For example, do not ask when it is convenient, but say you will be in the area next Tuesday and Wednesday, so which of those would be easier. When you do meet, take charge of the interview. An energetic but contained enthusiasm can carry you through the first few minutes – long enough to engage the potential buyer's interest. Forget the introductory small talk – you cannot afford that initial wheelspin before getting going. If you generate a momentum, it can carry you through the initial scepticism. Have all the information about the product in your head: specifications, price, discounts, delivery, variations to order and so on.

Dealing with excuses not to buy is one of the tests that shows the talented salesmen. Manuals and courses on this are full of the standard ploys. To illustrate, when a customer says he wants a bigger discount, the answer is that it takes only a slightly larger order to earn the extra discount. There is little point trying to remember all the attitudes and counter-plays like memorizing classic games of chess. Far more important is to learn the attitude: every excuse to avoid placing an order, or a large enough order, has a rebuttal if you are alert and bright enough. Two points of caution, however, are omitted from these manuals and courses of gung-ho inducements to get out there and knock them dead. One is that the aim of selling is to make the company money, so do not negotiate orders that will produce little or no margin. The second is to know when no means no and therefore not to outstay your welcome or you will never get an order from that buyer.

Selling through sales reps means the principal contact with customers is through the sales team. Accordingly, choose your team carefully. It is not nearly enough that they be good at selling. They have to be ethical, pleasant, polite, tidy, clean, knowledgeable and loyal. This means careful selection and plenty of motivation. Bear in mind that sales reps have been out there getting rebuffed time and again and still have to dredge up enough energy to bounce back and coax an order out of a reluctant customer. Their egos are bruised every day and they need lots of encouragement, praise and rewards to keep them going. Sales forces are generally on some form of incentive system linked to performance, but in such a dispiriting occupation a kindly word has almost as great a motivating effect.

Direct selling

Selling direct to the public cuts out the intermediary and has a wide variety of routes, for instance:

- doorstep selling
- mail order
- direct mail
- via an Internet site
- market stalls
- via owned showrooms
- telephone selling.

Businesses can start as market traders and progress to bigger things – Marks & Spencer and Amstrad did, for example – but this book is probably not for them. Doorstep selling is becoming relatively rare in

Britain, partly because it has been exploited by cowboys selling double glazing and concrete drives, and customers are becoming wary. Owning your own showrooms is an expensive foray into the property market and may need to be a second step in the company's expansion.

Direct mail

This topic could have come under the advertising section, which shows how closely all aspects of the company's marketing have to be integrated into a consistent system aiming at the one goal: getting more sales. Each aspect must have a variant of the same message and support all the other marketing efforts.

Getting leaflets to the right people depends on a good mailing list. Those are scarce and expensive to buy or rent. The Institute of Direct Marketing has the names of list brokers. Costs vary depending on how valuable the customers are, how easy it is to compile the list, and how much the list has been 'cleaned'. Mailing lists rapidly fall out of date as people die, move or change their names. Most are also compiled in a fairly haphazard way and contain duplications and mistakes. That means they must be regularly checked, updated and overhauled. Rents of £250 per thousand names are not uncommon. The alternative is to compile your own. That is time-consuming, with the results likely to be incomplete and inaccurate. That does not apply to previous customers, who of course should be told of any developments that might interest them.

A response rate of over 2 per cent is thought reasonably good so do not be over-hopeful of results. And this is when you have the mailing right, which is an art in itself.

There are design costs, printing, return pre-paid envelopes and postage costs all coming on top of the list rental. The moral is that it had better be right. This means testing the package and offer on a small number of people, and working out if the exercise is worth it even if the return is only 1 per cent, say (it could be even less).

Whether the response is by a reply-paid envelope or a fax-back sheet (likely to be more effective with businesses), make sure they have a code number on them to test the effectiveness of the exercise.

Exhibitions

How do you meet attractive people of the opposite sex? Obviously you go where they congregate and then find a pretext for starting a conversation. You go to art galleries, clubs, parties, or evening classes, depending on the type of person being sought. The logic is much the same for companies trying to meet compatible people with whom to start a meaningful business relationship.

One obvious venue is the exhibition. Before spending money on making yourself sexy and gaining an entry ticket, reconnoitre the show to see what sort of people go there, and what the normal visitor is like. There are also regulations and administration. Some exhibition organizers insist on standard shells, and an exhibitor might have to ship in displays and perhaps catering as well as people (who will need accommodation). There are other decisions, like the method of fitting out, whether to have decorative assistants to attract the eye but who might be unable to answer the questions; and where to find people patient enough to answer the same question 230 times a day to people who are as likely to buy as become prime minister. Yet the salesmen have to avoid prejudice: the tyre-kicker dressed like a tramp may actually buy, while the smoothie in Savile Row togs may be a competitor.

Take advice the first few times because there is much to learn, ranging from providing the right sort of stationery (order and message pads, and plenty of visiting cards), and ways of being rescued from obsessive bores keen to discuss every last detail of the product.

The Internet

The Web has been grotesquely over-touted as a means of selling worldwide. On the one hand, there are the teenage e-trade millionaires as examples, plus ministers telling us to get started or die; on the other, there is a steadily growing heap of spectacular Internet insolvencies, and a deafening barrage of e-everything, from e-mail to e-commerce. It is hard to resist the temptation to panic or say e-nough.

In practice, as you would expect, neither is right. Business remains business: you still need a decent product, have to find customers, fend off the competition, and sell at a price that will produce a profit. New Net ventures fell over because they overlooked one or more of those factors. Nevertheless, the computer is not a passing fad like the hula-hoop – there may be disagreement about when and how much, but nobody disputes the Internet is big and getting bigger.

One area in which it is absolutely right to be sceptical is statistics, especially with any connection to the Internet. Figures about the Web and the activity on it are bogus, including numbers of subscribers, amount of trade, companies on-line, and so on. Nobody knows, and there are no reliable ways of finding out. Thus, numbers should be treated with extreme caution, whatever their source. Projections are, therefore, doubly suspect. The actual figures are, however, almost irrelevant. For instance, one of the lowest estimates puts the current Internet trade at an annual rate of around £7 billion, and in four years' time that will be 40 times as much, and there are some researchers adding noughts to even that. Similarly, there are said to be anything from 130 million to 350 million people on-line now with thousands more joining every day. Even if you allow a latitude of plus or minus 50 per cent, the numbers are eye-wateringly large and unquestionably growing all the time.

The Internet is consequently difficult to ignore. All the more so because other companies are bound to be there and could drain away the customers. One major American corporation is said to have set up a separate e-commerce subsidiary with the instruction to get out and take all the business it could from the parent before the competitors did.

The Net does not only provide access to a new range of customers, but, at the very least, a new way of selling. This is because the most immediate and obvious effect of going on the Net is the visibility. This is often said to be a major boon since you are, in theory, immediately available to hundreds of millions of people all round the world – a tremendous number of potential customers. Nonetheless, although most potential customers may never find the website, competitors will. As a result, one of the effects of the Internet has been that oft-repeated cry about business speeding up alarmingly. Visibility produces swift reaction, which means it becomes much harder to take things slowly, check the effects and then tweak it with gradual improvements. You have to run quite hard to remain in the same spot.

For new businesses trading only on the Net, this has produced the theory that it must become instantly dominant, and hence be comparatively immune to attack. Geoff Bezos, for instance, when setting up the Net bookshop Amazon, disregarded immediate profit and went for market share at almost any cost. In fact, that strategy does not make a company invulnerable because others can easily replicate the leader, and specialist browsers allow customers to compare prices from them. This can have the effect of depressing prices to the point of eliminating profits. The solution is to establish a reputation for service – swift reaction, reliable delivery, constant information, tailored offers, and so on – which might counteract the otherwise dangerous, downward pressure on prices.

Advantages and drawbacks

Adding an e-commerce function on to an existing business has the following advantages:

- improving customer relations through more frequent and easier contact
- another opportunity to sell
- gaining access to large businesses which have planned to buy more supplies only on-line – British Telecom plans to handle 95 per cent of orders and 20 per cent of tenders over the net; the Automotive Industry Action Group is linking 630 assembly plants and suppliers; Sears, Carrefour and Bentalls are all linking with suppliers on-line
- improving customer service by shortening supply chains
- reduced overheads – there is no need to keep expensive property for customers to visit, nor hordes of staff to look after them and grab their attention; some have estimated the savings of processing purchase orders at something approaching 90 per cent

- cutting costs through lower stock levels, and also through opportunities of building to order – IBM, Hewlett-Packard, Dell and Wal-Mart all do that
- making buying easier, cheaper and more efficient
- acquiring a reputation for being alert, modern and thrusting, which can influence stock market ratings as well as industry regard
- using the technology to make management systems more streamlined – for instance, Safeway gives suppliers direct access to its stock control and lets them manage stock levels
- making it easier to outsource specialist functions to experts who can reap the benefits of scale
- being able to break into new geographical markets without enormous capital expenditure
- allowing diversification into other products and services.

Predictably there are also disadvantages. Judging from the experience of recent years, the principal ones include:

- alerting competitors to your products, design and selling approach
- letting enthusiasm run away with the cheque book without calculating what is a realistic requirement
- diverting so much management time to the new medium that the core business is neglected
- making a comprehensive dog's dinner of the attempt, and so inviting ridicule
- not getting a grip of the system, and so losing the potential benefits
- constantly increasing customer expectations, which become less of a challenge and more of a burden.

What sells?

It is usual to distinguish between trading with other companies over the Net – business to business (B2B) – and selling to consumers, called business to consumer (B2C). Conventional wisdom is that the majority of e-commerce (anything up to 80 per cent depending on whose guess you believe) will be to businesses. Some of this e-commerce will be modern versions of electronic data interchange, some will be a transfer to the Net of current elaborate paperwork systems of trade, some will be generated by adding products, ranges and customers, and some will be via a new breed of marketplace where a buyer can browse among the comparable offerings of dozens of suppliers.

Sales made over the Net tend to be in fairly restrictive areas. In the consumer sector, the biggest sales are in goods that are specific commodities and cheaper than in the shops, such as books, CDs and airline tickets. These are sold on price, and the margins are dangerously slim and need a substantial volume to make up for the small profit. Unquestionably sales will grow and presumably the Internet will increasingly take over all the transactions that used to go through mail order catalogues.

However, some customers and some goods do not lend themselves to Net shopping. Many people, for example, would like to feel the material and try the clothes on before buying.

Starting on the Net

The first step is to decide how much of a Web presence to implement. For instance, it is possible to dabble a toe in the electronic pond by starting with no more than a Web page giving the company name, an address, and some indication of its business. That is relatively easy and cheap, and entails putting a series of 'pages' detailing the work and facilities, or the catalogue on-line. This acts as little more than another piece of marketing publicity, comparable with posters or direct mail, with the added convenience of giving customers instant access to the company's range of products and services. Orders can then come either by phone, e-mail, or more traditional routes.

It is possible to create full selling sites in Australia, Britain, Germany and France etc., each with its own methods, language and market approaches (despite hype to the contrary, we still have a fragmented world). Even for a major global corporation, that would be unwise at the start. Far better to see what works and enlarge gently. It is possible to graduate from nothing more than a page with the company's logo, through adding the catalogue, to receiving e-mails or orders, to the site eventually becoming fully interactive and accepting orders and money transfers, and providing acknowledgements and delivery details.

A computer powerful enough to act as a commercial server plus commissioning all the tailor-made software for it is reckoned to cost up to £50,000 for a small business. And it could cost up to £20,000 a year to run it. However, that depends on the size of the ambition. It is possible to buy a power server (a machine with enough processing power and memory to act as the hub of a computer network or to operate an e-commerce site) with four processors and terabytes of memory for about £1,500. Using an Internet service provider's tools and facilities could cost £2,000 upfront plus £1,000 a year.

Some of the same questions have to be asked of both the power server and the service provider. One of the most obvious is access, which is a function of the line capacity and the computer power. The capacity of both should be adjusted not for the average amount of trade, but for the peaks, with a degree of safety margin built in. Speed and reliability are vital on the Net – customers become very irritated if kept waiting for the connection to be made or the Web pages to appear on their screens, and even more cross at failing to get through to the website.

External hosts have a range of other services available, at a price. When picking one, the first criterion is dependability of good service – preferably with a warranty – and then the price for setting up, the annual subscription and the hosting fee. After that other services may be required, such as Web space, preferably at a reasonable cost. One needs to find out whether the host automatically forwards e-mail and Web communications; if information is provided on the number of visitors; whether there are penalties for early termination of a contract and (importantly) if the domain name can be transferred to another service provider without a fee.

Designing a Web presence

This book is not the place for elaborate and detailed instructions on how to design and set up a website, this is too large a topic, but some general rules apply in every case.

It is quite a challenge to make the website enticing. It has to look good for people to read what is on it, and appear to provide all they need in as efficient a way as possible – then they will stay to read further and perhaps even place an order (even though that might be by e-mail or telephone). The techie phrase for this is that the site is 'sticky'. Some companies hope to accumulate a mailing list by making users of the site log on and provide all sorts of personal details. Unless you have some really useful information that customers are desperate to have, this is probably a mistake. Visitors resent it, they can enter fake data, or they may just leave. Not very sticky. However, there is nothing wrong in inviting them to leave a comment by having a link to a message or order page.

If the company has some people experienced in using the Internet, it can probably design its own simple site – HTML programming language can be mastered over a weekend and is surprisingly easy for even non-technical people. An even simpler option is to use a facility built into Microsoft's Word program. There are also relatively simple software packages that promise to make it even easier and the results prettier. In addition, it is frighteningly easy to pinch ideas and even complete pages and clever tricks from existing websites. With all that help and plagiarism, even a fairly straightforward Web presence of half a dozen descriptive 'pages' can take a week or two to become acceptable – although it will be tweaked and improved continuously.

The disadvantage of this approach is that it may look like brochures that have been designed by manufacturers rather than designers: amateur, rather dull and obviously done on the cheap. Since the point of the Web is that everybody has access to some of the most sophisticated and experienced companies and their sites, there is a danger it will look so dangerously drab that it deters potential customers.

Worrying about this desperate fight to be attractive tempts novices to cram the site with gimmicks, florid graphics, flashing and moving images and sounds, and so overload it that visitors rush to the exit, if only for a rest. Before committing yourself try browsing the Net to see how others do it, and learn from their numerous mistakes. Many have a page that is too wide to fit on to the normal display, and has to be jiggled side to side to side to read the text. Some have such clever graphics and animated designs, you can go away and make yourself a cup of tea while it loads on to the screen. Some have text in such small type that some screens cannot reproduce it in readable form. Some make it so difficult to get around the site that even a determined user might want to look for a phone number as the quicker option. Worse still, some fail to provide the name, address, phone and fax numbers of the company.

There is the additional worry that the site has to be readily usable by a range of devices. With the blurring of technical boundaries, it will become increasingly common to access the Web through a hand-held device, on TV sets, or from a car. That means learning another programming language, WML, which can generate the sort of displays that the small and less sophisticated screens on mobile devices can use.

WAP phones have suffered from being so heavily hyped that the real thing with its small screen was bound to be a disappointment. Nevertheless, the system is still evolving and the next generation, on which the telecom companies have already spent a major fortune for the licences, is expected to be better and faster. HSBC bank, for instance, already allows payment from WAP phones.

Remember to allow for the future in terms of expansion, changes and growth of sophistication. That could include logging information about visitors, adding further pages of information, or enabling the use of 'smart' cards. If the site is to become not just a piece of publicity accessible from the Net, but a fully-functioning commercial point, the exercise gets much trickier.

Professional help

Avoiding the DIY approach means either recruiting professionals or going to one of the hundreds of outfits offering to help. Like other aspects of design, it is probably best to use a professional, and preferably one without too grand an idea of what can be done. The cost can be considerable – creating a website can start from a few thousand pounds but could easily rise to millions. And there is a continuous maintenance need to keep the site interesting, add new facilities, and improve the working.

Picking the contractor requires the same process as hiring any other professional. Look at what they have done before and how good those sites are, how impressive the people are, and how far they understand the business and the approach aimed at. In addition, are they practical people or bent on hype and sales patter? There are also service providers and small-business portals that register the name, organize the domain and its visitors, and help with the design of the site.

It is a good rule never to take even the best professional's diktat about anything – test and question everything. Consequently, it is up to the managers of the business to visit the site and judge whether it is attractive and easily usable. There are simple tests: does it prominently display the company's name, address, telephone number and line of business; and does it come up on the screen quickly – do large pictures, sound and video slow down access until the visitor loses patience? This is why some sites with such fancy entertainment often offer the alternative of by-passing the clever stuff for quicker access to the content. You need to test whether it is easy to navigate around the pages for information, and back to the start again, and if each page concentrates on a comprehensible and limited topic, or rambles on so that one has to scroll up and down enormous lengths of text. And, most importantly, does it convey the message with the minimum of distractions or gimmicks?

The site and the software also have to cope with the vagaries of customers. They may come on with a query about the progress of their order; they may want to change time or place for delivery; they may ask questions like 'Can I change the colour?', 'Can I add to the number?', 'Is it too late to alter the specifications?'

A site is 'sticky' when customers stay with it, and like returning to it. There are many ways of achieving that, including good design, ease of use, and providing services or information beyond the original purpose of the business. This could be generalized news feeds, specialized industry gossip, or useful data about global or industry production. Some sites even provide competitions with small prizes. The point is to get visitors to keep coming back. Whoever designs the pages should make provision for that.

Software that logs how many visitors come to the site, how long they stay, which pages they visit and for how long, and how often they return can show what is popular. That can subsequently be enhanced. Alternatively, you could have a page that asks for comments. Internet users are free with their views.

A range of other software has to be bolted on, depending on the range of services the site offers, including accountancy packages that meld in with the existing systems and stock control.

It is also possible to piggyback, or form alliances as the trade prefers to call it. Toys-R-Us used Amazon as an outlet, and the bookseller gained another line to make its site more comprehensive.

How to get known

A danger is getting lost in the millions of traders with websites. This is surely going to get worse as the numbers on the net multiply and companies all learn the techniques of being picked by the search engines. When every backstreet shop from Aberfeldy to Abadan can get its own website, and every artisan from Asturias to Arkansas is selling over the Net, it is difficult to get noticed. The problem is particularly acute for the small and poor businesses. As with other routes of contact to the customer, the large companies can flex their budgets and use spot advertising and, if necessary, integrate the system into their other marketing spending.

The right name helps. People make assumptions: they expect a company called Steelbroadfield to have a website called www.steelbroadfield.co.uk or perhaps .com at the end. Having something wildly different loses many potential visitors. Nominet, the UK registry for Internet domain names, has a list of the names already registered. The system operates on the first come first served principle, and if somebody has already registered your preferred name for a site, tough luck. The only chance is if the holder is an obvious cybersquatter with no good grounds for registering or holding the website except to extort money from the rightful holder. Then he can be evicted.

The name can be registered either directly through Nominet, or rather more cheaply through one of the scores of agents, including most Internet service providers. Some companies consider the Web address so important they have registered every possible variant, and also secured the name in other areas. The other sites – such as .com and all the country variants – automatically route visitors to the company's main site. It does not have to be expensive, and the annual fee in Britain can be under £10 for a site.

That, however, is only the start. Then comes the tougher task of ensuring that people know you are there, and making the site so good that they will enjoy visiting and want to return. One essential element is that the Net presence has to be constantly up to date.

Most obviously, all the stationery should carry the name of the website, and so should any publicity material. In addition, your site can be linked to other compatible websites, but they will agree only if they get an advertising fee, a percentage of achieved sales or a reciprocal presence on your site. There may be official or semi-official bodies, trade associations and others which might help. Being recognized by the main search engines such as Google, Yahoo Alta Vista, Jeeves, Lycos, etc. is a specialized art and may take continuous effort.

At a later stage, you might consider making sales over the Net. This will need quite a lot of additional investment in the website itself and for additional software to ensure security, accept credit cards and log transactions.

Organization

For anything but the simplest site, separate management is needed. If the site is taking orders and trading, give it full autonomy.

There are staffing questions about whether the business has the skills already, and the people to spare to manage suppliers and customers on-line. If not, they can be hired or some parts of the process can be subcontracted to specialists. Either way the Net business disrupts existing methods or it has failed. For instance, somebody will have to think through whether the Net presence changes pricing and payment arrangements.

Getting on to Net trading might also entail setting up a delivery procedure. Since there is going to be extra business from the site – or somebody has failed – there will have to be transport capacity. E-customers are more finicky than most partly because they have got used to the speed of computer activity, and partly because there is a lingering mistrust of a business you cannot see and touch. This means that delivery must be exactly as promised, and preferably with continuously updated information for the customer. Some businesses have handed the whole of the despatch and transport part to an outside logistics contractor, although surveys have shown the service to be generally worse than the in-house departments.

Security

Embarking on full trading via the Net involves a new set of requirements. For example, if dealing with the public, the site will need a credit/debit card trading facility and, in every case, it will need guaranteed user authentication and encryption of sensitive data. It might also be possible for the final part of the transaction to be completed on the telephone instead.

Although there are now encryption systems that are, even in theory, uncrackable – making the police and other intelligence services extremely nervous – day-to-day security is evolving. There are certification companies providing an electronic signature guaranteeing the person at the other end of the deal is who he claims to be, and there are intermediaries offering to act as payment contractors or card guarantors, but all want a share of the spoils.

Protecting the system from computer glitches, software bugs, human error, fraud, fire and flood is achieved with software, hardware, careful procedures and common sense. Getting this or any other level of security wrong can be very expensive.

Marketing

The whole point of spending all this time, trouble and money to get on to the Net is to attract people to the site. The most obvious way is to put the site address on all stationery including the managers' cards, and on any advertising material, from brochures to posters. In addition, a special mailing to customers, actual and potential, to alert them to the new facility might help.

It is also crucial to get the site and its offerings registered with all the major search engines and directories. Work out what categories it is best to list the site under, and also include 'meta tags' to the page – these are invisible to the casual visitor but are clues for search engines. There are specialists, such as Submitit, that will do the comprehensive task for a fee.

It is worth exploring collaboration with other people on the Net. For example, a florist might try for a 'hotlink' connection from the sites of wedding organizers, caterers and undertakers.

There are advertising possibilities of various types and costs on other people's sites. Once again, this can be effected by some offset agreement or exchange.

There have been studies of the various parts or components of the market by ActivMedia Research, AMR Research, Andersen Consulting (now Accenture), Booz Allen & Hamilton, Crédit Lyonnais, Durlacher & Co, Forrester Research, Gartner Group, Goldman Sachs and KPMG.

INDIRECT SELLING

In some sectors it is possible or even usual to use agents and distributors to get to the customer, and this is quite a common way to start in overseas markets. The advantage of using an agent is the absence of overheads and administrative worries; the drawback is the lack of control. Finding someone suitable is likely to be harder than recruiting your own staff. Good agents are scarcer than hen's teeth and even mediocre ones are hard to find. One way to find an acceptable one is by asking trade associations and chambers of commerce and contacting as many companies with compatible products as possible. For instance, a company making car parts can ring round others in the same field but without competing products and ask if they can recommend anybody. Managers say they seldom get it right the first time.

11 Managing a business

Starting a business is fun. It is stimulating, the exploration is exciting, the novelty is refreshing, and the constant negotiations intellectually challenging. Running a business by contrast is protracted, unremitting labour, suffering implacable stress, constantly firefighting as crises hit with monotonous irregularity, and a never-ending series of frustrations. One soon learns that people do not do what they promise to, and fate clearly has you down to replace Jonah as the paradigm for bad luck. That is the reason for the prolonged self-examination in Chapter 1 because it does take a special sort of personality to be able to cope with that sort of life.

Of course, running your own business does also provide enormous rushes of adrenaline and sheer euphoria, for instance, when you win a major contract against much stronger opposition, do a sizzler of a presentation, or really get a product as you want it. On top of that there is enormous fun in creating something, in being independent, in solving really tricky problems, and generally in being challenged and feeling your capabilities are tested. And if you get it right, you will be rich.

With all that, however, comes a long slog of sheer routine management. No rules are reliable when it comes to this. Nobody can really explain how to cope with the multifarious challenges that managers face. It is this very vagueness that may account for every year producing yet another dazzling crop of panaceas and more glitzy best-selling solutions to all management problems. Regularly they come, providing just one more system to transform the company. Some may help, none is ever the whole answer.

Management gurus aside, there are certain age-old practices that may not be a fail-safe route to uncounted riches, but they can help prevent the business from collapsing. Almost by definition, every business insolvency is a management failure. Even if it appears to derive from some completely unforecastable event, it means the business did not have the safety nets. To be specific, the corporate undertakers – accountants specializing in receivership and liquidation who prefer to call themselves recovery specialists – find most failures stem from sheer incompetence in financial control.

That is the first focus of attention. There are others.

The Max Planck Institute for Psychiatry in Munich did a long and methodical study many years ago to discover the characteristics of successful managers. It hoped to find a predictive device to help recruit the right people and push them to the head of businesses. For many years, the researchers tried to find some characteristic common to success. Their first problem was defining success (e.g. was that manager so good because he happened to have a brilliant sales manager under him, was that other one a star because she happened to hit the market as it took off?). Once they got past that, they tried everything from IQ tests to graphology, psychometry to horoscopes, social background to education.

The first surprise was that there is no correlation between management success and intelligence. The IQ distribution of the good managers was almost identical with that of the population at large. The second surprise was that nothing else worked either. The only guide was that somebody who was successful in the past was likely to be successful in the future.

They did not test for common sense, however, partly because it is well nigh impossible to define and it would be fiendishly difficult to measure. It is the one indispensable attribute needed by someone expecting to run a business.

There are few general principles of management that stand up to close scrutiny. All the same, there are some indications that seem to work:

- Test every action and rule against common sense, and treat everything you are told with scepticism.
- Never take your eye off the ball – the moment you relax your watch on any aspect of the business, it turns nasty.

- Encourage, goad, praise, reward employees, and get them to produce ideas for making things better.
- Be viciously ruthless in refusing to accept second best – trying is not enough, you have to succeed.
- Care about customers – keep finding out what they want and why, and then give them something better.

In addition, find the 'driver'. As Hugh Aldous of accountancy firm RSM Robson Rhodes pointed out, every company has a number of characteristics that drive the business. 'Some of them come from the market, some of them are to do with constant development of the product so it is always ahead of expectations, some of the drivers come from building networks which recognize the value of your product in particular markets.' Consequently, a key to success is establishing exactly what does drive demand for what the business provides, and then evolving a plan for managing those key drivers.

The trouble with those rules, as with every other set of guidance notes, is that they are very easy to set down, but can look glib and remote on the page. There seems no way to explain why these have actually been found to work. It is even harder in a book like this which is forever warning against the easy answer, the management school's clever formula, and the management expert's glossily packaged solution. Managers who remain sceptical can find their own rules, or even do without them, provided they know what the important aims are for a business.

VISIBLE MANAGEMENT

Several of the principles of management can be encapsulated in being a visible manager. There is only one reliable way to find out what the business and the workers are doing, and that is to get into it. A company looks very different from the bottom up than from the top down. Get down there and talk to the employees, and ask what is going on.

Many years ago, when one of the insolvent Welsh television

manufacturing plants had been taken over by a Japanese company and had turned profitable almost immediately, one of the workers was interviewed on television. So what was the new management like, he was asked. 'Pretty tough,' he said. 'Arrive late and your pay is docked an hour; arrive late three times and you are docked a day.' And do the new managers understand the plant and the people, the interviewer asked. 'Well,' said the Welshman, 'every man jack of them regularly comes down and works a full shift on the assembly line. They know how it works and what goes on – you can't pull the wool over these fellows' eyes the way you could with the old lot.'

If anybody doubted the point of that interview, they had only to watch the television series *Back to the Floor*. Chief executives faced with doing the job of their subordinates suddenly came to realize with a shock just how massively unorganized, inefficient and tacky their businesses can be. And how much ill will that can generate and, as a result, lose employees and customers. Quite apart from anything else, getting among them and showing you exist and care, really bucks up the workers – they feel the top brass takes an interest.

Another confirmation of this is one of the classic cases in industrial psychology, which has given rise to the phrase the Hawthorne Effect. The Western Electric company decided to use a plant outside Chicago to test the optimum lighting level for factory production. So the light level was increased and the workers were asked what they felt. Output rose. Lighting intensified further. The same result. Several more times the lighting level grew and so did the output, despite the effect becoming almost blinding. So they decided to lower the level, and still output increased. Gradually the level lowered until it was below the original illumination, and still work improved. Western Electric was understandably puzzled and called in some experts to explain what was happening. It was simple. For the first time since the workers had been employed there, management was taking an interest in their welfare, trying to improve their lot, and actually asked them what they felt. Morale flourished and so did production.

When managers get too remote from the workers and the product, a dangerous detachment from the market can eventually lead to disaster. In addition to getting down to the shop floor or the main office space, senior executives also need to get out and talk to customers, especially their buyers. Are the salespeople good and knowledgeable, is quality up to the mark, are deliveries on time, are customers treated with care and courtesy? How does it all compare with the competition? This can, in fact, be one of the best ways of getting advance warning of what the others are up to, what new products they have in the pipeline, how they deal with complaints, and what their prices are in practice. It is also illuminating to become a shopper, ring the company, and try to order some goods.

This is relatively easy when there are half a dozen employees and the business is six months old. It needs to be maintained when the business has grown and the employees are not all personal friends.

Quality

For manufacturers, a vital figure to watch is repairs under warranty. That will show not only the quality of production, but also where it is failing. This is not only immediately expensive but long-term suicide in the way it irritates customers. Word of unreliability soon gets around and it is a label that takes many years to lose.

Complaints

There should always be a log of all complaints and a well-rehearsed system of dealing with them. People will be reluctant to log these because it will reflect on their own performance or those of their friends in the business. This is one area where management actions rather than words will count. It is not enough to say no blame attaches to a mistake unless it has been caused by gross negligence; it is much harder to act that way and avoid shredding the worker who made a mistake. Everybody is allowed a mistake, even a silly one, but not twice. Management must also emphasize – and believe – that complaints show where things can be made better.

Customers always complain, sometimes with justification. Nothing disarms even the most curmudgeonly grouser quicker than a swift apology. Unless the complaint is obviously wrong or stems from some crass folly by the customer, say sorry. If it makes the lawyers nervous on the grounds that you might be conceding liability, at least say that you are sorry the customer feels like that. And then offer to help. Everybody makes mistakes. Tell the customer it was a stupid thing somebody did and you intend to check immediately nothing like it can happen again, and you are very grateful to have the error pointed out – it will make the customer feel really good. Apologizing right at the start without equivocation and offering to put right any mistakes will produce a customer even happier than one who never had a problem in the first place. It is curious but true.

That does mean, however, that the mistake must not happen again. It takes a culture-setting programme to make sure all employees do not consider customers to be ignorant nuisances – even when they are. People should be treated courteously and helped as far as human patience will permit. A careful analysis of the complaints will show where the main weaknesses lie. If very few complaints are logged, somebody is probably not keeping a record.

This applies to service companies as well. Even if customers do not complain, it is instructive to have an occasional check on what they thought of the deal they got. Get somebody to ring, or better still do it yourself and ask if everything was satisfactory. Not only might you learn where things can go askew, but the customer will be really impressed.

Product mix

Chapter 8 explained the range of measures used to keep an eye on how the company is doing. Here, the internal detail rather than the company as a whole is the point of focus.

It is a good idea to produce more than a grand overall figure for the company's cash-flow out-turns, unless there is only one product and one form of sale. The more the total is broken down into components, the more a manager can do to tweak the business into a more profitable avenue. If one route for getting orders seems to be generating more for less, concentrate on it. If one product is making a markedly bigger profit than the others, it is worth concentrating on it. Even if the decision goes the other way in the end, because it is a temporary blip or the other line has major long-term prospects, it is worth considering.

All of that may be supplemented by market research from time to time to check whether demand is shifting, what the competition is up to, and whether the mix and type of product needs to be changed, updated or redesigned. It is one of the paradoxes of business that if you wish to stay the same, you have to keep changing. Producing the same service or product for decades assumes that tastes do not change, competitors are absent, and the company is already perfect. Unlikely, and the predictable route to decline.

Marks & Spencer did not get into trouble because it started selling rubbish but because its formula of good quality at an above-average price was no longer unique. The company found the going tougher in many of its sectors. In women's clothing for instance the competition had caught up and added style and panache to the formula. Like others before it M&S found it quite a struggle to fight back and reclaim lost ground.

The moral is that every business has to improve product, service, ambience and value continuously or someone will snatch away the customers. In the same way, there has to be a steady flow of new products, or greatly improved versions of the old ones, to keep the fickle consumer interested.

Honesty and greed

Just as workers who see the boss knocking off at 4 p.m. to play golf are unlikely to be strongly motivated to work unpaid overtime, so financial honesty starts at the top. If the directors work a fiddle, word will get round. If they start putting private petrol on the company account, putting girl friends on the payroll, getting the company to pay for redecorating the home, or they take samples of company products, it will not be long before the staff are doing it in greater style.

Similarly, it is short-term greed that makes some managers milk the new business right from the start for maximum income. It will not last long.

CORPORATE GOVERNANCE

A long list of preferred conduct drawn up and extended over recent years is intended mainly for quoted companies. However, a few of the precepts may improve the approach of even a small company, and will have to be put in place well before any public listing for the shares (see Chapter 12).

Legislation has spelled out (including in the Directors and Insolvency Act) that directors are responsible for their company's actions. The definition of director is wider than it seems, including not only executive and non-executive members of the board, but also 'shadow' directors (people who tell board members what to do or give advice that is normally followed). All of these have to take full responsibility, and no excuse of incompetence or ignorance is acceptable. They are assumed to know what the company has done and to have approved it. It is rare for a non-executive to be able to demonstrate that the rest of the board had so efficiently concealed information that he could not have found it out with a little determined effort.

Board members failing in their duties can incur fines, imprisonment and disqualification from acting as director in future.

PROCEDURES

Responsibilities

There was a brief summary of the responsibilities of company directors in Chapter 3. The responsibilities are not unreasonable considering a board is handling other people's money and is in a position of trust. However, the responsibilities do involve extensive penalties from which the limited liability of a company structure will not protect directors.

Overtrading means allowing the company to continue in business when it should have been obvious it is incurring extra liabilities without any rational likelihood of being able to settle them. This covers the sort of wishful thinking that overtakes desperate managers who see the enterprise sinking beneath them. Like gamblers, they make one more throw of the dice in the forlorn hope the winnings will eradicate the accumulated losses. It can land a director with unlimited personal liability for the company's debts, and that in turn may produce bailiffs distraining personal possessions, and result in bankruptcy.

If the company is used as a cover for personal fraud, the victims can still come after the perpetrator. If the company itself commits a criminal offence, the directors who permitted that will be held liable. In addition the company itself can sue its own directors for failing to exercise reasonable care and skill in their duties, or indeed for committing the business to liabilities without authorization from the full board.

As accountants keep pointing out when fending off lawsuits over audits, it is the directors who are responsible for preparing the company's accounts from proper records and presenting them for audit (if necessary), sending to shareholders, and filing at Companies House.

All directors are presumed to know what the company is up to and what decisions have been taken in their name, and that includes the non-executive directors. Ignorance is no excuse.

Contracts

Contracts do not have to be in writing to be valid and enforceable. There are a few exceptions such as bills of exchange, marine insurance, sale of land, or some deal that falls under the Consumer Credit Act. But all contracts do have to meet legal requirements to be valid:

- what is on offer must be clear and certain
- both sides must intend to form a contract
- both sides must be able to form a contract
- there is 'consideration' – some form of payment
- the offer is accepted unconditionally
- the aim of the contract is legal.

The third of those tests (having the capacity to form a contract) means in general that both sides must be over 18 years old, unless the deal is for necessaries such as food. Displaying some goods in a shop window is not 'offer' by these legal definitions, and if the wrong price is put on it a consumer cannot demand to have it sold at that rate. In legal language, the display is merely an 'offer to treat' – that is, the retailer is prepared to entertain offers for the goods at that price without obliging himself to accept.

Documentation

Company law requires a record be kept of directors and shareholder meetings, either in a minute book (a place for recording minutes) or on a sheet of paper, and filed. Decisions at company meetings are recorded and signed by the chairman, and are legally binding. This is a convenient way of supplementing the memorandum and articles of association, although those take precedence. However, these minutes can, for example, specify the specialist responsibility of each director, who is authorized to sign the cheques, and so on.

A wide range of other documentation needs to be kept for commercial or legal reasons. Accounting records for a private company have to be kept for three years, and six if it is public. The Taxes Management Act, Limitation Act and VAT Act, and PAYE regulations mean it might be best to keep it all for six years anyway. Some things like minute books and certificate of incorporation have to be kept permanently, while contracts to buy back shares have to be retained for ten years.

Credit control

This really belongs under the heading of financial control, and it is dealt with more extensively in Chapter 8. The main reason for mentioning it here is to remind the top executives that even the most important aspects of the business, from quality control to collecting the money, tend to slip unless continuously monitored.

CONTINGENCY PLANNING

Murphy's Law famously states that if anything can go wrong it will. And, as if that were not bad enough, there is also Riley's Extension which holds that Murphy was an optimist. Or, to put it another way, you can depend on the unexpected happening.

A survivor prepares for it. Obviously, it is not possible to allow for every specific contingency, but there must always be a safety margin to take up the slack when things go wrong. A comparison would be with drivers who take every corner to the absolute limit of the vehicle and tyres. One day they are bound to encounter an oil slick round the corner, some loose chippings, an ancient couple halfway across the road, or a bend that gets even tighter. Without the spare safety margin, somebody will eventually get killed.

So it is with business. It is subject to all the natural disasters, from lightning to flood, hurricanes to blizzards. In addition, there are possible workforce problems such as strikes and flu epidemics. Then there can be disruption to the environment, such as foot and mouth disease, transport strikes and power failures. Plant can break down, the computer can fail through a bug in the program, a virus, or the usual inexplicable malfunction. An inadvertent breach of the law provokes a prosecution for pollution, health and safety failure. And there are hazards in the supply chain on either side: a supplier is afflicted with one of these problems or just goes bust, or a major customer goes out of business (still owing money) or takes the business elsewhere. Some way to keep going has to be found even if several of these happen at once.

Risk assessment

The initial business plan contained a risk assessment section (see Chapter 4), but once the business is running a different set of criteria are used to judge vulnerability, and there are well-known actions to take to ward off disaster. For instance:

- You still need to allow for changes in interest rates, and limit variable rate borrowings to levels that can be serviced even if rates increase.
- If exporting, the business protects itself against changes in exchange rates by hedging currencies, invoicing in sterling or getting paid upfront.
- Similarly, changes in the costs of raw materials, semi-manufactures, and components are offset by buying forward, organizing long-term contracts.
- Allowing for the vagaries of fashion (and that applies not just to clothes) is possible only by being watchful, having a feel for what is going on, and reacting quickly.
- Changes in technology can make products obsolete or produce cheaper and more effective rivals, and this too demands permanent alertness.
- Competition is a constant challenge and a well-managed company is always examining rival offerings, reverse-engineering them, and trying to beat the best.
- If the computer is vital – as it usually is – there must be a standby machine with continuously updated data, or a bureau that can take over.
- If everything grinds to a halt as the result of a power cut, a standby generator is an obvious precaution, at the very least for the computer.
- Being heavily reliant on one customer is obviously worrying, no matter how benevolent he is; the aim is always to keep the biggest buyer to below 20 per cent of output.
- Similarly, a supplier accounting for a substantial volume always needs an alternative, and preferably two or three, either to start supplying now or to be available in case of shortages.

Individual companies have their own specific dangers on top of those, such as the loss of key people like designers, copywriters or sales managers. Then there are public relations disasters such as an airline suffers the crash of a fully-loaded plane, a food manufacturer's output is adulterated, or any company's top person is charged with something deeply disreputable. To some extent, a few of the risks can be covered by insurance (see Chapter 6), but the consequent damage and disruption are unlikely to be adequately insurable at an acceptable cost.

Therefore, as indicated in the list, the first course is risk reduction. The second is to analyse the dangers. For instance, in the case of a public relations problem, who says what and to whom? For a prolonged power cut is there a chance of shifting to another site or would the generator be sufficient? If the premises were flooded, where would everyone go?

As Chapter 10 explained, it is a good idea to build up good relations with the media from the start, and this will come in handy when things go wrong. That is also the time when the management's mettle is tested. Contrast the prolonged prevarication and misleading reassurances from the government over BSE with the immediate, open and considerate reaction of Michael Bishop of British Midland when one of his planes crashed on to a motorway. The ministerial attempts to pretend the animal epidemic was small, local and unlikely to affect people bred suspicion, rumour and mistrust which rumbled on for many years. Mr Bishop's honest and open reaction, and the instant insistence on an open inquiry ensured his airline did not suffer.

OUTSOURCING

Entrepreneurs are often too busy managing to run the business. If the business is successful, that dilemma continually gets worse. The more the enterprise grows, the more staff have to be added, the more specialisms are required, and the more unwieldy it becomes. Yet the odd thing is, it is usually only the largest companies that use outsourcing as a way to reduce the administrative burden. At the very least it is an option worth exploring, especially for the question of cost and security of service.

EXPORTING

Governments have always been keen to encourage businesses to export, but it is not the safe and easy option politicians would have us believe. Considering the extensive extra work and the greater risks involved, managers need to be sure it is worth it. This means overseas trade has to be profitable or necessary enough (for a strategic balance of customers; to offset the oscillations of any one economy and so on) to counteract:

- the political dangers
- extra transport costs
- high levels of administration
- greater problems of obtaining your money
- exchange fluctuations.

We are told the EU is a single market, but of course it is nothing of the sort. Not just languages, but habits, preferences, legal requirements, safety regulations and bureaucracy ensure the market remains fragmented for almost every type of good and service. Even the markets closest to hand, and the ones with a converging set of rules provide a challenge. Not least with languages. British businessmen are notoriously inept at languages, but even in places like Holland and Sweden, where everyone seems to speak faultless English, it makes life easier if the brochures are in the local language. Many other European countries not only feel flattered or friendly towards someone speaking their language, but might have difficulty communicating business requirements in English. It is also easy to assume that Germans, say, have a great command of

English, when in fact they have merely mastered fluent social language. Curiously, even countries such as Australia and America which seem to speak the same language, probably need separate literature to meet local legislation and to conform to domestic styles and approaches.

A safe assumption is that an approach that works in Britain will not work in a foreign country. Many huge industrial and retailing corporations have learnt that at substantial cost.

For a young or small business, the problems are even greater. It has to decide whether to sell from its home base, to find a suitable agent, or to set up an overseas office. All options involve some extra expense. A rapidly growing number of small businesses is getting involved in exports as a result of overseas buyers contacting them through their Internet sites.

Exporters also have to keep track of the documentation, including the complexities of VAT. Sales to VAT-registered businesses in the EU are zero rated, but the VAT number must be shown on all the documents. It might be worth hiring a specialist experienced in weaving a way through the paper trail. The job could also be taken over by a freight forwarder, which can collect the money as well, obviously for a fee. The British International Freight Association can provide a list of members, but do run a check by contacting a selection of customers and talking to small business associations before picking one.

Collecting money from overseas can be a problem circumvented by obtaining irrevocable letters of credit, getting insurance for the debts from organizations such as the Export Credits Guarantee Department, or better still by getting paid upfront through a pro-forma invoice.

Starting to export is hard work and always inherently riskier than home trade, yet there are countervailing advantages. It is worth at least considering whether these more than offset the drawbacks. The benefits include:

- larger volume of sales producing lower unit costs
- reducing reliance on the UK economy

- thicker margins in places where sterling is cheap
- a general increase in the business
- being able to travel on expenses.

12 Success and what to do with it

There is absolutely no obligation to grow the business. Many people start out as sole traders and remain that way until the day they retire. Others become large enough to maintain the 'lifestyle' business that supports the family in adequate if not sumptuous comfort, and yet others establish a small business that employs, say, a couple of dozen people and are happy to keep it at that level. Mike Sheehan of Alt-Berg boots, for example, employs 13 people in Richmond, Yorkshire, and plans not to get too much bigger since his explicit ambition is not to make a million but to ensure that boots are still being made there in 100 years' time.

If one of those approaches is the sort of thing that appeals, and your picture of the future, disregard this chapter. The only section that could be of interest is the one on how to sell the business in the absence of a satisfactory successor to run it.

EXPANSION

From sole trader

Much of this book has worked on the assumption that the business being set up starts as an incipient corporation with several people already on board and expecting to take on more. As the statistics show, this is not that common a pattern. A vast number of businesses, running into millions possibly, are sole traders. They represent the majority. They can be anything from a plumber or decorator working alone, through a management or marketing consultant, to a small publisher or a freelance journalist.

Although any of these might obtain help from others in the trade if confronted with a really big job, they are not planning to hire anybody. They have a roster of contacts and business specialists used in the past. These people are brought in for specific tasks on a set basis or as subcontractors, just to complete a major job.

If growth does come, normally the first transition is to recruit somebody on a part-time basis to help with the correspondence, book-keeping and administration. That can turn into a full-time job if the venture continues to thrive, but a growing number of people would rather opt for a smaller income than let themselves in for the miles of red tape and oceans of regulations when they become a multi-person business. They prefer stagnation to stress.

Although there are additional formalities the moment you start employing somebody, they are relatively manageable. It is only when there are more than five employees that the administration takes on legal complexities.

There is, however, a third option in some cases: outsourcing. Chapter 11 also mentioned this, but in this context the main point is that there are specialist companies that can take on almost any surplus job you want to subcontract. Storage, delivery, research, manufacture, computer running, or maintenance, even sales and accounts can be shunted on to experts who may even be able to do it cheaper through getting the economies of sale. Major corporations have taken this route with such enthusiasm that some of them, like British Airways for instance, have practically turned into virtual corporations with nothing but the board of directors and key planning staff as full-time employees, and everything else bought in. Outsourcing has become a multi-billion-pound business.

Growth

Even if the company started with a handful of friends collaborating to create a business, or the entrepreneur has had a few staff from the beginning, there are problems of growth. The first reaction is to prefer the problems of success to the trials of disaster, but many a business has foundered from mishandling the transition from a tiny business to a medium-sized corporation.

One of the most painful questions the founder has to face at this stage is whether he is the right person to manage the next level of corporate structure. To create a business from nothing, it takes a very different sort of personality from the sort of person who is good at managing an established and growing operation and is more of an administrator than a charismatic initiator. A classic example was Sir Clive Sinclair, an inventor of genius and a visionary who initiated a range of wholly novel products into the market, but was temperamentally unsuited to the detailed processes needed for ensuring a business prospers, which resulted in most of his efforts disappearing.

It is not just the founder who may need to rethink his role. The buccaneering, casual way small businesses may be run is helpful in keeping them flexible and reactive in the early stage, as well as focused on what matters: establishing the business. However, that sort of attitude can make life difficult in larger companies. The clever companies, especially in advanced technologies, keep such mavericks around but make sure they are not part of the mainstream organization. They are needed for innovation and iconoclastic new thinking, but they would be too disruptive and so are kept on tap, rather than on top.

Buying other businesses

It can take a long time to reach the sort of size considered sensible for getting a stock market listing. One way to accelerate it is through acquisitions. That process does not just add size but can also reduce competition through buying another supplier to the same market; it can increase geographical or product coverage; it can improve purchasing power; and it can bring an additional crop of good managers.

The main problem is that people tend to have the same attitude as Groucho Marx had to clubs: I would not want to buy the sort of company someone wants to sell. The first point to investigate is why the organization is up for sale. There are some perfectly valid reasons, for example, retirement and a lack of successors, the need to cash in on a business not large enough to float on the stock market, selling off part of a business to concentrate on the other bits, ill health, emigration and disenchantment with the business.

There are many ploys in selling a business and the buyer should not fall for them. These include all the clever devices listed in this chapter in the section dealing with how to sell a company (p.249). Have a look at those and check whether there are any symptoms of such devious tricks in the businesses being examined as potential purchases.

Sellers sometimes try to inject a note of drama and tension into the sale procedure as a way of stampeding a careful and hesitant buyer. Part of this process is to set up a real or pretended auction to hike the price, and try to unsettle buyers into feeling they are losing a much-desired bargain, or hustle them into an accelerated early decision by setting deadlines. The correct response to the former is to have worked out in advance the absolute maximum you are prepared to pay (although subject to a wide variety of non-financial conditions) and on no account to go above that. If somebody else is fool enough to pay more, that is their lookout. The right response to the second tactic requires strong nerves and saying the timetable suggested by the seller is not convenient. If the deal falls through as a result, you will be no worse off than before negotiations started. If this transaction does not go through, there are always others.

Always remember, it is not the good deals you miss that hurt, it is the bad ones you do.

It would take a high order of arrogance to dispense with the help of professionals in this process. The seller knows more about the company than the buyer, even if they are in the same sector business, and sometimes it can take protracted investigation to unravel the full state of the finances. This is the 'due diligence' examination by accountants to assess not only that the business is as the sellers say it is, but how to put a sensible valuation on the enterprise.

Finally, ensure that there are restrictive covenants in the deal to prevent the sellers setting up across the road and fetching back all their old clients.

Buying insolvent businesses

One way to pick up the occasional bargain is through buying a crashed company from the receiver or liquidator. What distinguishes a roaring success from a dismal failure is principally management – just because incompetent managers have caused a business to fail does not mean there is no demand for its products.

Stripped of debts, pared down to its essentials, a company with a nice collection of products can be made successful, especially when integrated into another to give it the benefit of size. The ones to beware of are service sector organizations. These are essentially people businesses and all the main assets of the company can leave in a week or two, leaving you with nothing but a name. By a strange irony, however, you cannot do the same in reverse. Transfer of Undertakings (Protection of Employment) regulations (generally referred to as Tupe) prevent someone who has bought the company from stripping out any dead wood and surplus staff.

Swift action is vital in buying an insolvent undertaking. As word gets round that the business has foundered, customers immediately abandon it and it can take a long time to entice them back. Fortunately, the UK legal system is geared to that and a receiver can dispose of a company in 24 hours if need be.

This works to the buyer's advantage because receivers realize they have an asset with a precipitously declining value. The buyer can bluff, if faced with a high price, by saying that he demands some time to think it over. The only danger is somebody else stepping in.

Reverse takeover

A reverse takeover is when a smaller but active and well-managed company buys a larger, more sluggish outfit to bring the former's energetic management to the head of the combined business.

SUCCESSION

On the Continent there is still a well-established expectation that the founder's children will take on the business, and their children after them. Since the Victorian years, this practice seems to have faded in Britain. If the business has grown truly large, there may be some thought of succession at the top, but often the question is how the founder can realize the maximum value for the business. This attitude is also fostered by the other investors who have less emotional connection with the business than with money.

Well-established businesses, however, may be able to buy out the short-term investors and promise dividends to the rest as a way of avoiding sale or flotation. Parallel with that must be some sensible anticipation of eventual retirements. For the founder, this is as painful as stepping sideways when professional managers have to move in to administer growth. The baby, built up over many years and nurtured through innumerable problems, must now be handed over to somebody else's tender care.

One answer is to bring in somebody young to be groomed for succession several years before the founder retires, as a gentle way of easing the new generation into the business.

BEING BOUGHT OUT

Getting a stock market listing is such a prolonged, time-consuming and expensive process there has to be a very good reason for going through it. The main reason is usually to get a better price, and sometimes as the road to further growth through acquisition. With a public listing, the company can use its shares rather than cash to buy other companies. This is made easier if the shares are highly valued, but the drawback is that small companies in the main attract little interest on the exchange – analysts cannot be bothered with them, fund managers have difficulty investing in them, and small shareholders have not heard of them. As a result, they languish unloved unless they happen briefly to be in some sector that becomes startlingly fashionable.

A much cheaper and less problematic route for buyout is a trade sale. In general, the price is likely to be higher from a quoted company for two reasons: it can use its own shares either to raise the cash or to offer as payment and, therefore, it can command greater capital resources; and quoted companies of any reasonable size have a higher price earnings ratio than unquoted companies. Consequently, the market value of an unquoted company can rise by say a third simply through becoming part of a quoted business.

HOW TO SELL A COMPANY

The preparations for a sale have to start two or three years before the negotiations open. Just as when you sell your house everything is tarted up to look its best, it is perfectly legitimate to make the company look good. However, window-dressing, creative accounting, massaging figures and the like have always had an illegal aspect. As a result of some spectacularly burnt fingers and loud scandals of recent years, people have become rather more inquisitive and careful about business details and accounts. It is like selling anything else: it is wrong to lie, but there is nothing either illegal or immoral about making what you sell look its best. And there is a wide range of ways to make a business seem as attractive as possible.

There is little point in leaving everything to a rush at the last moment. Sweeping untidy bits of inconvenient business under the accountancy carpet is unlikely to fool even the most naive buyer, especially as most will send in investigating accountants for a 'due diligence' examination. Everything about the business must seem attractive. For instance, businesses quite often jettison their small local firm of accountants and lawyers, and hire well-known names. It will inspire confidence in buyers that nothing shady is being perpetrated.

It also takes time to untangle personal and business finances – areas which tend to get blurred in family-held businesses. Furthermore, there are many ways in which a private business is carefully tuned not to make the maximum taxable profit, and that has to be turned around. Bear in mind that if the business is being sold on a price/earnings ratio (P/E) multiple of five to eight, making an extra £100,000 profit puts an additional £500,000 to £800,000 on the price.

One system for improving the appearance has always been to reduce expenditure to maximize profits. That means curtailing travel, entertainment, family members in sinecures, research and development, and building maintenance and refurbishment. In addition, it involves being more cautious about purchasing new plant, and one allows computers, company cars and office equipment to continue a little longer, and so on. Chasing payments harder and reducing stock levels to the bare minimum will also help the process. Some accounting policies can be adjusted, such as depreciating machinery or transport equipment over a longer period. All of this needs to be done years ahead or the prospective buyer is bound to balk at the wide range of discontinuities in the accounts.

There are some indicators that make a company attractive to buyers. These will give the managers some idea of what needs to be done in the years running up to a sale. Buyers like companies which have:

- a good share of their market
- good management below board level
- some top management staying after the sale
- a wide spread of major customers
- consistent growth for the previous year
- up to date and uncomplicated accounts
- margins above the sector average.

Most of these are within the capacity of good management to improve and, indeed, if the managers are good will already be true. The hardest is probably the first, but that can be remedied by making acquisitions some years before the sale.

As for the mechanics of the deal, it might be wise to bring in a merchant bank and/or a firm of accountants and perhaps a firm of solicitors at a fairly early stage, to advise on how to lick the business into an attractive package, and how to construct the contract of sale. They would also be able to approach potential buyers in a much more confidential way, and so prevent the enterprise collapsing as rumours get out that it is in trouble or up for sale.

Trade sale

The most obvious buyer is another business in the same line of business, and the next most obvious is one looking for vertical integration. That makes finding a buyer rather easy – the biggest competitor is likely to be the most interested.

Even then there are many decisions involved. For instance, if the business owns its own property, will that go with the company or will the managers strip that out first and either keep or sell it separately? What will happen to the other separate assets like company cars and overseas sales offices? What about the name? If that belongs to the person starting the business, there may be some reservations about leaving unfettered use of it to someone else. If a subsidiary is sold, it may have to forfeit the parent company's name.

The next question is when to sell. At the top of the market is the obvious answer, but it is easier to say than to do. Stockbrokers, estate agents, Internet companies and telecoms businesses have all gone through periods when outrageous prices were being paid for very little because the fashion said that was the place to be. It is too much to hope that your little niche company will suddenly command a P/E of 60 or more as it comes into vogue, but it can be part of a more highly regarded sector from time to time. This is the other reason to start to plan well ahead and get the company into a state of readiness – to ride the rising tide.

Management buyout, buy-in

When the founders want to cash in their profits, the existing management may be potential buyers. After all, the managers know the business best, are credible when it comes to raising venture capital backing to finance the deal, and between them may be able to muster a handsome price for the business. This is an area so much liked by venture capitalists that the managers can probably get several of them to bid for backing the deal. Their preference is understandable: the risks are small since there is a well-established financial record, the people wanting backing are experts in the field, and the prospects for a later sale are good if recent experience is anything to go by.

Managers are finding an increasingly aggressive competitor in the form of the venture capital houses that once used to back them in the purchase. Instead, the fund managers are now bidding on their own account and installing their own recruited managers or getting together with professional managers in a joint effort to acquire a company. Several of the larger funds like Apax and 3i have been aggressive in this field.

In addition to the management buyout (MBO) and the management buy-in (MBI), there are ever-growing armies of hybrid deals with their own sets of acronyms. For example, there is the BIMBO – a buy-in with a management buyout. That is to say that the entrepreneur selling his creation is replaced by a new expert chief executive (usually backed by a venture capitalist) who comes in from outside the business and buys it in collaboration with the other existing management.

Selling to the workers is rare, but does occasionally happen.

Setting the price

Negotiating is a more complex art than it first appears. The haggle in the souk stage of fixing the price is only the final manifestation of a long and carefully manipulated process, and even that has more levels in skilled hands than you would realize without training and expertise.

The first stage is careful preparation. This involves knowing as much as possible about the people on the other side of the deal: their strengths and weaknesses, preferences, temper, reasons for wanting to buy, the state of their finances, and their attitude to timing.

Decide what you want in detail: break it down into what would be nice to have; what is essential; and what is tradable for some compensating benefit given by the other side. Never make a concession without an offsetting advantage granted by the opposition. It is usually a mistake to think you can win their good will by making a generous gesture. The chances are they will take it as a sign of weakness.

Never disclose the price at the start of talks if you can possibly avoid it.

After the sale

Some managers are content to get their profits, meld the company into a larger unit that can provide the muscle to make it grow to the next stage, and go on working for the larger enterprise. Others prefer to take the cash and try their luck elsewhere, while a third group wants a quiet retirement in the sun. All these dreams can be shattered by the terms of the sale. If the demands for post-sale performance are too onerous, and the payment is contingent on subsequent years' profits, the seller can find himself poor and out of work. That is even truer in cases where company performance is more determined by the new owner than the inherent profits of the company. That emphasizes why it is best to get good negotiators on board early on.

GETTING A STOCK MARKET LISTING

The main reasons for flotation are to realize the original investors' profits, to raise a large chunk of additional financing, and to enable the business to make acquisitions by issuing more share rather than having to find cash. Flotation also makes it easier to make share incentives more valuable. Lesser and perhaps more suspect reasons are to burnish the egos of the directors, to improve status and to gain extra publicity.

Working up to a listing or public quotation of shares takes long preparation. This is partly because the record being presented for the initial investors has to show a smooth rising curve of improving finances, culminating in the latest figure of at least £5 million of pre-tax profit. Other aspects may also need tidying. The management team and the board may have been good enough to have brought the company this far, but that may not be enough for the market. Quite apart from the specific demands of the corporate governance rules, there might have to be added people with the gravitas and experience to command respect, and the board may grow with the addition of some high-prestige, non-executive directors.

Flotation is also an extremely expensive business. There are accountants, stockbrokers, lawyers, merchant banks and perhaps even separate underwriters all demanding large chunks of cash.

Getting a share on to the stock market may be a useful way for the investors, including the founding managers, to realize their investments and make a handsome profit, but everything has a price. The price for a quote is that the company is under permanent public pressure, there is a much increased range of regulatory and reporting requirements, and surveillance, and the range of management options is much reduced.

To illustrate, a private company may decide a piece of research that could take ten years to complete and a further five years before the product reaches the market is a worthwhile investment in its future. The obsession with short-term performance indicators of public companies would make that extremely difficult if it took a substantial portion of the company's investment, and hence prejudiced profit growth and dividends in the interim.

In addition, a company with a relatively small market capitalization (the total value of the shares at the prevailing price) is not much loved. Being outside the FTSE 350, which covers the 350 largest UK companies by market capitalization, means institutional investors will almost certainly avoid it, and stockbrokers' analysts are unlikely to take much interest. That in turn means newspapers will mention the shares less often, which leads to fewer investors buying, and hence to the price being low. All of that is intensified the further down the scale you go. Any company with a market capitalization of under £100 million will struggle to be noticed, and under £50 million will be largely ignored.

One of the stock market requirements is continuous growth: of turnover, of sales, of profit margins. This is one of the factors driving the takeover fever so prevalent in Britain: no company can continue to increase like that through organic growth, so many are driven to buying their enlargement to keep the analysts and fund managers happy. On top of that, the share price reflects not only what the company does or achieves but also the expected direction of the economy and the performance of other companies in the sector. Therefore, for instance, a computer distribution business may be thriving and have cash in the bank, but if several of its competitors have recently reported a downturn in orders and a squeeze on margins, shares in every comparable company will fall, the good ones included.

In theory, it should not matter to the business what the current share price stands at, since trade is unaffected by that. In practice, if the shares are very cheap it means a business cannot make acquisitions for shares because it would have to issue too many to make a sound deal. A depressed share price also makes the business vulnerable to being bought by a predator who can pick up the assets at a low price. This becomes a Catch-22 because what makes a business interesting to the managers of investment funds is a record of growth, but organic growth is seldom fast enough for those people. Theoretically, the way out of this impasse is to produce spectacular organic growth, and to set up wonderful and clever lines of communication with stockbrokers, fund managers and journalists. However, in the real world it is not that easy.

Another part of the price of being listed is the amount of management time it eats up. If the company does grow to be large enough to be of interest to stockbrokers' analysts, then twice a year at the time of the results the board must brief them and explain precisely what has been achieved and how, and what the future holds. Then the directors have to go through it all again with financial journalists. In addition, the regulatory requirements do demand board supervision. And there are continuing fees to professionals.

All in all, it is not a decision to be taken lightly. To add further doubts, the recent years have produced a long catalogue of companies deciding that flotation was not worth the candle, and buying themselves back to private status.

Advisers

Flotation needs a sponsor or nominated adviser to take the company through the process. One of these may be a merchant bank, though the larger accountancy firms are grabbing a share of the business as well. For its hefty fee, the sponsor will prepare the prospectus, advise on pricing and organize an underwriter for the shares. This often produces a paradoxical position: the adviser will generally suggest a fairly low issue price to ensure that all the shares are taken up, and to give the company a good send-off on the market by starting with a healthy jump in the price on the first day of trading; yet at the same time it will organize the issue to be underwritten so that any shares not taken up are bought in and the company gets its money.

It takes an experienced and strong-minded board to opt for only one of these courses by, for instance, saying it would be prepared to accept some of the shares not being taken up and so save itself the large underwriter's fee.

There is also the need to have a house stockbroker to provide additional advice on pricing, timing and the best method. After the flotation, the broker stays on board to act as intermediary between the company and the stock exchange authorities.

A reporting accountant produces the figures for the prospectus and for the advisers by going through the company books and doing another diligent assessment of the figures (hence the label for those checks of 'due diligence').

There are also solicitors to check the memorandum and articles of association and the directors' contracts are all they ought to be, and to go through the prospectus to make sure it meets all the legal requirements. Sometimes a second set of lawyers for the sponsor will go through that again.

Quite often a financial public relations company is hired as well. This will organize distribution of the documents to relevant journalists, set up a press conference, write press releases, and try sweet-talking journalists into writing laudatory comments about the issue.

Now you can see why it is expensive, even before paying the stock market fees.

The method of flotation

One of the main routes to a flotation is a public offering. This means distributing prospectuses, taking advertisements in the newspapers, holding press conferences and so forth to drum support from all the potential investors, institutional and private. The company's stockbroker will also help to find potential shareholders. The other route is through placing with institutional investors.

Public offering

This is the most expensive route to a public quotation. It involves creating and printing a prospectus, which is a fat document giving so much detail about the business and its managers that few private investors would have the time or expertise to absorb it. To prepare that, the reporting accountants and merchant bankers have to crawl all over the business to ensure nothing is omitted and everything is accurate. The issuing price is set low to give the quotation a good send-off with a large initial price rise. Despite that, advisers usually also insist on an underwriter to the issue – a bank which will buy any shares that failed to sell in the market, and so ensure the company gets the money it planned for.

Placing

In a private placing, all the shares issued by the company at the time of coming to the market are sold by a stockbroker to its wealthy clients, generally speaking the major institutions, such as insurance companies and pension funds. Some of the shares must also be offered to the public at large.

Issue by tender

A much rarer way of selling the shares is to invite tenders. The offer document normally gives the minimum acceptable price and the shares are then allocated to the highest bidders.

Choice of stock market

Companies valued much under £250 million will feel unloved on the main London stock market. They will have few if any stockbrokers preparing reports on them, institutional investors will seldom take an interest, and the share price will struggle on a low rating. Consequently, other markets have sprung up to nurture the tiddlers.

Ofex

Strictly speaking Ofex (contraction of 'off the exchange') is not really a stock market at all. It is a computerized trading facility owned by a firm of stockbrokers. It has fewer tough regulations than any of the other markets, including AIM, and is therefore much cheaper to join or to be traded on. Being a little specialized, it has less 'liquidity' than the more mainstream stock markets (there is less trading and small amounts of money available for dealing), so the trade in any particular company may be only intermittent. All the same, it can provide not only a toe in the water in the hope of moving into the deeper pools of the main markets, but can help some existing holders who need to find a value for their shares.

Companies joining Ofex will be raising money from private individuals, rather than from institutions as is the case with the other markets.

AIM

The Alternative Investment Market (AIM) was created to make it easier for small companies to get a listing by reducing the barriers to entry. The cost advantages have been much eroded by the demands of the City. The sponsors and advisers want to protect themselves against blame if things go wrong and require extensive examination by professionals, and that costs money. It is still cheaper than the £500,000 of raising money and getting a full listing.

Since many financial institutions prefer to invest in companies with a full listing, AIM may suffer. The fact that it nevertheless has a value for small companies is shown by the hundreds that have decided to get a quote on it. Among the attractions are that the company is not obliged to release any minimum proportion of its shares for public ownership. There is also an absence of demand for a record either of the managers or the company, and the market capitalization is considered irrelevant – in practice it ranges from £2 million to about £100 million.

Techmark

This is really a sub-group of companies, collected from the main market to create a separate index and group as a way of trying to draw attention to the smaller high-technology businesses. It also includes some well-established computer-related companies, but it allows young, fast-growing companies to get in rather more easily.

New arrivals for the sector still need at least three years of financial record, except by special concession.

London stock market

Unless the company has a record and expectation of spectacular growth, is likely to be valued at over £300 million, and is in a well-considered sector, this is probably the least favoured market to start in.

Among the demands for a full listing are that the company unbelts at least a quarter of its issued equity for market trading, and that it has at least three years' financial record (preferably of high and rising profits).

Euronext

The merged stock exchanges of Paris, Brussels and Amsterdam.

Nasdaq

This giant New York-based market is the main US forum for trading in shares of advanced technology companies. It is second in size only to the main Wall Street stock exchange, the Big Board. Most of the companies quoted are American, but a steady sprinkling of more substantial European technology shares have been getting a quote there, in part to get access to the huge American investment capital, and in part because companies tend to be more highly rated in New York.

It is getting increasing competition from other exchanges trying to get its market, such as the New York-based American Stock Exchange, the Cincinnati exchange (a virtual market on the computer), and the Boston stock market.

Nasdaq Europe

Set up to be a pan-European market for technology and fast-growing companies, on the model of the New York-based Nasdaq, this market has attracted far fewer companies than AIM. However, they tend to be larger and with larger ambitions. The cost of joining is high.

VirtX

In a pan-European exchange, based in London, this market was created from a merger of the Tradepoint electronic trading with the Swiss stock exchange. It is trying to increase its presence through low charges for being listed there, for trading, and for settlement.

Jiway

An on-line cross-border stock market owned by OM Gruppen, which owns the Stockholm stock exchange.

European new markets

All stock exchanges want a steady flow of new companies obtaining a listing, and so encourage small companies to join. The equivalents to London's Alternative Investment Market are the French Nouveau Marché, and the multinational Euro NM. British companies are welcomed there, although there has to be a good reason for not getting a quotation in your home market, where financial people and customers are more likely to know the business.

Acknowledgements

Adrian Furnham, professor of psychology at University College, London, made helpful suggestions and lent me a pile of books to try to prevent the checklist in Chapter 1 being total nonsense. I am also grateful to Hugh Aldous of accountancy firm RSM Robson Rhodes for helpful suggestions. Mike Warburton of accountancy firm Grant Thornton said he merely missed some boring television to check and revise the chapter on tax, and I would like to thank him for performing an ever less enticing task with such cheerfulness. But above all, it was Kay Broadbent of market research and brand development business Broadbent Associates, who read through the whole text and provided an invaluable insight into running her type of business, and also helped to remove many of the ambiguities and follies of the book. Charlie Mounter of Macmillan went through the text with a diligence beyond the call of duty – she tightened flabby writing, clarified confused passages and tried to edit it where I would allow her to change the text. They all did their best to improve the book, so any mistakes that remain are my own fault.

Appendices

A Sources of information, help and advice

In addition to the following organizations you can also find help and information from trade associations, newspapers and libraries.

Accenture
60 Queen Victoria Street
London EC4N
Tel: 020 7844 4000

Advertising Standards Authority
Brook House, Torrington Place
London WC1
Tel: 020 7580 5555

Advisory Conciliation and Arbitration Service (ACAS)
180 Borough High Street
London SE1 1LW
Tel: 020 7396 5100
www.acas.org.uk

Alternative Investment Market
Tel: 020 7797 4404
www.londonstockexchange.com

AMR Research
540 Chiswick High Road
London
Tel: 020 8996 8200

Association of British Insurers
51 Gresham Street
London EC2V 7HQ
Tel: 020 7600 3333
www.abi.org.uk

Beer & Partners
14 Frenchs Hill
Cambridge CB4 3NP
Tel: 01223 508846

Better Payment Practice Group
www.payontime.co.uk

Booz Allen & Hamilton
7 Savoy Court
London WC2R
Tel: 020 7393 3333

Bristol Business School
Tel: 0117 976 2544

British Chambers of Commerce
22 Carlisle Place
London SW1P 1JA
Tel: 020 7265 2000
www.britishchambers.org.uk

British Exporters Association
Broadway House, Tothill Street
London SW1 9NQ
Tel: 020 7222 5419
www.bexa.co.uk

British Franchise Association
Thames View, Newton Road
Henley on Thames
Oxon RG9 1HG
Tel: 01491 578050
www.british-franchise.org.uk
www.franinfo.co.uk

British Insurance and Investment Brokers' Association
14 Bevis Marks
London EC3A 7NT
Tel: 020 7623 9043
www.biba.org.uk

British International Freight Association
Radfem House, Browells Lane
Feltham
Middx TW13 7EP
Tel: 020 8844 2266
www.bifa.org

British Rate and Data
www.brad.co.uk

British Venture Capital Association
12–13 Essex Street
London WC2R 3AA
Tel: 020 7240 3846
www.bvca.co.uk

Business Clubs UK
Tel: 01302 771763
www.onlinebusinessclub.net

Business Information Service
British Library
96 Euston Road
London NW1 2DB
Tel: 020 7412 7454

Business in the Community
137 Shepherdess Walk
London N1 7RQ
Tel: 0870 600 2482
www.bitc.org.uk

Business Links
Tel: 0845 600 6006/756 7765
www.businesslink.org
Also with premises in: Accrington, Ashington, Bierton, Birkenhead, Bridgwater, Brierley Hill, Burgess Hill, Carlisle, Cheltenham, Chesterfield, Chippenham, Durham, Edgbaston, Fareham, Leeds, Leicester, Leyland, Lincoln, London, Luton, Manchester, Middlesbrough, Newbury, Northampton, Reading, Rotherham, St Albans, Salisbury, Stoke-on-Trent, Sunderland, Swaffham, Swindon, Telford, Trowbridge, Warrington, West Malling, Wigan

Business Money£acts
see Money£acts

Business Pages Directory
www.businesspages.co.uk

Business Sale On-line
www.businesssaleonline.net

Business Statistics Office
Government Buildings
Cardiff Road
Newport
Gwent NP10 8XG
Tel: 01633 815696
www.statistics.gov.uk

CCN
Tel: 0115 941 0888

Chartered Institute of Patent Agents
Staple Inn Buildings, High Holborn
London WC1V 7PZ
Tel: 020 7405 9450
www.cipa.org.uk

Commission for Racial Equality
10–12 Allington Street
London SW1E 5EH
Tel: 020 7828 7022
www.cre.gov.uk

Companies House
Crown Way
Cardiff CF14 3UZ
Tel: 029 2038 8588/0870 333 3636
www.companies-house.gov.uk

37 Castle Terrace
Edinburgh EH1 2EB
Tel: 0870 333 3636
www.companies-house.gov.uk

55–71 City Road
London EC1Y 1BB
Tel: 020 7253 9393
www.companies-house.gov.uk

Confederation of British Industry
Centre Point, New Oxford Street
London WC1A 1DU
Tel: 020 7395 8247
www.cbi.org.uk

Cooperative Development Agency
Coach House Workshops
Upper York Street
Bristol BS1 5BB

Cranfield School of Management
Cranfield
Bedfordshire MK43 0AL
Tel: 01234 751122

Crédit Lyonnais
5 Appold Street
London EC2
Tel: 020 7588 4000

Customs and Excise
22 Upper Ground
London SE1 9PJ
Tel: 020 7620 1313
www.hmce.gov.uk

Disability Rights Commission
Tel: 0845 7622 633
www.drc-gb.org

Dunn & Bradstreet
38 Finsbury Square
London EC2A
Tel: 020 7256 8733
www.dnb.com

Durlacher & Co
4 Chiswell Street
London EC1
Tel: 020 7628 4306

E-Centre
www.eca.org.uk

Employment Appeal Tribunal
58 Victoria Embankment
London EC4Y 0DS
Tel: 020 7273 1041
www.employmentappeals.gov.uk

52 Melville Street
Edinburgh EH3 7HS
Tel: 0131 225 3963
www.employmentappeals.gov.uk

Employment Tribunal
44 The Broadway
London E15
Tel: 0845 795 9775

Engineering Employers' Federation
Broadway House, Tothill Street
London SW1H 9NQ
Tel: 020 7222 7777
www.eef.org.uk

Enterprise Zone
www.enterprisezone.org.uk

Environment, Transport & the Regions, Department of
Eland House, Bressenden Place
London SW1E 5DU
Tel: 020 7944 3000
www.detr.gov.uk

Equal Opportunities Commission
Arndale House, Arndale Centre
Manchester M4 3EQ
Tel: 0161 838 8312
www.eoc.org.uk

Equifax
25 Chapel Street
London NW1
Tel: 020 7298 3000

Euler Trade Indemnity plc
1 Canada Square
London E14 5DX
Tel: 020 7860 2541

Euronext
Portbus 19163
NL 1000 GD Amsterdam
Tel: 00 312 0550 5555

Palais de la Bourse
B1000 Bruxelles
Tel: 00 322 509 1211

39 rue de Cambon
F75039 Paris Cedex 01
Tel: 00 331 4927 1000

European Union/Commission
8 Storeys Gate
London SW1
Tel: 020 7973 1992
www.europa.eu.int

33 Queen Street
London EC4R 1AP
Tel: 020 7512 7000

European Venture Capital Association
Tel: 00 322 715 0020
www.evca.com

Experian Ltd
38 Houndsditch
London EC3
Tel: 020 7623 3860/0115 934 4548

Export Credits Guarantee Department
2 Exchange Tower,
Harbour Exchange Square
London E14 9GS
Tel: 020 7512 7887
www.ecgd.gov.uk

Factors & Discounters Association
Boston House, The Little Green
Richmond
Surrey TW9 1QE
Tel: 020 8332 9955
www.factors.org.uk

Federation of Small Businesses
2 Catherine Place
London SW1
Tel: 020 7928 9272
www.fsb.org.uk

Finance & Leasing Association
15–19 Kings Way
London WC2B 6UN
Tel: 020 7836 6511
www.fla.org.uk

Financial Ombudsman
POB4, 183 Marsh Wall
London E14 9SR
Tel: 0845 766 0902
www.financial-ombudsman.org.uk

Forrester Research
9 Windmill Street
London W1
Tel: 020 7631 0202
www.forrester.com

Forum of Private Business
Ruskin Chambers, Drury Lane
Knutsford
Cheshire WA16 6HA
Tel: 01565 634467

Gartner Group
The Glanty
Egham TW20 9AW
Tel: 01784 431611

Goldman Sachs
133 Fleet Street
London EC4
Tel: 020 7774 1000

Health & Safety Executive
2 Southwark Bridge
London SE1 9HS
Tel: 020 7717 6000

Immigration & Nationality Directorate
Lunar House, Wellesley Road
Croydon
Surrey CR9 2BY
Tel: 0870 606 7766
www.ind@homeoffice.gov.uk

Industrial Common Ownership Movement
20 Central Road
Leeds LS1 6DE
Tel: 0113 246 1737

Information Commissioner
Wycliffe House
Wilmslow
Cheshire SK9 5AF
Tel: 01625 545740
www.dataprotection.gov.uk

Inland Revenue
Tel: 0845 607 0143
Electronic business tel: 0845 605 5999
Employers tel: 0845 714 3143
Self-assessment tel: 0845 900444
www.inlandrevenue.gov.uk

Instant Search
Tel: 01254 822288

Institute of Direct Marketing
1 Park Road
Teddington
Middlesex TW11 0AR
Tel: 020 8977 5705

Institute of Directors
116 Pall Mall
London SW1 5ED
Tel: 020 7839 1233
www.iod.co.uk

Institute of Export
Export House,
Minerva Business Park
Lynch Wood PE2 6FT
Tel: 01733 404400
www.export.org.uk

Institute of Patentees and Inventors
189 Regent Street
London W1B 4JY
Tel: 020 7434 1818
www.invent.org.uk

Institute of Trade Mark Attorneys
2–6 Sydenham Road
Croydon
Surrey CR0 9XE
Tel: 020 8686 2052
www.itma.org.uk

Interforum
83 St Jude's Road
Egham TW20 0DF
Tel: 01784 473005
www.interforum.org.uk

j4b
www.j4b.co.uk

Jiway
131 Finsbury Pavement
London EC2A 1NT
Tel: 020 7065 8000

Kelly's Directory
Windsor Court
East Grinstead House
East Grinstead
West Sussex RH19 1XA
Tel: 01342 326972
www.kellys.co.uk

Kompass Directory
Windsor Court
East Grinstead House
East Grinstead
West Sussex RH19 1XA
Tel: 01342 326972
www.kompass.com

KPMG
8 Salisbury Square
London EC4
Tel: 020 7311 1000

Learning & Skills Council
24 The Quadrant
Bantons Lane
Abingdon OX14 3YS
Tel: 01235 556101

London Stock Exchange
Throgmorton Street
London
Tel: 020 7588 2355
www.londonstockexchange.com

Money£acts
66–70 Thorpe Road
Norwich NR1 1BJ
Tel: 01603 476476

Nasdaq
www.nasdaq.com

Nasdaq Europe
Exchange Towers
Old Broad Street
London EC2N 1HP
Tel: 020 7786 6400

Box 15
56 rue des Colonies
B1000 Brussels
Belgium
Tel: 00 322 227 6520
www.nasdaqeurope.com

National Business Angels Network
40–2 Cannon Street
London EC4N 6JJ
Tel: 020 7329 2929/4141
www.bestmatch.co.uk

National Minimum Wage
DSS Longbenton
Gateshead NE9 1YX
Tel: 0845 600 0678

Nominet
www.nic.uk, www.nominet.org.uk

Occupational Pensions Regulatory Authority
Invicta House
Trafalgar Place
Brighton
BN1 4DW
Tel: 01273 627600
www.opra.gov.uk

Ofex
1 Goodman's Yard
London E1 8AT
Tel: 020 7423 0800
www.ofex.com

Office for National Statistics
1 Drummond Gate
London SW1V 2QQ
Tel: 020 7533 6207
www.ons.gov.uk

Patent Office
Concept House, Cardiff Road
Newport
Gwent NP10 8QQ
Tel: 01633 814000/0645 500505
www.patent.gov.uk

Pensions Advisory Service
11 Belgrave Road
London SW1V 1RB
Tel: 020 7233 8080
www.opas.org.uk

The Prince's Business Trust
18 Park Square East
London NW1 4LH
Tel: 020 7543 1200
www.princes-trust.org.uk

Quoted Companies Alliance
56 Gresham Street
London EC2
Tel: 020 7600 3745
www.qcanet.co.uk

Race Relations Employment Advisory Service
2 Duchess Place
Birmingham B16 8NS
Tel: 0121 452 5447
www.dfee.gov.uk/rreas

Recruitment & Employment Confederation
36–38 Mortimer Street
London W1W 7RG
Tel: 020 1462 3260

Regional Development Agencies
Contact the Department of Trade and Industry
Tel: 020 7215 2612
www.dti.gov.uk./assistedareas

Advantage West Midlands
Tel: 0121 380 3500
www.advantage-westmidlands.co.uk

East Midlands Development Agency
Tel: 0115 988 8300
www.edma.org.uk

East of England Development Agency
Tel: 01223 713900
www.eeda.org.uk

North West Development Agency
Tel: 01925 644734
www.nwda.co.uk

One NorthEast
Tel: 0191 261 2000
www.onenortheast.co.uk

Scottish Enterprise
5 Atlantic Quay
Glasgow G2 8LU
Tel: 0141 248 2700
www.scottish-enterprise.com
Also offices in: Aberdeen, Clydebank, Dumfries, Dundee, Edinburgh, Galashiels, Glenrothes, Kilmarnock, Paisley, Stirling.

South East England Development Agency
Tel: 01483 484226
www.seeda.co.uk

South West of England Regional Development Agency
Tel: 01392 214747
www.southwesternengland.co.uk

Yorkshire Forward
Tel: 0113 243 9222
www.yorkshire-forward.com

Scottish Business Shop Network
5 Atlantic Quay
150 Broomielaw
Glasgow G2 8LU
Tel: 0141 228 2000
www.scottish-enterprise.co.uk

Small Business Service
St Mary's House, Moorfoot
Sheffield S1 4PQ
Tel: 0114 259 7788/0345 567765/ 020 7072 4072
www.businessadviceonline.org.uk

Southampton University
Tel: 02380 592217

Standard & Poor's
Garden House, Finsbury Square
London EC2
Tel: 020 7826 3800
www.standardandpoors.com

Start in Business
www.startinbusiness.com

Strathclyde University Business Information Sources on the Internet
www.dis.strath.ac.uk

Techmark
see London Stock Exchange

Thomson Directories
296 Farnborough Road
Farnborough
Tel: 01252 555555
www.thomweb.co.uk

Trade and Industry, Department of
1 Victoria Street
London SW1H 0ET
Tel: 020 7215 5000
www.dti.gov.uk

E-commerce advice
Tel: 0845 715 2000
www.dti.gov.uk/infoage

Trade Partners UK
66–74 Queen Victoria Street
London SW1E 6SW
Tel: 020 7215 5444
www.tradepartners.gov.uk

UK Business Incubation
Aston Science Park
Love Lane
Birmingham B7 4BJ
Tel: 0121 250 3538
www.ukbi.co.uk

UK Taxation Directory
www.uktax.demon.co.uk

Welsh Development Agency
Pearl House, Greyfriars Road
Cardiff CF1 3XX
Tel: 029 2082 8730

Westminster University
35 Marylebone Road
London NW1 5LS
Tel: 020 7911 5000

Work and Pensions, Department for
1–11 John Adam Street
London WC2N 6HT
Tel: 020 7712 2171
www.dwp.gov.uk

Pensions
Tel: 0845 731 32323
www.pensionguide.gov.uk

Yellow Pages
Queens Walk, Oxford Road
Reading RG1 7PT
Tel: 0800 605060
www.yell.co.uk

B Glossary

ACAS Advisory Conciliation and Arbitration Service; a government agency to reconcile warring parties, for example, in disputes between management and unions.

accounting reference date The date of a company's financial year end; the date of the balance sheet; Companies House assumes it is the last day of the month in which it was incorporated, but that can be changed by returning a form to Companies House.

ADSL Asymmetric digital subscriber line; a system for getting more data down existing copper telephone cables which can, in theory, provide data at 8Mbps (megabits per second) to the subscriber and 1Mbps going to the Internet. In practice, the rate falls well short of that; ADSL is useful for consumers wanting to download video or programs.

angels Somebody backing a theatre or film production with their private cash; **business angels** are, therefore, the people who put up funding to get a business off the ground.

applets Small computer programs for specific tasks; they are embedded in Web pages to activate animations or perform calculations.

articles of association The rules set by the company for its own conduct.

authorized capital The value of shares the company is allowed to issue, although not all have to be issued.

averaging In the context of insurance, this means the reduction of a claim by the proportion the risks have been underinsured.

B2B Business to business; selling to other companies.

B2C Business to consumer; selling to individual end-users.

bad debt Money owing to you that is unlikely to be recovered.

bankruptcy Strictly speaking this means a person going bust and the legal procedures that take over his assets to pay off as many of the debts as possible; a company goes through a different set of procedures including administration, receivership and liquidation.

base rate The interest level set by the Bank of England from which banks calculate the interest they pay and demand.

browser A computer program that allows users to look for information on the **WorldWide Web**; best-known names are Netscape Navigator, Opera and Microsoft's Internet Explorer.

burn rate The rate at which a company consumes cash; high-technology start-ups normally have a very high burn rate while expensive people are recruited and there is work on the products before any sales have started.

business angel A person prepared to back a business with private cash; angels often get directly involved with the business either by providing advice or becoming non-executive directors.

capital gain The rise in the value of an asset, part of which may be caused by an inflation in that sector or in the economy generally.

charge In the context of corporate finance, this means the legal security of a lender against some asset.

cif Abbreviation of cost, insurance and freight. The exporter pays for transport and insurance cover for the goods to the destination overseas (see also **fob**).

company secretary The person legally responsible for keeping company records required by law and for filing the annual return.

constructive dismissal When the conditions of work for somebody have been so much worse than it would be reasonable to expect someone to tolerate, the employee can resign and claim constructive dismissal for being forced out.

cookies Small files transmitted by a website to visitors' computers so they are recognized the next time, and the website knows their passwords, credit card information, their preferred layouts and pages; the subject of controversy between people concerned about privacy and companies wanting to provide customized friendly service.

corporate venturing Large corporations backing infant businesses with funds; more popular in America than Britain where there are two main categories: the big company which helps the development of new products or technologies that may become useful; and the funding of bright young employees who want to go off and start out on their own.

debenture Written acknowledgment of a loan (a form of corporate IOU), generally secured against the assets of a company.

direct response Also called 'off-the-page'; advertising, often with a coupon, that tries to persuade consumers to respond directly to the advertiser.

direct selling Transactions directly with the consumer instead of the more conventional distribution through wholesalers and retail outlets.

dividend A payment to shareholders as their share of the company's profits; the company is not obliged to pay dividends no matter how large the profit, and may not pay them from capital.

domain name The equivalent of an address on the Internet that is more than just a destination for e-mail; the ones ending in .com and so forth are called top-level names because they have no country designation; the British addresses have an ending to designate the country of registration, such as .co.uk, .org.uk. etc.

due diligence A shorthand term for a buyer or investor exercising the care that legislation requires in managing a business, by diligently investigating the claims of a business before investing in it.

earn out Part of the payment for a company may be deferred to ensure it is all as claimed, with the seller getting staged payments, sometimes for several years; the amounts in some deals are linked to the financial performance of the business.

EDI A computer-based system used by several industries, e.g. car manufacturing, for linking suppliers to manufacturers to allow ordering, invoicing etc. to be all done on-line; now being adapted from the dedicated network to the Internet.

elasticity of demand A measure of how much sales depend on price: if sales change proportionately more than a change in price, the demand is called elastic; if less, inelastic.

equity Another word for ordinary shares in a company.

European Economic Area This extends beyond the 15 EU member states (Austria, Belgium, Denmark, Finland, France, Germany, Greece, Ireland, Italy, Luxembourg, the Netherlands, Portugal, Spain, Sweden and the United Kingdom), and includes Iceland, Liechtenstein and Norway.

factor In the context of corporate work, this is a company that buys the outstanding credits of a company by taking over its sales ledger for immediate payment and then collects the debts from customers itself; the amount of discount (i.e. percentage of the face value of the invoices) depends on the sector and that company's experience.

firewall A system of software and hardware to provide a barrier between the computer that deals with the outside world through the telephone lines, and the company's own system with its software and data files that have to be kept secure.

floating charge Security for a loan over any assets of a business including stock; the more usual method of specifying the item or building which acts as collateral.

fob Abbreviation of free on board – the normal basis for pricing overseas sales, meaning the exporter pays transport and costs as far as the ship's hold (see **cif**).

gateway Link between two otherwise incompatible Internet systems.

gearing The ratio of borrowing to issued share capital; a company with a large percentage of debt is called highly geared.

going concern The basis on which accounts are prepared. In other words, the assumption is that the business will continue and its assets are valued on the use to the business rather than the price they would fetch on the second-hand market; if the auditor's report emphasizes that the accounts have been made on this basis, it is a hint that the enterprise is rocky.

goodwill In the business context, this is a balancing item: when a company is taken over the price is usually above the book value of the assets and well above the break-up value of the business; that difference is called the goodwill.

host A company, normally an **Internet service provider**, that provides computers, software and transmission links for websites; there are also some specialist businesses in the field.

hostile takeover A slight misnomer since the offer is friendly, but it is greeted with distinct hostility by the target, which either does not want to be bought, or not at that price.

HTML Hypertext mark-up language – a computer programming language usually used for creating Internet presence pages.

hyperlink Cursor-sensitive places on a Web page that allow you to jump to another page or website.

intellectual property Intangible assets, such as know-how, patents, copyrights and trademarks.

Internet A global network of computers linked over the telephone lines.

Internet service provider The company that provides individuals access to the Internet; usually also providing a range of other services, ranging from e-mail to specialist Web pages.

ISDN Integrated services digital network; faster data transmission rate across the telephone system.

issued share capital The number of shares that have actually been allotted to shareholders.

Java A computer programming language.

joint and several liability Each one in a group, such as partners, sharing the liability of all the others, and being responsible for their debts.

liquidity The availability of cash to meet the need for it; in one sense it means the amount of cash or near-cash a company has for paying its immediate debts, and in the context of a stock market it means the amount of cash available for dealing in a particular share or class of shares.

listing Another word for a quotation on the stock market.

market capitalization The total value of the shares on issue at the share price at the time; if the company has issued 1 million shares and they are trading at 243p, the market capitalization of that business is £2,430,000.

memorandum of association The document that sets out the company's name and what it was set up to do.

nominal share capital The amount of shares a company may issue, even if it actually issues only five of them.

portals Internet sites that provide access to a range of others; they range from the massive ones run by the big search engine companies, to industry-specific collaborative sites.

price/earnings ratio (P/E) The ratio of the market value of a business as related to its profits; for instance a company with profits of £250,000 and a value of £2 million, has a P/E of 8; for quoted companies it is generally calculated on the basis of after-tax profits per share compared with the share price.

private equity Shares in a company that has not been floated on a stock exchange.

reservation of title The seller continues to own the goods until payment for them has been received.

reverse engineering Taking apart an existing product to see how it was constructed and put together, usually with a view to replicating it or producing something better.

Romalpa clauses A 1976 legal case, Aluminium Industrie Vassen v Romalpa Aluminium, approved a contract clause by the seller of raw material to retain rights not only to the goods, but to the items manufactured from them and, if sold, to the proceeds from the sale. However, for the clause to succeed the precise wording is crucial.

search engines A specialist service for net users that looks for information on the Web by homing in on key words; the big names include Yahoo (strictly speaking a directory), Lycos, AltaVista, Google and Hotbot.

server A powerful computer, usually used as the central machine in a network.

snailmail Internet users' scornful word for traditional post.

Stakhanovite Somebody exceptionally hard-working and productive; it comes from Alexei Stakhanov, a Russian coal-miner who broke all Soviet records with his prodigious production.

underwriter The person who takes on the insurance for a fee. When it is life, household, or car etc., the underwriter is an insurance company or a Lloyd's syndicate; when it is to ensure all the shares in a new issue are bought and not left with the company, the underwriter is commonly a merchant bank.

URL Universal resource locator, the technical name for **domain name** or Web address.

venture capital Finance for a fairly young business in return for unquoted shares. It can range from start-up finance to get a business going, development finance for expansion, or later investment as for a management buyout; also called private equity finance.

Wap Wireless application protocol; the standard that allows the Internet to get on to GSM (Global Systems Mobile) mobile phones.

website A collection of web 'pages' under a common **domain name**.

WML Wireless mark-up language; a programming language for creating Internet sites that can be viewed easily on mobile devices.

WorldWide Web The area of the Internet used by business and consumers and which is searched by **browsers** and **search engines**.

C Reading Matter

A to Z of Finance, Michael Becket (Kogan Page)
Accounts and Accounting Reference Dates (Companies House, free)
Annual Return (Companies House, free)
British Venture Capital Association Directory (BVCA, free)
Business Moneyfacts (monthly)
The Business Property Handbook (Royal Institution of Chartered Surveyors)
Code of Practice (Commission for Racial Equality)
Code of Practice on Equal Pay (Equal Opportunities Commission)
Code of Practice on Sex Discrimination (Equal Opportunities Commission)
Companies Act 1948 (HMSO) useful for its table A which has specimen articles of association
Company Formation (Companies House, free)
Company Names (Companies House, free)
Company Secretary's Handbook (Butterworth Tolley)
Contracts of Employment (Trade Department)
Directors and Secretaries Guide (Companies House, free)
Discipline at Work (ACAS)

Employing People: a handbook for small firms (ACAS)
Employment Handbook (Butterworth Tolley)
First Steps as a New Employer (Inland Revenue, free)
Guidance Booklet for Limited Liability Partnerships (Companies House, free)
Guidelines for Directors (Institute of Directors)
A Guide to Export Services (Department of Trade and Industry, free)
A Guide to Producing a Business Plan (Ernst & Young, free)
Health and Safety Laws: what you should know (Health and Safety Executive)
Health and Safety Regulations: a short guide (Health and Safety Executive)
How the Stock Market Works, Michael Becket (Kogan Page)
Mental Well-Being in the Workplace (Health and Safety Executive)
Recruitment and Induction (ACAS)
Setting Up a Limited Company, Mark Fairweather and Rosy Border (The Stationery Office)
Sex Equality and Advertising (Equal Opportunities Commission, free)
Small Business Factbook, with three supplements a year (Gee Publishing)
Starting in Business (Inland Revenue, free)
Tackling Work-Related Stress: a manager's guide (Health and Safety Executive)
Thinking of Taking Someone On? (Inland Revenue, free)
Workplace Health, Safety and Welfare: a short guide for employers (Health and Safety Executive)
Written Statement of Employment Particulars (Department of Trade and Industry)

D Legislation

Chapter references indicate either where the particular legislation is mentioned explicitly, or where it is relevant even if not specifically referred to.

Access to Medical Records Act 1988 (Chapter 7)
Asylum and Immigration Act 1986 (Chapter 7)
Business Names Act
Collective Redundancies and Transfer of Undertakings (Protection of Employment) (Amendment) Regulations 1999 SI1999/1925
Companies Act 1948, 1985
Consumer Credit Act 1974 (Chapter 11)
Consumer Protection Act 1987

Consumer Safety Act
Contracts (Applicable Law) Act 1990
Contracts of Employment Act 1972
Control of Misleading Advertisement Regulations Act 1988 (Chapter 10)
Control of Substances Hazardous to Health Regulations 1988 (Chapter 7)
Copyright Designs and Patents Act 1988 (Chapter 3)
Data Protection Act 1998 (Chapters 7 and 10)
Defective Premises Act 1972
Directors and Insolvency Act 1985 (Chapter 11)
Disability Discrimination Act 1995
Employment Acts 1980, 1982, 1989, 1990
Employment Protection (Consolidation) Act 1978 (Chapter 7)
Employment Relations Act 1999
Employment Rights Act 1996 (Chapter 7)
Equal Pay Act 1970 (Chapter 6)
Factories Act 1961 (Chapter 7)
Fair Trading Act 1973
Financial Services Act 1986
Fire Precautions Act 1971
Fire Prevention (Metropolis) Act 1774 (Chapter 6)
Health and Safety at Work Act 1974 (Chapter 7)
Health and Safety (Consultation with Employees) Regulations 1997 (Chapter 7)
Human Rights Act 1998 (Chapter 7)
Income and Corporation Taxes Acts 1970 and 1988 (Chapter 9)
Income Tax (Employment) Regulations 1993 SI1993/744 (Chapter 11)
Industrial Tribunals Act 1996
Insolvency Act 1986
Landlord and Tenant Act 1954 (Chapter 6)
Late Payment of Commercial Debts (Interest) Act 1998 (Chapter 11)
Limitation Act (Chapter 11)
Management of Health and Safety at Work Regulations 1999 (Chapter 7)
Maternity and Parental Leave etc Regulations 1999 SI1999/3312 (Chapter 7)
National Minimum Wage Act 1998 (Chapter 7)
National Minimum Wage Regulations 1999 SI1999/584 (Chapter 7)
Occupiers Liability Act 1957
Offices, Shops and Railway Premises Act 1963 (Chapter 7)
Partnership Act 1890 (Chapter 3)

Part-Time Workers (Prevention of Less Favourable Treatment) Regulations 2000 SI2000/1551 (Chapter 7)
Public Interest Disclosure Act 1998 (Chapter 7)
Race Relations Act 1976 (Chapters 6 and 7)
Regulation of Investigatory Powers Act 2000
Rehabilitation of Offenders Act 1974 (Chapter 7)
Safety Representatives and Safety Committees Regulations 1977 (Chapter 7)
Sale of Goods Act (Amendment) Act 1995
Sex Discrimination Acts 1975, 1986 (Chapter 7)
Social Security Contributions and Benefits Act (Chapter 7)
Statutory Sick Pay (Medical Evidence) Regulations 1995 (Chapter 7)
Supply of Goods and Services Act 1982
Taxation of Chargeable Gains Act 1992 (Chapter 9)
Taxes Management Act 1970 (Chapter 11)
Telecommunications (Lawful Business Practice) (Interception of Communications) Regulations
Trade Marks Act 1994 (Chapter 3)
Trade Union and Labour Relations (Consolidation) Act 1992
Trades Description Act 1968
Transfer of Undertakings (Protection of Employment) Regulations (Chapter 7)
Unfair Contract Terms Act
VAT Act 1983 (Chapter 11)
Wages Act 1986
Weights and Measures Act 1985
Working Time Regulations SI1998/1833 (Chapter 7)
Workplace (Health Safety and Welfare) Regulations 1992 SI1992/3004
Young Workers Directive

Court cases

Aluminium Industrie Vassen v Romalpa Aluminium 1976 WLR676 (Chapter 11)
Chief Constable of Lincolnshire v Stubbs (Chapter 7)
Clough Mill v Martin 1984 1 WLR111 (Chapter 11)
Edwards v National Coal Board 1949 (Chapter 7)
Furniss v Dawson 1984 STC153 (Chapters 5 and 9)
Ramsay v IRC 1981 STC174 (Chapters 5 and 9)

Index

WENDY GROSSMAN

The Daily Telegraph Small Business Guide to Computer Networking

MACMILLAN

Can I hook together my new and old computers?
Do I want broadband?
How should I back up my systems?

This accessible guide by a leading technology writer will help you navigate the choices available, overcome the jargon and troubleshoot your network once it is up and running. Covering such basic advice as what hardware and software you might need, whether to go wireless and how to set up cable modem, DSL or ISDN connections so that they can be shared by several machines, this invaluable handbook also addresses all the crucial security issues you will face.

Written for those who run a small business or even a home network themselves, this book will help you make those necessary but time-consuming decisions, leaving more time to focus on the business itself.

NIKI CHESWORTH

The Daily Telegraph Guide to Paying Less Tax

MACMILLAN

Everything you need to know about cutting your tax bill.

Taxes are an inescapable fact of life, but many people overpay their tax either through apathy or because they don't realize how they can easily – and legally – avoid paying it. This authoritative guide offers comprehensive and detailed advice on the tax system and how it works, to ensure that at whatever level you pay tax, you're not paying more than you have to.

Thousands of people pay too much in tax every year. This guide will make sure that you're not one of them.

JOHN ADAIR

Effective Time Management

PAN BOOKS

Time is a precious resource, both irreplaceable and irreversible. But how can you learn to save time and spend it wisely? Effective Time Management will help you make the most of every hour. In this unique guide John Adair focuses on managing time using a wide range of examples and case studies. These will help you to:

- identify long-term goals and middle-term plans
- plan the day and make the best use of your time
- learn to delegate and acquire time effectiveness in the office and at meetings

Effective Time Management will show you how to eliminate time-wasting activities, leaving you with more time for your real priorities.

JOHN ADAIR

Effective Leadership

PAN BOOKS

The art of good leadership is highly prized and demands a keen ability to appraise, understand and inspire both colleagues and subordinates.

Effective Leadership is carefully structured to ensure a steady, easily acquired insight into leadership skills, helping you to:

- understand leadership – what you have to be, know and do
- develop leadership abilities – defining the task, planning, briefing, controlling and setting an example
- grow as a leader – making certain your organization encourages leaders to emerge

Drawing on numerous examples – commercial, historical, military – *Effective Leadership* is the ideal passport to the development of leadership.

JOHN ADAIR

Effective Motivation

PAN BOOKS

Understand what motivates you and your staff and become aware of how you can increase energy and motivation to achieve your goals.

People are the most important asset in any business today. Great results come from great people. Every manager needs to be able to motivate or draw out the best from others, which is not easy in times of corporate change and personal uncertainty.

Effective Motivation is a practical guide to this key leadership skill. Based on a careful evaluation of the research into motivation, John Adair presents a set of strategies for motivating high-performance teams.

JOHN ADAIR

Effective Innovation

PAN BOOKS

Innovation – the process of taking new ideas through to satisfied customers – is the lifeblood of any organization today. Nothing stultifies a company and the individuals working in it more than a lack of interest in positive change. You cannot stand still: you either go backwards or move forwards.

In *Effective Innovation*, John Adair looks at both creativity and innovation, generating new ideas and bringing them to the marketplace. His 'seven habits of successful creative thinkers' provide a compelling framework for developing your own productive-thinking skills. This readable book also covers leadership of creative teams and discusses how to build an innovative climate in organizations.

OTHER TITLES AVAILABLE FROM PAN MACMILLAN

WENDY GROSSMAN

THE DT GUIDE COMPUTER NETWORKING	1405006773	£10.99

NIKI CHESWORTH

THE DT GUIDE TO PAYING LESS TAX	0333908457	£9.99
THE DT GUIDE TO PLANNING YOUR RETIREMENT	1405006382	£9.99

JOHN ADAIR

EFFECTIVE TIME MANAGEMENT	0330302299	£6.99
EFFECTIVE LEADERSHIP	0330302302	£6.99
EFFECTIVE MOTIVATION	0330344765	£6.99
EFFECTIVE INNOVATION	0330344757	£6.99